INTERNET
Concepts & Activities

Karl Barksdale
Technology Consultant
Provo, Utah

Michael Rutter
Christa McCauliffe Fellow
Brigham Young University

Benjamin A. Rand
Technology Consultant

JOIN US ON THE INTERNET
WWW: http://www.thomson.com
EMAIL: findit@kiosk.thomson.com   A service of I(T)P®

South-Western Educational Publishing
an International Thomson Publishing company I(T)P®

Cincinnati • Albany, NY • Belmont, CA • Bonn • Boston • Detroit • Johannesburg • London • Madrid
Melbourne • Mexico City • New York • Paris • Singapore • Tokyo • Toronto • Washington

Team Leader: Steve Holland
Managing Editor: Carol Volz
Marketing Manager: Stephen Wright
Editor: Mark Cheatham
Art Coordinator: Mike Broussard
Consulting Editor: Cinci Stowell
Production House: Litten Editing and Production

Internal Photos: Image Copyright © 1998 by PhotoDisc, Inc.

ISBNs: 0-538-72088-3 (spiral bound)
          0-538-72166-9 (perfect bound)

1 2 3 4 5 6 7 8 9 10   WCB   02 01 00 99 98

Printed in the United States of America

International Thomson Publishing

South-Western Educational Publishing is a division of International Thomson Publishing, Inc. The ITP® registered trademark is used under license.

The names of all commercially available software mentioned herein are used for identification purposes only and may be trademarks or registered trademarks of their respective owners. South-Western Educational Publishing disclaims any affiliation, association, connection with, sponsorship, or endorsement by such owners.

Preface

The Internet has put the information of the world literally at our fingertips. With a few mouse clicks, you can access planet earth, even outer space.

The Net is the door to what some have called the *information superhighway*. The information of the world is connected by a group of computers and computer systems. This *web* is joined, or networked together, and is accessible to anyone with a computer, modem, and phone line. So, almost anyone can access the Web from home, from the office, or even from an automobile. Your computer has become a window to the world. In seconds you can visit a museum; dissect a virtual frog; discover the weather in Moose Jaw, Saskatchewan; visit a library; or peruse the home page of your favorite catalog.

But, you ask, how does this all apply to me? How will the Internet affect what I do at school or at work? What practical use is all this information, and how can I find what I need? How can the Internet help me study or do research? How is the Internet used in business—how might it affect the way I do my job?

This book can answer your questions. Each chapter presents an ongoing business project (*Net Project*), so you can experience how the Internet is commonly used in the business world. Each chapter presents basic Internet concepts and language. Then, it builds upon this new understanding with hands-on activities that will enable you to learn operating system functions and file maintenance and how to use and customize a browser, download software, use e-mail and newsgroups, and conduct searches.

Once you develop your new knowledge and skills, you will learn how the Internet is dramatically affecting the way many companies do business through online catalogs and selling online services. You will feel confident using the Internet for research by locating online reference materials and sites relating to specific academic areas such as math or journalism as well as government sites.

Using *Internet Concepts and Activities*, you will learn how to master the Internet. Cyberspace is more than a playground; it's the future, and you should be a part of it. Mastering the Net isn't hard, but there are tools that will speed up the task. You will learn how to use these tools so you'll be in control.

Internet Concepts and Activities is divided into sections and chapters, arranged from the general to the specific. You will learn a concept and then apply it through hands-on activities. The book will take you through each step in a logical, easy-to-follow manner.

In *Section 1: Tools of the Trade*, we will help you master your Web browser, and we will take care of a few messy file and folder issues, so you won't drown in a worldwide tidal wave of information. We will also teach you a few tricks that Net veterans use to speed things up on the Net, such as compressing and decompressing files.

In *Section 2: E-Communication: E-Mail and Newsgroups*, you will learn how the world communicates electronically. E-mail and newsgroups are the two most active communication tools. Although e-mail and newsgroups are extremely easy to use, you will discover some handy tricks of the trade in these pivotal chapters.

In *Section 3: Finding a Needle in the Global Haystack*, you will learn how to find almost anything on the Internet. In the process, you will get a taste of the vast variety of information that is the Internet.

In *Section 4: Exploring the Net for Information and Fun*, you will learn how to use the Net as a research tool for work or school projects. The Web is the most up-to-date resource for science, math, writing, journalism, humanities, business, and government. In every academic area, the Web has you covered. Then, after a hard day at work on the Internet, you will be ready for some fun. We'll show you how to locate information about movies in your area, your favorite TV shows, and even music to match your tastes, no matter what they are.

In *Section 5: Sprechen sie Internet? How the Internet Speaks*, you will ease into the technical side of Web communication systems, protocols, and languages. In this section, you will learn how HTML organizes Web information and explore the uses of Java, JavaScript, push technology, VRML, Active X, Shockwave, and other tools that are changing the shape of the online world. You will even create your own simple Web page!

Throughout the book, you will learn to locate specific information quickly and efficiently. The Net offers a mountain of information. In the last few years, the information available on the Web has multiplied exponentially. There is a lot to sift through, and the navigational skills you will gain from this book will help you do it.

Search engines are more powerful and easier to use now than ever before. With just a little practice, you can use any search engine like a pro. You will learn how to use Boolean operators that will supercharge your search engine. You'll also learn how to use online libraries and encyclopedias or search for a long, lost friend.

HOME PAGE SUPPORT

This text is supported by a Web page at the South-Western Educational Publishing site *computered.swep.com*. At the Computer Education opening screen, click the *Resources* button. Scroll down the list until you locate the Web page for this book.

The Web page contains current hotlinks to most Web sites for the text activities. If, for some reason, a Web page cited in the book goes down permanently, visit our Web page to find a replacement site, since we'll update these links. If you bookmark our Web page, you can use it to go directly to your assigned activities and Web sites.

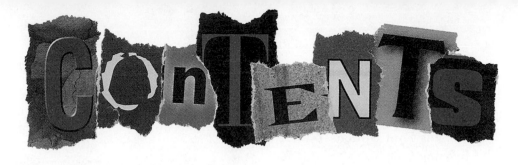

SECTION 1—TOOLS OF THE TRADE 1

CHAPTER 1
Quick Operating System Know-How 2

    Activity 1.1   A Few Pull-Downs to Warm Up 3
    Activity 1.2   Changing Your Window's Size 6
    Activity 1.3   Scrolling Around 8
    Activity 1.4   Copy and Paste 10
    NET PROJECT: Create Your Own Personal Network . . . 13
    NET PROJECT TEAMWORK: Expanding Your Contacts 14
    WRITING ABOUT TECHNOLOGY: Who Should Control the Information? 14

CHAPTER 2
Virtual Filing Cabinet: Save It for Later 15

    Activity 2.1   Exploring Explorer and Finder 17
    Activity 2.2   Creating Folders 20
    Activity 2.3   Saving, Moving, and Deleting Files 22
    NET PROJECT: Organize Your Virtual Filing Cabinet . . . 25
    NET PROJECT TEAMWORK: Sharing Files with Others 26
    WRITING ABOUT TECHNOLOGY: Getting Organized 26

CHAPTER 3
Through the Looking Glass: A Browser Primer 27

    Activity 3.1   Introduce Yourself to a Web Browser 28
    Activity 3.2   "Address Please"—Entering Internet Addresses 30
    Activity 3.3   The Toolbar: One-Click Commands 32
    Activity 3.4   Using the History Folder 34
    Activity 3.5   Adding to Favorites/Bookmarks 36
    Activity 3.6   Cleaning House—Organizing Your Favorites 39
    NET PROJECT: Organizing Your Bookmarks 43
    NET PROJECT TEAMWORK: Narrowing Down Your Lists 44
    WRITING ABOUT TECHNOLOGY: Browsers, Bookmarks, and the Net 45

CHAPTER 4
WWWhat? Understanding Net Addresses 46

    Activity 4.1   Understanding Hyperlinks 47
    Activity 4.2   Understanding Internet Addresses 49
    Activity 4.3   Internet Domain Names 50
    NET PROJECT: Start Your URL Collection 55
    NET PROJECT TEAMWORK: Collecting URLs Together 56
    WRITING ABOUT TECHNOLOGY: The Impact of the Web 56

CHAPTER 5
Beyond the Looking Glass: Your Dream Browser 57

Activity 5.1   Toggling the Toolbar and Status Bar 58
Activity 5.2   Changing Font Options 60
Activity 5.3   Changing Colors 62
Activity 5.4   Toggling Multimedia Options 64
NET PROJECT: The Net Means Business 66
NET PROJECT TEAMWORK: Present Your Top Sites. 67
WRITING ABOUT TECHNOLOGY: Summarize Your Findings . . . . . : 67

CHAPTER 6
Bringing It Home: Downloading Files 68

Activity 6.1   Finding Shareware 70
Activity 6.2   Decompressing Files 72
Activity 6.3   Downloading FTP Software 74
NET PROJECT: Train Your Colleagues 77
NET PROJECT TEAMWORK: Build a Training Program as a Team. 78
WRITING ABOUT TECHNOLOGY: The Advantages of Teams 78

SECTION 2—E-COMMUNICATION: E-MAIL AND NEWSGROUPS 79

CHAPTER 7
Goodbye Snail-Mail: An Intro to E-Mail 80

Activity 7.1   Compose and Send a New Message 83
Activity 7.2   Read a Message 85
Activity 7.3   Creating Folders to Organize Your Mail. 86
Activity 7.4   Send an Attachment 87
Activity 7.5   Using Your Address Book 89
NET PROJECT: Prep for Your Big Presentation 92
NET PROJECT TEAMWORK: Tag-Team E-Mail. 92
WRITING ABOUT TECHNOLOGY: E-Mail's Impact on Writing 92

CHAPTER 8
What's New(s)? An Intro to Newsgroups 93

Activity 8.1   Subscribing to and Unsubscribing from a Newsgroup 94
Activity 8.2   Reading and Downloading Newsgroup Posts 96
Activity 8.3   Posting a Response 98
NET PROJECT: Newsgroups as Sources for New Product Ideas 101
NET PROJECT TEAMWORK: Consensus and Recommendations 102
WRITING ABOUT TECHNOLOGY: Newsgroups as a Business Resource 102

SECTION 3—FINDING A NEEDLE IN THE GLOBAL HAYSTACK 103

CHAPTER 9
"I Think I Can!" The Little Search Engine That Could 104

Activity 9.1   And/Or/+ 106

Activity 9.2   Not/-.   107
Activity 9.3   Near/Adj   108
Activity 9.4   Parentheses   109
Activity 9.5   Natural Language and Phrase Searches   110
NET PROJECT: Fly Fishing for Computer Geeks   113
NET PROJECT TEAMWORK: Fly Fishing as a Team Sport   113
WRITING ABOUT TECHNOLOGY: Succeed with Search Engines   113

CHAPTER 10
Virtual Library: Using Online Resources **114**

Activity 10.1   Virtual Libraries   115
Activity 10.2   Virtual Encyclopedias   116
Activity 10.3   Virtual Museums   117
Activity 10.4   People Finders   119
NET PROJECT: Freestuff   122
NET PROJECT TEAMWORK: Teaming Up to Compile Useful Resources   122
WRITING ABOUT TECHNOLOGY: Privacy versus National Security   122

SECTION 4—EXPLORING THE NET
FOR INFORMATION AND FUN 123

CHAPTER 11
Exploring Sciences and Math **124**

Activity 11.1   Meteorology   125
Activity 11.2   Astronomy and Space Exploration   128
Activity 11.3   Biology   130
Activity 11.4   Math   131
NET PROJECT: Plan an Educational CD-Rom   134
NET PROJECT TEAMWORK: The Space Race   135
WRITING ABOUT TECHNOLOGY: The Internet's Role in Science Education   135

CHAPTER 12
Exploring Writing, Journalism, and History **136**

Activity 12.1   Writing   137
Activity 12.2   History   140
Activity 12.3   Journalism and News   142
NET PROJECT: News on the Run   145
NET PROJECT TEAMWORK: Team Up for the Big Push   145
WRITING ABOUT TECHNOLOGY: Is the Internet the End of Traditional News Media? . . .   145

CHAPTER 13
Exploring Business **146**

Activity 13.1   Economics   147
Activity 13.2   Online Shopping   149
Activity 13.3   Look Up Stock Prices   151
NET PROJECT: Online Investing   155
ADVANCED NET PROJECT: Tycoon   156

NET PROJECT TEAMWORK: Team Stock Competition 156
WRITING ABOUT TECHNOLOGY: Online Security 156

CHAPTER 14
Exploring Government 157

Activity 14.1   Government 158
Activity 14.2   Law 160
Activity 14.3   Political Issues 162
NET PROJECT: Keeping Up with the Government 166
NET PROJECT TEAMWORK: E-Mail Your Senator 166
WRITING ABOUT TECHNOLOGY: The Internet's Impact on Government 166

CHAPTER 15
Movies, TV, Music: The Web's Got You Covered 167

Activity 15.1   Let's Go to the Movies!. 168
Activity 15.2   Couch Potato's Guide to TV 171
Activity 15.3   Music—Lyrics, Shopping, What's Next? 173
Activity 15.4   Sports for the Armchair Quarterback 174
NET PROJECT: Movie Critic 178
NET PROJECT TEAMWORK: Games Debate 178
WRITING ABOUT TECHNOLOGY: Unofficial Web Sites and Copyright Protection 178

SECTION 5—SPRECHEN SIE INTERNET? HOW THE INTERNET SPEAKS 179

CHAPTER 16
Your First Web Page: Your Parents Will Be So Proud. 180

Activity 16.1   Understanding Tags 181
Activity 16.2   Create a Simple Web Page 184
Activity 16.3   Advanced Web Page Design 187
NET PROJECT: Plug In Your Creativity for an Effective Web Site 193
NET PROJECT TEAMWORK: Web Site Hardware 193
WRITING ABOUT TECHNOLOGY: Doing Business on the Web 193

CHAPTER 17
The Many Languages of the Internet 194

Activity 17.1   Java—What Can You Do for Me Today? 196
Activity 17.2   A Walk in the Virtual Park 198
NET PROJECT: A Virtual-World Site for GreatApplications, Inc.. 201
NET PROJECT TEAMWORK: Web Technologies for the Future 201
WRITING ABOUT TECHNOLOGY: The State of the Internet. 202

GLOSSARY 203

INDEX 208

USING THIS BOOK

Introduction

Section Openers provide a brief overview of each chapter and are written in a conversational style that is easy to understand.

Finding a Needle in the Global Haystack

By the time you have finished the activities in this section, you will be able to find almost anything on the Internet.

Locating the specific information you need was easier a few years ago than it is today, because the number of documents on the Web have multiplied exponentially. There is simply more information to search through before you find what you need.

Fortunately, search engines are improving every month, allowing you to narrow searches more expertly and with less effort than ever before.

Chapter 9 will introduce you to the world of search engines. You will learn how to use Boolean operators to give your searches real power. Chapter 10 will familiarize you with electronic versions of the more traditional sources of information: the library and the encyclopedia. Also, you'll see some of the world's greatest museums and search for a long-lost friend.

Chapter 9 "I Think I Can!" The Little Search Engine That Could. 104

Chapter 10 Virtual Library: Using Online Resources 114

Section 3

CHAPTER 10

Virtual Library: Using Online Resources

Chapter Objectives:
In this chapter, you will learn about many of the online resources at your disposal. After reading Chapter 10, you will be able to:

1 locate online libraries and look up information in them.

2 locate and use encyclopedias online.

3 locate and look around online museums.

4 find people's e-mail and street addresses using search engines.

Net Terms

people finder

e-book

mirror site

A Virtual World of Information

The Internet contains literally a world of information. You've just learned about using search engines to locate information. Did you know there are more traditional sources of information available on the Net as well?

Online (or on-line) encyclopedias are also valuable sources of information. The world is accumulating information at such a tremendous rate that printed materials can no longer stay up to date. Online versions can be updated with new information and statistics as soon as they are available.

As the world becomes digitized, libraries are making more of their content available online. You can "check out" a book at any time, since there are enough copies for everyone. And no books ever get lost.

The Louvre in France is one of the world's greatest museums. Millions of people visit it every year. But billions more have never had the opportunity—until now. You can take a virtual tour through many of the world's finest museums. You don't have to spend thousands of dollars getting there, or worry about finding a place to park.

Ever have a problem finding someone's phone number? How about someone who has moved away, but you don't remember where? A **people finder** is a search feature provided by search services on the Internet that helps you find addresses and phone numbers, and we'll show you how to use it in this chapter. ■

Chapter Opener

Chapter Openers provide Objectives, Terms, and an introduction to chapter content. Each chapter builds upon the skills and understanding learned in previous chapters.

Activities

Step-by-Step Instructions provide hands-on reinforcement and simplify the process of working through each activity. (When necessary, instructions are provided for both Netscape and Internet Explorer browsers.)

Activities are written to support each chapter objective. These activities cover the Web topics that are most relevant to today's classroom and workplace. Each activity begins with a brief explanation of key concepts.

Screen Illustrations of both Netscape and Internet Explorer and both Windows and Macintosh platforms, when necessary, make activities easy to understand.

Virtual Libraries

One day, the world's books will all be available from virtual libraries via the Internet. But digitizing all that content takes time and money. Most organizations responsible for putting content online are nonprofit. They are working tirelessly with a lot of volunteer effort to accomplish a Herculean task.

The selection of titles at online libraries is growing steadily. But collections are far from complete. For example, one online library features 5,500 works, with authors as diverse as Shakespeare, Jane Austen, and Plato. However, the library has nothing by Ernest Hemingway or John Steinbeck.

Let's find a few online libraries and take a look at where the future of libraries is headed.

1. Go to your favorite search engine.

2. Key in *libraries AND (online OR on-line)*. You may need to be in the search engine's *Advanced Search* area to use Boolean operators.

3. Browse through the hits until you find a public library. Look for the bigger libraries, such as the Internet Public Library, The Library of Virginia, or the Houston Public Library.

4. Search the resources at the library you selected. For example, at the Internet Public Library lobby (Figure 10.1), you can visit the *Online Texts* link. Here you can search for an "e-book" by author or title, or browse by Dewey decimal categories. An **e-book** is a book that has been digitized and put into online libraries for public use.

5. Try looking up your favorite author. If he/she isn't there, look up a book you read for an English class. Find an e-book to read.

6. Go back to your search engine and locate the WWW Virtual Library or another major library. Perhaps you can even visit the Library of Congress!

7. Browse through your new library selection and compare it to the first library you visited.

THINKING ABOUT TECHNOLOGY

The WWW Virtual Library seems to embody the very reason the Internet was invented. The articles and links found in the "library" are maintained by experts in each field from around the world. Truly, it is a collaborative effort. Does it work? How do you think it will evolve in the future?

ACTIVITY 10.1

Objective:
In this lesson, you will learn to locate online libraries and look up information in them.

Figure 10.1
The Internet Public Library lobby

Read Offline

If you intend to read an e-book, save the page to your computer. Then exit your browser and read the book offline, to avoid unnecessarily taking up valuable Internet access lines that your fellow Netizens could use.

Thinking About Technology is designed to develop critical thinking skills as it asks the user to assess the impact that Web technology is having on everyday life.

Sidebar Features

Special Features occur throughout the text to present important concepts in a brief, easy to read format.

Netiquette discusses the common practices within the online community.

Net Ethics

Net Ethics provides a forum for discussion of important ethical and legal concerns in relation to the Internet.

Net Life

Net Life presents the culture of the Net and is designed to enhance understanding of the Net community.

Internet Milestone presents significant historical benchmarks in the development of the Internet.

End-Of-Chapter

Net Vocabulary reinforces key concepts presented in the text in the form of a vocabulary exercise.

Net Review short answer questions test the retention of important chapter information. This serves as an excellent review for the chapter test.

CHAPTER Review

NET VOCABULARY

Define the following terms:

1. *people finder*

2. *e-book*

3. *mirror site*

NET REVIEW

Give a short answer to the following questions:

1. *What are some of the issues surrounding online libraries?*

2. *What is Project Gutenberg and why is it important?*

Net PRoject

FREESTUFF

GreatApplications, Inc., needs a customized list of library, governmental, and other free research-oriented resources that employees can use when they are doing their business research. Compile a list of libraries, encyclopedias, and e-books that employees would find useful. Save this list of resources in an electronic file in your *Resources* folder. Include at least 25 resources on your list. Call this list *freestuff*.

NET PROJECT TEAMWORK   Teaming up to compile useful resources

As a team, combine *freestuff* resource lists together into a mega-list of over 100 resources that employees in a company like GreatApplications, Inc., would find beneficial. Save this list of resources in your common folder. If one team member knows HTML, that person can create an active hypertext version of your research.

Look back through previous Net Projects and find links that relate to this list. Consolidate and organize your list by topics, as Yahoo! and many other search services have done.

WRITING ABOUT TECHNOLOGY   Privacy versus National Security

With what you have learned about PGP and the national encryption security debate, prepare a 100-word essay, on a separate piece of paper, supporting one of the following opinions. Use your searching skills to find information that supports your point of view.

Option 1: Encryption technology should only be in the hands of the government.

Option 2: Encryption technology should be available to every Net user in the United States, but shouldn't be given to anyone in a foreign country.

Option 3: The Internet is an international tool, not subject to the laws of any one country. Therefore, encryption software should be available to all.

Option 4: Since the government funded the development of the Internet, it should control the use of encryption on the Net.

· PORTFOLIO · PROJECT

Your winter or spring dream vacation is just a snowball throw away. Plan ahead. There will still be lots of snow in the Rockies. Search for one of these ski resorts in Colorado: Aspen, Breckenridge, Copper Mountain, Crested Butte, Snowmass, Steamboat, or Vail.

Net Project puts the user's new tools and skills to work by applying them to an ongoing Web-based business project. Each project focuses on topics such as the following: doing online research, making online purchases, investigating push technology, and maintaining folders and bookmarks.

Net Project Teamwork is a team option for the Net Project designed to emphasize the importance of working in teams to accomplish common goals.

Writing About Technology emphasizes the importance of developing writing and critical thinking skills within the emerging, complex world of Web computing. Each of these end-of-chapter assignments provides an opportunity for building a personal portfolio.

Net Fun is intended to show that with the Internet, it *is* possible to learn and have fun at the same time!

See These Other Texts About the Internet!

Internet Explorer 4.0 by Dennis O. Gehris

This product is an introductory text to the Microsoft Web browser Internet Explorer 4.0.

Product	ISBN
Student Text	0-538-68597-2
Electronic Instructor Package	0-538-68598-0

Table of Contents

Chapter 1: Introduction to the Internet and the Internet Explorer Browser
Chapter 2: Downloading and Configuring Internet Explorer
Chapter 3: Browsing the World Wide Web
Chapter 4: Searching the Internet
Chapter 5: Finding and Downloading Files
Chapter 6: Using Multimedia Tools
Chapter 7: Sending and Receiving E-Mail Using Outlook Express
Chapter 8: Internet Newsgroups Using Netmeeting
Chapter 9: Authoring Web Pages Using FrontPage Express
Chapter 10: Using Other Internet Tools
Appendix A: Internet Explorer Keyboard Shortcuts
Appendix B: Major Web Sites for Exploration
Glossary of Internet Terms
Index

FrontPage 98 by Mark Ciampa

This text provides an introduction to the basic features of Microsoft® FrontPage 98 and allows users to create Web pages with ease.

Product	ISBN
Student Text	0-538-68601-4
Electronic Instructor Package	0-538-68602-2

Table of Contents

Section I: GETTING STARTED WITH FRONTPAGE
Chapter 1: FrontPage Basics
Chapter 2: Making It Look Good
Section II: ADDING PIZAZZ TO PAGES
Chapter 3: Images
Chapter 4: Elements and Components
Chapter 5: Tables
Section III: NOW YOU'RE A PRO
Chapter 6: Managing Files and Webs
Index

Understanding & Using the Internet by Bruce McLaren

This text provides a comprehensive overview of the Internet from a history of its development to the importance it plays in business today.

Product	ISBN
Student Text	0-538-72132-4
Electronic Instructor	0-538-72133-2

Table of Contents

Unit 1: Development of the Internet
Unit 2: Connecting to the Internet
Unit 3: Electronic Mail—The Basic Internet Tool
Unit 4: Hypertext and World Wide Web
Unit 5: Searching for Information on the Web
Unit 6: Discussion Groups: News Groups and Mailing Lists
Unit 7: FTP—File Transfer Protocol
Unit 8: Creating HTML Documents
Unit 9: Electronic Commerce on the Internet
Unit 10: The Future of the Internet
Appendix
Glossary
Index

Internet Custom Modules

Need to include Internet topics in your curriculum? Our Internet modules offer an up-to-date, concise overview of Internet technology topics with introductory concepts. Illustrated with screen captures and figures, each short (30-to-60-page) module also includes glossary terms and exercises. The modules you choose will be combined into a custom textbook available within days of your order. Or, bundle one or two modules with another South-Western title for even more versatility. Call 1-800-245-6724 for more information.

Instructor support materials available on Web site (for instructors only; password protected) include approximately 4 pages per module of teaching tips, lecture notes, background information, and answers to the student exercises.

Internet Custom Modules:

1.	The Internet: An Introduction	0-538-68621-9
2.	Web Design Basics Using PageMill	0-538-68623-5
3.	Web Design Basics Using FrontPage	0-538-68622-7
4.	Netscape Basics	0-538-68625-1
5.	Internet Explorer Basics	0-538-68624-3
6.	Lotus Notes Basics	0-538-68626-X
7.	AOL Basics	0-538-68630-8
8.	Introduction to Internet Research Using Search Engines	0-538-68631-6
9.	Using a Web Browser and FTP	0-538-68632-4
10.	Intranet Basics	0-538-68643-X
11.	Internet Graphics Basics	0-538-68633-2
12.	Internet Multimedia Basics	0-538-68634-0
13.	HTML Basics	0-538-68627-8
14.	Web Design Basics Using Home Page	0-538-68635-9
15.	Web Page Maintenance	0-538-68636-7
16.	Java Basics	0-538-68628-6
17.	Writing for the Internet	0-538-68637-5
18.	Using the Internet for Career Exploration	0-538-68638-3
19.	Internet Business Applications Using Microsoft Office	0-538-68639-1
20.	Ethics and the Internet	0-538-68640-5
21.	MSN Basics	0-538-68629-4
22.	Internet Activities	0-538-68641-3
23.	Internet Business Simulation	0-538-68642-1
24.	Advanced Internet Business Applications	0-538-68644-8

South-Western
Educational Publishing

Join Us on the Internet
WWW: http://www.swep.com

Tools of the Trade

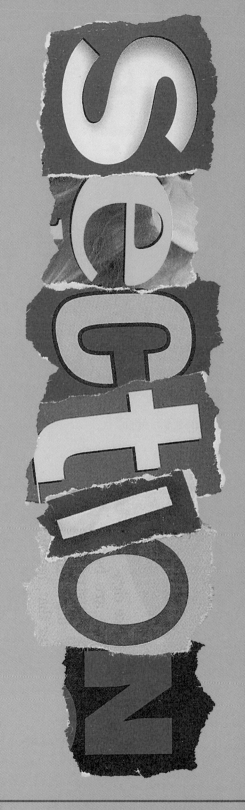

Welcome to the Internet.

Or better yet, welcome to "cyberspace," a term often used to describe the Net and the World Wide Web. The word *cyberspace* was coined by the science fiction author William Gibson in his book *Neuromancer* (New York: Ace Books, 1984). Gibson describes a shadowy world in which computers and people interact in a futuristic silicon society.

Cyberspace can be a troublesome, if not a complicated, place for beginners. In fact, newly initiated users of the Net are often described as *newbies*. The designation indicates that Net rookies make a lot of mistakes as they first explore the cyber world. In this section, we will show you how to avoid the mistakes rookie Net users make when they launch into cyberspace.

Your primary Internet tool will be your Web browser. Your browser is your looking glass to the Net. Two Web browsers dominate: Netscape's Navigator (now part of the "Communicator" suite of tools) and Microsoft's Internet Explorer. These two Net interfaces are changing the way we use our personal computers. We will help you become very comfortable with your browser. And, it doesn't matter anymore if you are on a Windows, Macintosh, or Unix computer system. Browsers work in a similar way on nearly every computer system.

Chapter 1 will familiarize you with the graphical user-interface tools you will need to use the Web. Chapter 2 gives you the skills to organize your cyber files and folders. Chapter 3 will orient you to the basics of your Web browser. Chapter 4 will help you interpret Internet addresses, so you will always know where you are going and where you have been. Chapter 5 gives you the knowledge to customize your browser to fit your own personal style. Chapter 6 is perhaps the most important chapter in Section 1. This chapter will help you pull important information from the Web and use it on your desktop.

Chapter 1	Quick Operating System Know-How	2
Chapter 2	Virtual Filing Cabinet: Save It for Later	15
Chapter 3	Through the Looking Glass: A Browser Primer . .	27
Chapter 4	WWWhat? Understanding Net Addresses	46
Chapter 5	Beyond the Looking Glass: Your Dream Browser.	57
Chapter 6	Bringing It Home: Downloading Files	68

Quick Operating System Know-How

Chapter Objectives:

In this chapter, you will learn some of the basic functions of an application window. After reading Chapter 1, you will be able to

1 use pull-down menus.

2 minimize, resize, and restore your application window.

3 use the scroll bars.

4 cut, copy, and paste.

Communicating with Your Computer

The Internet is improving the way we use our computers. A new Web-like interface is appearing on millions of new computer systems every year. Web-based operating systems and Net computers are making it easier and easier to find your way around the Internet. This chapter will introduce you to this user-friendly Web interface.

The activities in this chapter will provide good background knowledge, give you a little more familiarity with your Web-computer environment, and put your browser to good use as we go exploring. All of the lessons will be useful to you whenever you use the computer, not just when you're surfing the Internet.

If you are familiar with a **GUI**, this chapter will be very easy for you. GUI, pronounced "gooey," stands for **graphical user interface**, a system that allows users to communicate commands to the software by clicking on pictures or icons. Most of you are already working in either a Windows or a Macintosh environment. Both use GUI interfaces. Click a GUI icon (picture) with your mouse and something happens. For instance, click the Print icon, and your document will print. ■

Net Terms

graphical user interface (GUI)

network

network interface card (NIC)

peer-to-peer network

workgroup

client

server

server-client network

pull-down menu

toolbar

ellipses

dialog box

ARPANET

maximize button

zoom box

minimize button

taskbar

active server pages

click and drag

scroll bar

Internet service provider (ISP)

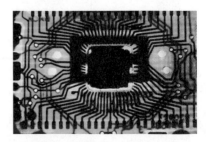

A Few Pull-Downs to Warm Up

Pull-down menus and toolbars are the easiest way to access the commands that make a program do something. A **pull-down menu** is a bar displayed usually at the top of the program screen that lists options from which you can select. Once you select an option by a mouse-click, a vertical list opens, giving you a choice of commands. A **toolbar** is a bar of GUI icons that usually provide one-click access to frequently used commands. A well-organized program will carefully place each option in a menu or toolbar, so that all are easy to remember and find. Figures 1.1a and 1.1b illustrate menus in Windows and on a Macintosh computer.

Menu options with **ellipses** (three little dots . . .) will pull up a dialog box when selected. A **dialog box** is a window that requires you to enter information before the software can execute a command. For example, the Open File Dialog Box asks you to specify the drive, directory, and file name for the program you want to open.

ACTIVITY

1.1

Objective:
In this lesson, you will learn to use pull-down menus.

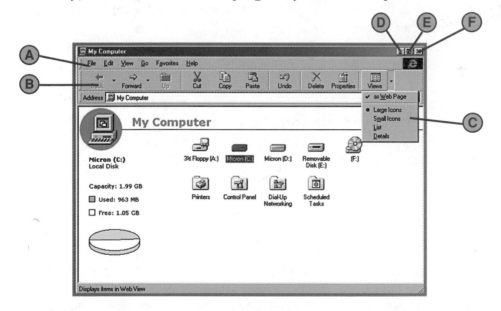

KEY

A	Menu Bar
B	Toolbar
C	Pull-Down Menu
D	Minimize
E	Maximize
F	Close

Figure 1.1a
Menu bar and toolbar in Windows Web View

KEY

A	Menu Bar
B	Toolbar
C	Pull-Down Menu
D	Zoom
E	Size
F	Quit

Figure 1.1b
Pull-down menus and toolbar on a Macintosh browser

Internet Explorer

Figure 1.2a
Internet Explorer icon

Netscape Communicator

Figure 1.2b
Netscape Communicator icon

Most Web software programs share at least three common pull-down menus. These are the File, Edit, and Help menus.

Let's look at a File menu before we go any further.

1. Open your browser by double-clicking its icon on your desktop, as shown in Figures 1.2a and 1.2b.

2. Using your mouse, move your pointer until it is over the *File* menu item on your menu bar.

3. Click on the word *File* to display the menu. As you move your mouse pointer around the menu, different options will highlight, and in some cases spring open. Notice how some menu items, usually with arrows, cause other submenus to appear. These are called "cascading" or "pop-out" menus.

4. You have several ways to close menus that are pulled down. You can
   a. click outside the menu list to "unclick" the menu.
   b. press ⟨Esc⟩ (in Windows).
   c. click or drag your mouse to the menu heading again and pick another option.
   d. select an option from the pull-down menu (this will carry out a command or open a new dialog box).

There are subtle differences between the way the Windows and Macintosh GUI interfaces work. However, if you can use one of these operating systems, you will have no trouble switching to the other if you need to.

NET FACT

How Networks Work

A **network** is a group of computers that can communicate or "talk" to each other through connections or links. This term is not limited to computers. In the business world, "networking" can refer to the process of making friends and meeting new people who may be beneficial to you or your company in the future.

In the computer world, a network of computers is linked together usually with some type of cabling and a **network interface card (NIC)**. A NIC is a circuit board that connects your computer to the other computers on the network, so that the computers can exchange information. Some networks are called **peer-to-peer networks**, which means that every computer on the network or in the workgroup has access to the resources of every other computer, including drives, files, and folders. A **workgroup** is a smaller network within the larger network. The computers of the people in the workgroup are linked together so that they can share resources to accomplish group tasks. Peer-to-peer networks are usually used in small offices of less than 10 computers.

Larger companies tend to use server-client networks. In a server-client network, each personal computer is a **client**. A **server** is a high-speed computer that stores information to be shared and provides it to requesting clients. A **server-client network,** then, is a network of clients sharing information distributed by servers. This is the type of network on which the Internet system is based. It is kind of like going to a fancy restaurant. You, the customer (or client), look at the menu and give your order to a waiter. The waiter takes the order to the chef (the server), who prepares meals for everyone who has ordered. The waiter then brings the meal back to you, the (by now) hungry client.

In Windows there is another way to access your pull-down menus. Did you notice that most menu items have one underlined letter? Let's see what they do.

5 Press and hold the ⟨Alt⟩ key and then the letter *F*.

6 You can use your arrow keys to cycle through the menu items.

7 To close the pull-down menu, press the ⟨Alt⟩ key again and let go.

You might ask, why not use your mouse? What happens if your mouse quits working? You'll be happy you learned this keystroke method.

8 Select the *File* menu and choose *Quit,* or *Exit.* The Macintosh command is usually Quit, as shown in Figure 1.1b on page 3. The Windows command is traditionally Exit, as illustrated in Figure 1.3.

NET TIP
Web Addresses

Note that current links to most Web sites presented in this book can be found on the Internet Concepts and Activities *Home Page. Choose* Resources *at* **computered.swep.com**. *Remember that a Web address may change at any time. An address given in this book as an example may no longer be valid. If this is so, either access the Home Page for the current link or do a search to find a similar site (see Chapter 9 for a discussion of search methods).*

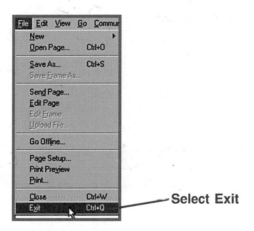

—— **Select Exit**

Figure 1.3
The File pull-down menu

THINKING ABOUT TECHNOLOGY

Think about your "network" of friends. What does each contribute to make your life better or easier? What do you contribute back to each of them? In what ways do you think networking (computers and people) might help the business world to run better? How can the Internet keep you in closer contact with your personal network of friends or future business contacts?

Internet Milestone

ARPANET

The forerunner of today's Internet was a 1960s project called **ARPANET**, the Advanced Research Projects Agency Network. This was a network established for military and scientific use. Its main purpose was to maintain communications in case of a nuclear war or a natural disaster that might destroy large sections of communication lines. The theory was that if any part of the network went down, the ARPANET could automatically reroute and keep at least part of the network "alive."

This theory was tested during the Gulf War. Despite precision bombing of key communication centers by the American and coalition forces, the Iraqis were able to maintain communications, thanks to an ARPANET-style computer network.

Today's Internet has inherited many of the survivalist technologies from ARPANET. These technologies help make the current Internet very durable.

ACTIVITY 1.2

Objective:
In this lesson, you will learn how to manipulate your application window.

Changing Your Window's Size

Application windows come in many shapes and sizes. You can change the size of many of them, but not all. Most application windows can be **maximized** or **zoomed** (enlarged to fill the screen), **minimized** (made much smaller), or somewhere in between. The buttons (also called "boxes") to control these operations are usually located in a corner of your Web browser window. The Windows buttons are shown in Figure 1.1a on page 3 and Figure 1.4a below. The Macintosh buttons are shown in Figure 1.1b on page 3.

Clicking the minimize button shrinks your window. In Windows, it shrinks the window down to a button and puts it on the taskbar, where it is out of the way, as shown in Figure 1.5. The **taskbar** is a toolbar that displays the applications (tasks) that you currently have running. Clicking on a taskbar button restores the application to its previous size.

A maximized window can take up the whole screen. The *close* button exits the program.

Figure 1.4a
From left to right: the minimize, maximize, and close buttons

Figure 1.5
The Windows taskbar with minimized applications

Click to reopen a minimized application.

1. With your Web browser open, click the *minimize* button in Windows or the *zoom* box on your Macintosh.

2. On the taskbar, click the button for your minimized application. On a Macintosh, resize your window with your zoom box again.

3. In Windows, after your application resizes, click on the *restore* button. The restore button looks like overlapping windows and is located be-

Net **Life** *The Browser Wars*

Netscape Communications Corporation and Microsoft have developed today's two most commonly used browsers: Netscape Navigator and Microsoft Internet Explorer. They have waged war on each other for years, each trying to dominate cyberspace. They compete by adding significant new features and browser support for their cyberspace products. When Microsoft entered the browser wars in 1995, it was significantly behind Netscape, which controlled over 80 percent of the browser market. To cut into that lead, Microsoft has added some significant innovations, like **active server pages**. These are Web pages that allow you to change their appearance. You can resize pictures and move things around, just like you can in your own computer files—only on Web pages! Active server pages are sure to make life on the Net more exciting than ever. If you want to know where our online lives are heading, keep your eye on Microsoft and Netscape.

tween the minimize and close buttons when the window is maximized. Restoring a window makes it slightly smaller. Clicking the maximize button makes the window full size again.

You can also resize a window by dragging the borders and corners.

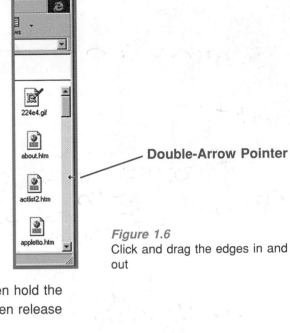

4 Move your pointer over one edge of your program window until it changes to a double-arrow cursor, as shown in Figure 1.6.

Double-Arrow Pointer

5 Click and drag the border to resize horizontally or vertically to any size you like. **Click and drag** means the use of a pointing device, such as a mouse, to latch onto an object on screen and move it to some other location. Place the pointer over the object you want to move—in this case, the border. Click the mouse button to grab it. Then hold the button down while you slide the object to its destination. Then release the mouse button.

Figure 1.6
Click and drag the edges in and out

6 Click a corner to resize the window in two directions at once, as shown in Figure 1.7.

7 Click and drag the edge to resize your window to any size.

Figure 1.7
Click and drag the lower corner in and out

8 When you are finished, click the *maximize* button to restore the window to its previous size.

Double-Arrow Pointer

9 Play with these options until you are comfortable with them.

THINKING ABOUT TECHNOLOGY

Think about all the ways you can change the appearance of your windows. Why might you want to change the "look" of your windows? What other ways would you like to change things on your computer screen? Check your computer's Help feature to see if you can do these things!

The Internet has been called a "Network of Networks." It is a system of local Networks that work together. No one owns the Internet. If no one owns it, then who controls it?

ACTIVITY

1.3

Objective:
In this lesson,
you will learn to use
the scroll bars.

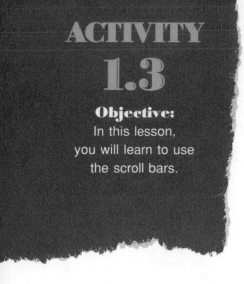

Scrolling Around

Scroll bars are helpful little tools. They are bars, with a small box in them, that appear along the side or bottom of open windows, or both, whenever there is too much information to show in one screen (see Figure 1.8). Clicking and dragging the small box allows you to slide around the window to view contents that were previously hidden. Scroll bars are smart enough to turn themselves off when all the contents of the window show on screen, so the scroll bars are not needed. You'll know when they're off because the arrow buttons will be grayed or the bar will disappear altogether.

If you are on a Web page and the scroll bars are enabled, try the following:

1 Click on the up or down (or the left or right) arrow once. How far did the page scroll?

2 Try clicking just above the down arrow. How far did the page scroll this time?

3 Now click and drag the rectangular box, or "floating bar," in the scroll bar. What happened this time?

All three scrolling methods are useful. Clicking on the arrow buttons scrolls the page a little bit at a time. Clicking in the scroll bar area "pages down" a screen full of information at a time. Using click and drag on the floating bar is a good way to skim quickly through a document.

NET FACT

How the Internet Works

In the Net Fact on page 4, we told you how networks work. The Internet is really the world's largest network. Computers from all over the world can share information.

Today's Internet is made up of a "backbone" of high-speed phone lines that carry computer data. Supercomputers located at different universities and businesses around the world are tied into this backbone structure. Other local educational systems and commercial **Internet service providers (ISPs)** can link their Web servers (remember what a server does?) to the supercomputers using specialized data phone lines. An ISP is a business that physically connects its customers to the Internet. When you buy Internet access from an ISP, you usually access their Web server through a modem connected to a phone line. How do *you* connect?

The World Wide Web is only part of the Internet. You can abbreviate the World Wide Web as WWW or W3, or you can just call it the Web. All cyber-geeks will know what you are talking about.

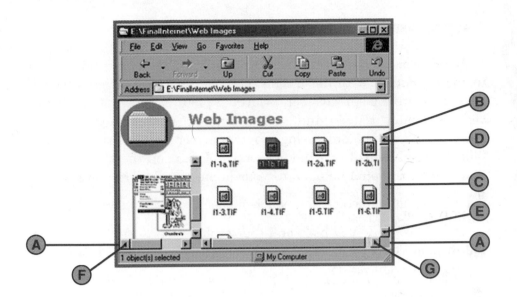

KEY

A Horizontal Scroll Bars
B Vertical Scroll Bar
C Floating Bar
D Up Arrow
E Down Arrow
F Left Arrow
G Right Arrow

Figure 1.8
This window has a bunch of scroll bars

THINKING ABOUT TECHNOLOGY

Why do you think scroll bars are necessary? Why not just limit the contents of a window to just what fits on the screen? Why do you think there are two horizontal scroll bars at the bottom of the screen shown in Figure 1.8? What might these two scroll bars allow you to do that one could not?

ACTIVITY 1.4

Objective:

In this lesson, you will learn to cut, copy, and paste.

NET TIP

Switching between Applications

Windows users already know how to switch between applications by using the taskbar. However, did you know about the keyboard shortcut? Try holding down the ⟨Alt⟩ key and then pressing ⟨Tab⟩. ⟨Tab⟩ will cycle through all of your open applications or documents until you select one by releasing the ⟨Alt⟩ key.

Macintosh users can easily switch from their Web browsers to their word processors by clicking the Application menu—you know, the little computer in the top right corner of the screen.

Copy and Paste

When you are out on the Web, you will find the copy and paste tools very useful. With these tools, you can select text from a Web page, cells from a spreadsheet, or even a picture, copy it to a virtual clipboard, and "paste" it into your document. Make sure your browser and a word processing program are both open. You can use WordPad or Notepad in Windows or SimpleText on the Macintosh. Your browser should be open to your home page before you start.

1. Open your word processor, and then open your Web browser. Your home page should appear.

2. In your Web browser, move your cursor over text you would like to copy. Any text will do.

3. Click and drag across the sentence or paragraph. Let go of the mouse button when you are finished selecting the material you want. The text should be highlighted as shown in Figure 1.9a in Internet Explorer and Figure 1.9b in Netscape Navigator.

4. From the *Edit* menu, choose *Copy,* as shown in Figures 1.9a and 1.9b, or press ⟨Ctrl⟩ + C in Windows or ⟨Apple⟩ + C on a Macintosh.

5. Switch to a new document window in your word processor or text editor.

6. On the *Edit* menu, choose *Paste* or use ⟨Ctrl⟩ + V in Windows or ⟨Apple⟩ + V on the Macintosh.

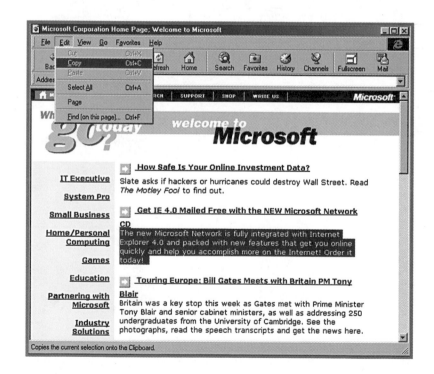

Figure 1.9a
Select text and copy in Internet Explorer

The text you selected in the browser now appears in your word processor or text editor, as shown in Figure 1.10. Remember that *Cut* removes your selection and needs to be repasted to save, while *Copy* maintains a copy in its original location.

Figure 1.9b
Select text and copy in Netscape Navigator

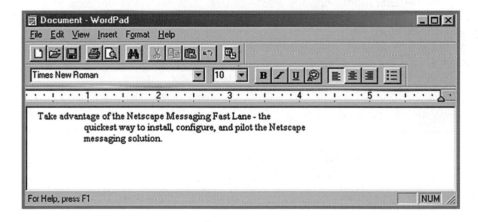

Figure 1.10
Paste text in your word processor or text editor

THINKING ABOUT TECHNOLOGY

In what ways have computers made life easier for you? How have they made it more difficult?

Net Ethics · *Using the Words of Others*

The Internet provides easy access to the ideas of others. As you can see in Activity 4.1, the Internet gives you the ability to cut and paste text or pictures into a document of your own in an instant. However, just because this information is easy to use, do not assume that you can present it to others as being your own. If you use the ideas of others in your own writing, you should include a note about where that information came from, just as if you had found it in a book. Why do you think it is unethical to present the ideas of others as being your own? What harm could result from doing this?

NET VOCABULARY

Define the following terms:

1. graphical user interface (GUI)

2. network

3. network interface card (NIC)

4. peer-to-peer network

5. workgroup

6. client

7. server

8. server-client network

9. pull-down menu

10. toolbar

11. ellipses

12. dialog box

13. ARPANET

14. maximize button

15. zoom box

16. minimize button

17. taskbar

18. active server pages

19. click and drag

20. scroll bar

21. Internet service provider (ISP)

NET REVIEW

Give a short answer to the following questions:

1. What is the Internet and how does it work?

2. Describe two ways that you can tell a computer program to do something.

3. Describe how you can change the shape of a window, using the click-and-drag method.

4. What tools would you use to put something from a Web page into your word-processing document? How do they work?

CREATE YOUR OWN PERSONAL NETWORK

You just started working at GreatApplications, Inc., a software company in Atlanta, Georgia. The first day on the job is always difficult and exciting. You quickly discover that you must depend on a number of other people to do your job effectively. You may need a report from the Marketing Department, statistics from Research & Development, a spreadsheet from the Accounting Department, or help from Network Support.

You quickly realize that you need to build a network of your own—a list of friends, colleagues, and business associates who can help you get your job done. Ultimately, a network of people will help you be a success at GreatApplications, Inc.

Build a network of school or business colleagues who can help you now and in the future. Interview at least five people. Fill out a Personal Network Contact Card for each person you interview. By the way, you must have a very diverse range of skills and interests in your group; so, interview people you don't know.

Personal Network Contact Card

Name of contact _____

Personal Web page address: http:// _____

Phone number _____ e-mail address _____

Interests _____

_____

Skills _____

Computer experience _____

Comments (How could this person be helpful?) _____

_____

Personal Network Contact Card

Name of contact _____

Personal Web page address: http:// _____

Phone number _____ e-mail address _____

Interests _____

_____

Skills _____

Computer experience _____

Comments (How could this person be helpful?) _____

_____

Net Ethics   *Sharing Personal Information*

When someone shares information with you, should you keep it confidential? When is it okay to share information you learn about another person? If people know that information they have shared with you in confidence is finding its way throughout GreatApplications, Inc., will they ever share with you again? How eager will they be to work with you in the future? What would *your* reaction be if someone were to break your confidence?

Personal Network Contact Card

Name of contact _____

Personal Web page address: http:// _____

Phone number _____ e-mail address _____

Interests _____

_____

Skills _____

Computer experience _____

Comments (How could this person be helpful?) _____

_____

Personal Network Contact Card

Name of contact _____

Personal Web page address: http:// _____

Phone number _____ e-mail address _____

Interests _____

_____

Skills _____

Computer experience _____

Comments (How could this person be helpful?) _____

_____

Personal Network Contact Card

Name of contact _____

Personal Web page address: http:// _____

Phone number _____ e-mail address _____

Interests _____

_____

Skills _____

Computer experience _____

Comments (How could this person be helpful?) _____

_____

NET PROJECT TEAMWORK Expanding Your Contacts

Form groups of three or four people. Do not group with your friends. Group with people that you perhaps have never talked to. Interview each other. Find out each person's skills, interests, and computer experience. Ask each of your new contacts, "How can we work together?" Create Personal Network Contact Cards for the newest members of your network!

WRITING ABOUT TECHNOLOGY Who Should Control the Information?

With what you know about the Internet at this point, write a 100-word answer, on a separate piece of paper, to one of the following questions:

Option 1. In your opinion, is it good or bad for so much information to be available to everyone? Give reasons to support your decision.

Option 2. How much control should the government have over Internet content? Should anyone have control over it? Support your position.

Option 3. How much do computers and the Net impact your life now? In what ways do you think that will change in the next 5 years? 10 years?

Virtual Filing Cabinet: Save It for Later

Chapter Objectives:

In this chapter, you will learn how to keep track of files you want to save. After reading Chapter 2, you will be able to

1 organize your computer using several file management functions.

2 make a new folder.

3 save and delete files.

Net Terms

files

data

folders

directories

drives

hard drive

network drives

File Transfer Protocol (FTP)

NSFNET

remote access

Organization—Computer Style

If you have ever had a school locker, you know how important a place it is. You can store your books and folders between classes. You can also store pens and pencils, a few pictures, and a few of your long-lost assignments.

Neat students arrange everything in logical order. Each class has its own notebook or folder, and all assignments are arranged by date or project title. Not-so-neat students simply throw one thing on top of another. Good luck trying to find today's assignment.

Your computer's hard drive is like your locker. It stores thousands of files. Some of those files run your computer's operating system, others run applications, and still others contain the data that you or someone else may have created, like the following:

- word processing files
- spreadsheet files
- database files
- CAD drawings
- graphics
- video files
- sound files
- Web pages

Imagine what an awful mess it would be if all of those files were thrown into random folders! With well over 200,000,000 computer devices expected to be on the Net by the year 2000, imagine what a chaotic place the Internet will be if Web users don't keep their files organized.

Computers don't like disorganization. They store information in different drives, folders or directories, and files. Just like you use folders and notebooks for different classes, the computer uses drives,

folders, and files to keep organized.

A typical Macintosh folder structure is pictured in Figure 2.1. A typical Windows Web view folder or directory organization is shown in Figure 2.2.

- **Files** are storage places for **data**, which are the pieces of information that a computer processes. Data can be in any form: numbers, text, images, and even voice and video. You can create files and name them using an application program.
- **Folders** or **directories** are simulated file folders that hold data, applications, and other folders. Folders are logical places to put related files.
- **Drives** are the storage places for data. A **hard drive** is the primary storage area on your computer. It offers a large storage capacity and fast retrieval.

It's important to understand the way computers store files, so that you can keep your own folders and drives organized. Windows computers assign each drive attached to it a letter. Floppy drives (where you insert the small recordable "floppy disks" you buy at the computer store) are usually assigned letters A or B. Hard drives (a computer often has several) start with the letters C and D. A CD-ROM drive might be assigned letter D, E, or F. Zip or Flash drives are usually drive E. **Network drives** (drives shared by a network of computers) are often assigned letters from F to Z and are treated the same as a hard drive.

As you will see in Activity 2.1, inside these drives you will find folders or directories. Inside directories you will find files of all kinds and additional folders. ■

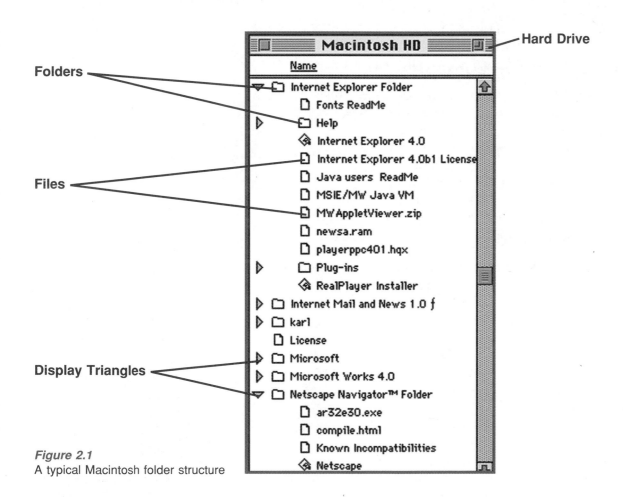

Folders

Files

Display Triangles

Hard Drive

Macintosh HD

Name

▽ 🗁 Internet Explorer Folder
  🗋 Fonts ReadMe
▷ 🗁 Help
  ◈ Internet Explorer 4.0
  🗋 Internet Explorer 4.0b1 License
  🗋 Java users ReadMe
  🗋 MSIE/MW Java VM
  🗋 MW AppletViewer.zip
  🗋 newsa.ram
  🗋 playerppc401.hqx
▷ 🗀 Plug-ins
  ◈ RealPlayer Installer
▷ 🗀 Internet Mail and News 1.0 ƒ
▷ 🗀 karl
  🗋 License
▷ 🗀 Microsoft
▷ 🗀 Microsoft Works 4.0
▽ 🗀 Netscape Navigator™ Folder
  🗋 ar32e30.exe
  🗋 compile.html
  🗋 Known Incompatibilities
  ◈ Netscape

Figure 2.1
A typical Macintosh folder structure

Exploring Explorer and Finder

You can learn a lot about people and their computers by looking at how they organize their folders and files. To understand how data is organized, look at the Windows Explorer illustration (Figure 2.2). It is split into two panes. On the right side is a list of available drives, which can include network drives, floppy and hard disk drives, removable Zip drives, and CD-ROM drives. On the left side is more detailed information about any drives, folders, and files that have been selected. These features are not exclusive to Windows. The Macintosh operating system has very similar features.

ACTIVITY 2.1

Objective:
In this lesson, you will learn how to identify drives, folders, directories, and files and how to change the file display status.

Tree File and Folder Organization

Views Pull-Down Menu

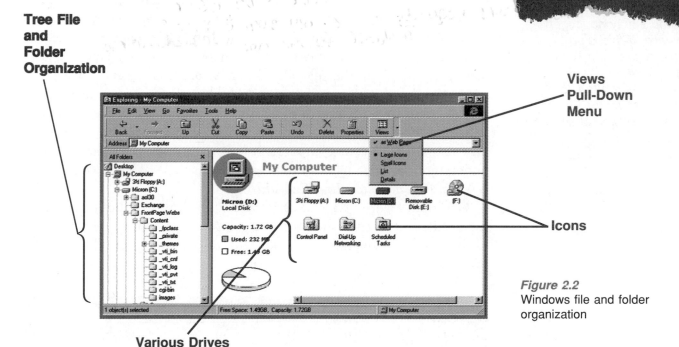

Icons

Various Drives and Folders

Figure 2.2
Windows file and folder organization

Try making the following changes on your computer:

1 For Windows users, click the *Start* button →*Programs* →*Windows Explorer.* Macintosh users, double-click on your Macintosh *Hard Drive* icon.

2 Move your mouse pointer to the + symbol next to the Windows folder and click it. On the Macintosh, click on the little triangles. The folder branches out, revealing more folders and files inside. Use your scroll bar to view some of the files in the folder.

3 In Windows, click the *Views* button on the toolbar and try the following options:
- As Web Page
- Large Icons
- Small Icons
- List
- Details

NET TIP
Windows Explorer

Windows users: Take a minute to notice how the Explorer screen is organized. Identify the following elements on your screen:
A Menu Bar
B Drive Selection Window
C Left Pane—displays available drives and folders
D Right Pane—displays drives, subdirectories or folders, files and other information

---

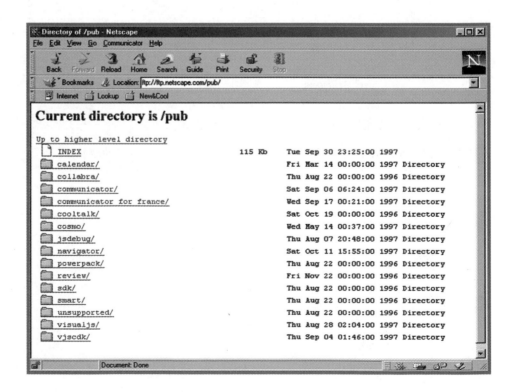

NET TIP
Web Addresses

Note that current links to most Web sites presented in this book can be found on the Internet Concepts and Activities *Home Page. Choose* Resources *at* **computered.swep.com**. *Remember that a Web address may change at any time. An address given in this book as an example may no longer be valid. If this is so, either access the Home Page for the current link or do a search to find a similar site (see Chapter 9 for a discussion of search methods).*

④ With your Macintosh, click the *Views* button in your Finder and try the following options:

- By Small Icon
- By Icon
- By Name
- By Size
- By Kind
- By Label
- By Date

Now that you know how your computer is organized, it is time to visit the Web and view how Net computers are organized. Figure 2.3 shows a typical file structure organization on a server on the World Wide Web. Figure 2.3a shows the folders at the Netscape FTP site, and Figure 2.3b shows folders at the Microsoft FTP site. You can download files from these locations. These are not as pretty or as fancy as regular Web pages, but underneath, all computers use this file or directory structure to organize information. And, the structure is essentially the same as the drive, folder, and file structure that you just examined on your computer. Knowing this will really help you understand how file names are organized on the WWW in *Chapter 4: WWWhat? Understanding Net Addresses.*

Compare Figures 2.1, 2.2, 2.3a, and 2.3b. How are the file structures different or the same in these samples? Remember, the first example is on a Macintosh; the second, on Windows; and the last

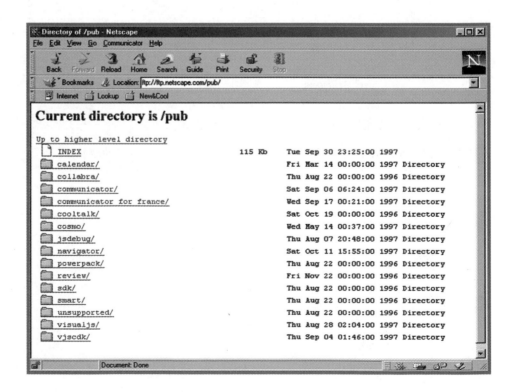

Figure 2.3a
Internet file and folder organization on the Netscape FTP site

two, on the Internet, probably residing on a powerful Unix, SUN, or WindowsNT computer. While these computers are very different, how are they similar?

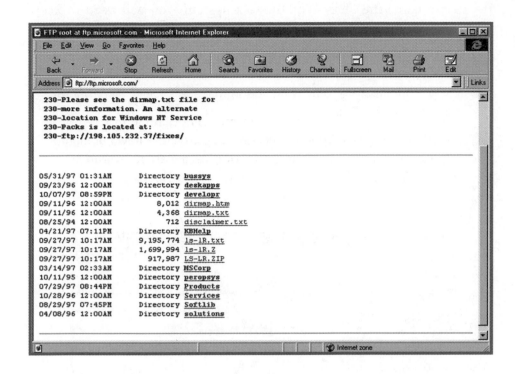

Figure 2.3b
Internet file and folder organization on the Microsoft FTP site

THINKING ABOUT TECHNOLOGY

What methods do you use to keep your schoolwork organized? Are they effective? What could you do to improve your organization? Can a computer help?

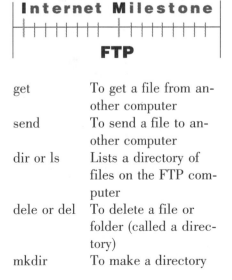

Internet Milestone

FTP

Knowing how files and folders (directories) are organized is very helpful when you are on the Net. When you move files from one computer to another, you will generally use a program called **FTP**, which is short for **File Transfer Protocol**. FTP is a program that allows you to move files from place to place on the Internet. FTP is older than the Web and goes back to the earliest days of Net history. In the old days, you used text commands to move files, including:

get	To get a file from another computer
send	To send a file to another computer
dir or ls	Lists a directory of files on the FTP computer
dele or del	To delete a file or folder (called a directory)
mkdir	To make a directory

A typical text command for FTP might be:

- open ftp.netscape.com
- get 30cd501.exe

Today you can drag and drop the files from one computer to another by clicking and dragging the files you want with your mouse...more on this in *Chapter 6: Bringing It Home: Downloading Files.*

ACTIVITY

2.2

Objective:

In this lesson, you will learn to create a new folder to store files.

Creating Folders

Let's make a folder to store your Web information. These instructions apply to Windows 95, Windows 98, and Macintosh computers. If you are using the older Windows 3.1 system, you will need to keep your folder names shorter—eight characters or less.

1 Click your *C drive* icon in Windows Explorer or your *Hard Drive* icon on the Macintosh.

Note: Your instructor may want you to make this folder somewhere other than in the C drive.

2 Select *File→New→Folder* in Windows Explorer, as shown in Figure 2.4a, or select *File→New Folder* on your Macintosh, as shown in Figure 2.4b.

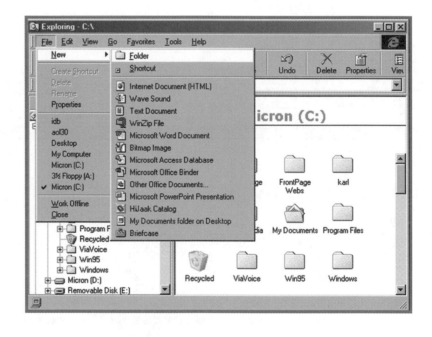

Figure 2.4a
Create a new folder in Windows

Figure 2.4b
Create a new folder on a Macintosh

3 Name the new folder with your name, as shown in Figure 2.5. Press ⟨Enter⟩ or ⟨Return⟩ when you are finished naming your new folder.

Figure 2.5
Name your folder and press enter or return

4 Double click your new folder to open it.

5 Create a new folder inside the *Your Name* folder.

6 Name this folder *Temp.*

7 Create another folder. Name this folder *ToTrash.*

Folders are a good way to organize your Internet discoveries. You might have a folder for pictures and another folder for text files. Another folder could be for programs you've downloaded. How you organize is up to you, but make sure that you can find things when you need them!

THINKING ABOUT TECHNOLOGY

Let's assume that you can put all the TV shows you like to watch into folders, so that you can pull one out and watch it anytime the mood strikes. If you pile them all together, then you will have to look through them at random for the one you want, cutting into your viewing time. How would you group the shows into folders so that you can find the one you want quickly? What would you name each folder? What folders could you put inside the larger folders to further subdivide your selections?

Internet Milestone

NSFNET

During the 1980s, the National Science Foundation (NSF) funded a system of supercomputers called **NSFNET** for scientific research. Located at several universities throughout the United States, these supercomputers were accessible to scientists through **remote access** from around the country. There are several kinds of remote access, but the most common is to dial in to another computer with a modem over phone lines.

As more and more scientists began working together over the NSFNET, other agencies like NASA and the Department of Energy (DOE) added their resources to the expanding network. Other schools and agencies eventually joined the infant Internet, laying the foundations for today's vast Internet superhighway of information.

ACTIVITY 2.3

Objective:
In this lesson, you will learn to save and delete files.

NET TIP
Crash!

Be absolutely certain you know what is in each file you want to move or delete. If you move a system or program file to a different location, you may cause your computer to crash. Since this tends to aggravate your teachers, it would be best to avoid the situation.

Saving, Moving, and Deleting Files

Net users tend to accumulate lots of extra files. It is important to know how to save information, but it is equally important to delete files and folders that you no longer use. Saving and deleting are simple tasks when you know what to do. It's also something that you will do all the time.

First, you need to create a file that you can practice with. If you get stuck on a step, ask for help. These are very common skills. Someone sitting nearby will know how to do them. Don't be shy—ask for help if you need it.

1. Open your word processor or text editor.

2. Type the words *"This is a test"* and save your file with the name *Practice* in the *Temp* folder you created in Activity 2.2.

3. Close your word processor or text editor.

4. Double click on the *My Computer* icon in Windows or on the *Hard Drive* icon on the Macintosh and locate the *Your Name* folder.

5. Double click the *Your Name* folder so you can see the *Temp* folder.

6. Open the *Temp* folder.

7. Select the *Practice* file and move it to the *ToTrash* folder that you just created in the previous activity. You can do this in a number of ways, depending on the computer system you have. Normally, you can click and drag the file from one folder to another. On some newer systems, you can also select the *Practice* file, click the *Cut* button, and then *Paste* the file to the new folder. (See Figure 2.6.)

8. Delete the *Practice* file. There are several ways to do this.
   • Click and drag the file to the *Trash* (Macintosh) or to the *Recycling Bin* (Windows).
   • Select the file and press the *Delete* button in Windows. (See Figure 2.6.)

9. Delete the *ToTrash* folder the same way you deleted the *Practice* file.

You have created a file, saved it, moved it, and deleted it, all in a few easy steps. This is an important skill, since Web users tend to download lots of files. Most of these files become obsolete after a few days and need to be deleted.

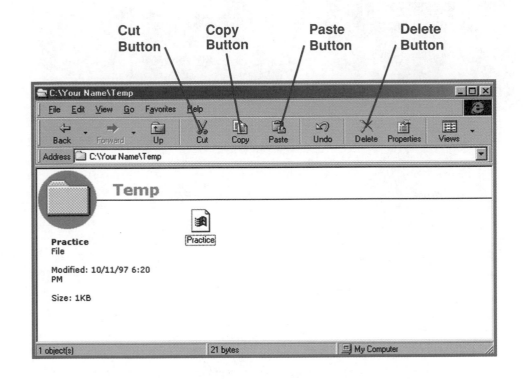

Figure 2.6
Select delete in Windows
Web view

THINKING ABOUT TECHNOLOGY

The Internet's basic structure was put together by people wanting to share information freely. That is why there are billions and billions of files in cyberspace. You may or may not have "rights" to save and delete files on your network computer at school or work or on most computers on the Net. What problems might arise in a network environment if everyone has unlimited access to all files? What if everyone could delete any files they wanted to delete on the Net? How can problems be prevented?

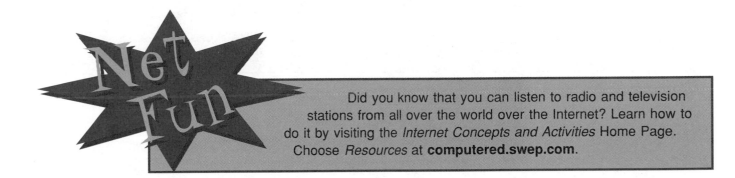

Did you know that you can listen to radio and television stations from all over the world over the Internet? Learn how to do it by visiting the *Internet Concepts and Activities* Home Page. Choose *Resources* at **computered.swep.com**.

NET VOCABULARY

Define the following terms:

1. files

2. data

3. folders

4. directories

5. drives

6. hard drive

7. network drives

8. File Transfer Protocol (FTP)

9. NSFNET

10. remote access

NET REVIEW

Give a short answer to the following questions:

1. In the chapter opener, your hard drive was compared to your locker at school. Assume that you need to explain how a hard drive stores files to a friend who knows nothing about computers. How would you do it? Compare it to something that helps you understand a computer's storage system.

2. Name three options in the Views menu of your Windows Explorer or Macintosh Finder, and explain what each option does to the "look" of the files and folders organization.

3. Explain how to create a new folder.

4. Why is it important to move only files that YOU have created?

ORGANIZE YOUR VIRTUAL FILING CABINET

Your first day on the job at Great Applications, Inc. has been a busy one. You have met the people in all the cubicles around you. Most of them are very friendly and helpful. The IS (information systems) manager (a nicer title for the company's head computer geek) has introduced you to the network resources and explained where you can and can't save files. You even got a directory on the network with your name on it, in which you can save your work files. You realize that you need to get organized quickly.

You have started creating a network of colleagues and vendors you'll be working with. The next thing you need to do is organize your virtual filing cabinet, so that you can store and retrieve the information you need to do your job well.

In the *Your Name* folder, you are going to create several subfolders to store the different types of information and documents you will be creating and accumulating in your work.

1. Create a file entitled *Notes.*
2. Create a file entitled *Research.*
3. Inside the *Research* folder, create two subfolders entitled: *Personal Research* and *Company Research.* (Windows 3.1 users must keep the names shorter, like *PerRes* and *ComRes.*)
4. Go back one folder to the *Your Name* folder and create two more folders called *Contacts* and *WebPages.*
5. Open the *WebPages* folder and create another folder called *Images.*

Your final tree structure should look like Figure 2.7 in Windows Explorer.

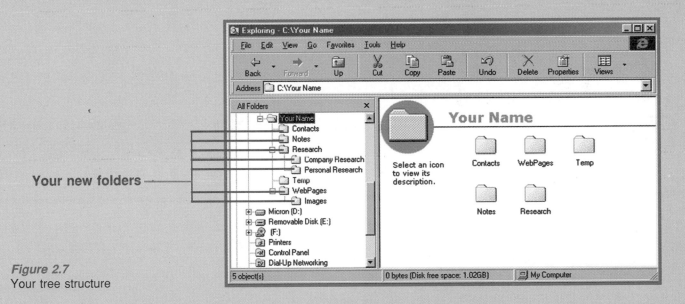

Your new folders

Figure 2.7
Your tree structure

6. Write a brief note thanking the IS people for helping you get set up in your new cubicle. (Hint: You want to be good friends with the IS department.) Use the technique you learned to create a new file and to save it properly. Two sentences will do. File the document in the *Notes* folder as *Thank You to IS.* (Windows 3.1 users use the name *ThanksIS.*)
7. Return to Chapter 1's Net Project. Create an electronic file of the data you collected from the five contacts. File this data in your *Contacts* folder.

Sharing Files with Others

Most companies have an area on their local network where employees can share files. Do some investigation with your instructor and find this common or sharable area on your school's local network. Ask for permission to use this common area to share assignments and files. Create a folder with a name that describes your team in this sharable area on the network. (Note: If you don't have a common network folder, you will need to share files with your team the old fashioned way—with floppy disks.)

Try a test file. Have all members of the team create an electronic Personal Network Contact Card for themselves, just like those found in the Net Project in Chapter 1. You can create your card electronically in something like Notepad or SimpleText. Save your team data into your common team network folder. Open your common folder and download the contact cards from the other team members to your personal *Contacts* folder. On some networks, you may need to open the file first and then use the *Save As* command to save the file to your *Contacts* folder. Report back to your team about whether or not you were successful. Discuss whatever problems occur and try to find a solution to any file-sharing problems you have.

WRITING ABOUT TECHNOLOGY **Getting Organized**

With what you know about computer organization, write a 100-word answer, on a separate piece of paper, to one of the following questions:

Option 1. Discuss why organization is so important on a computer, on a network, and on the Internet.

Option 2. Explain how your computer is organized. Describe its file, folder, and drive organization.

Option 3. Explain step-by-step how to create a folder and subfolder on your computer system.

Option 4. Research and explain step-by-step how you would change the name of an existing folder.

Through the Looking Glass:
A Browser Primer

Chapter Objectives:

In this chapter, you will learn about the different parts of your browser application. After reading Chapter 3, you will be able to

1 describe the different parts of a browser window.

2 use the Address box to enter Internet addresses.

3 use the toolbar.

4 view your history option and move back and forth between pages you've visited.

5 enter URLs.

6 organize your favorites/bookmarks.

Net Terms

user-friendly

Mosaic

hypertext

Address/Location box

Uniform Resource Locator (URL)

home page

netizen

History folder

virus

cookie

search services

Not So Long Ago in Cyberville

Not so long ago, the Internet was limited to scientists and military personnel who used difficult text-based commands to navigate from computer to computer. Since it was not **user-friendly**, only someone who really needed to use the Internet would use it.

In 1993, the world's first well-known browser, **Mosaic**, was developed at the National Center for Supercomputing Applications by students and professors of the University of Illinois in Urbana-Champaign. What Mosaic did was put a graphical user interface on the World Wide Web. Pictures could be seen using the browser, and different sites on the Internet could be linked using hypertext.

Hypertext is kind of like hyperspace on Star Trek. You click a mouse and suddenly you're transported from one place to another. Hypertext can jump you from one point on a page to another point on the same page—hardly exciting—or from one site in your hometown to a computer in Hong Kong—much more fun.

Part of getting the most out of the Internet is knowing how to use the tools at your disposal, such as the browser.

ACTIVITY

3.1

Objective:

In this lesson, you will learn to identify the different parts of a browser window.

Introduce Yourself to a Web Browser

Take a look at Figures 3.1a and 3.1b. Before you read the Net Tip, see if you can identify the lettered sections. Then look at the Net Tip to see how many you got right! When you feel like you can label a similar picture on a quiz (hint-hint), move on to Activity 3.2.

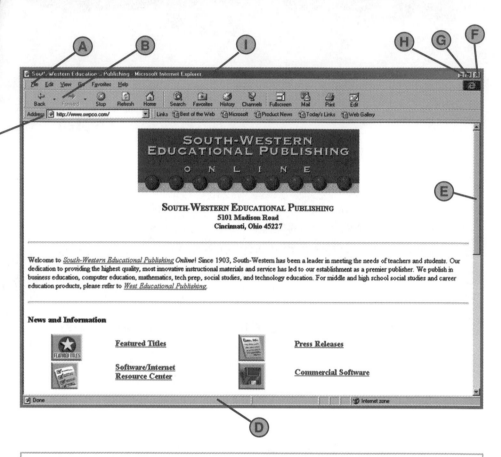

Figure 3.1a
Internet Explorer window

NET TIP

Browser Window Elements

Here are the labels for the parts of the browser windows shown in Figures 3.1a and 3.1b. Notice that the key elements are similar in Netscape and Internet Explorer.

A Pull-Down Menus
B Toolbar
C Address Box
D Status Bar
E Scroll Bar
F Close Button
G Maximize Button
H Minimize Button
I Title Bar

Why do you think that Netscape Navigator and Internet Explorer are so much alike?

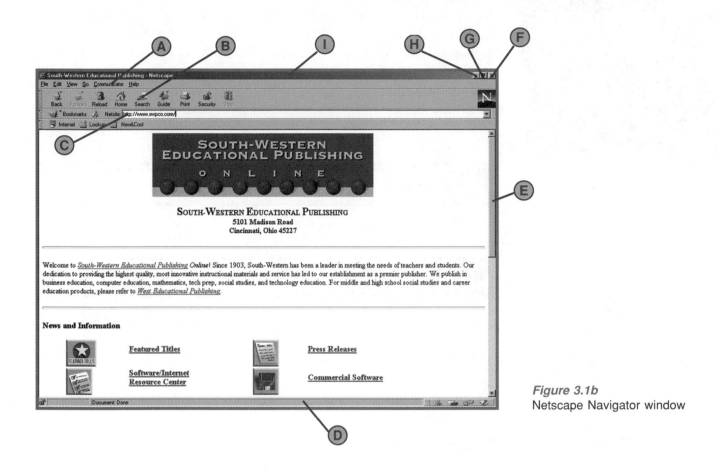

Figure 3.1b
Netscape Navigator window

Born at the National Center for Supercomputing Applications, Mosaic became the "killer application" that made the World Wide Web popular. Perhaps it is true that without Mosaic, the average person may never have heard of the WWW.

But, Mosaic was important in other ways. First, Mark Andreessen, the co-founder of Netscape, was a programmer on the original Mosaic software. Many of the other Mosaic programmers went to work for Netscape in 1994. Second, Mosaic never really died. A company called Spry bought the rights for the original Mosaic code. They improved Mosaic, then sold their code to Microsoft, which used it as the basis for the original Internet Explorer.

Mosaic's place in history is secure, even if its place on your desktop has been relinquished to more powerful browsers.

ACTIVITY
3.2

Objective:
In this lesson, you will learn how to use the Address box to enter Internet addresses.

"Address Please"—Entering Internet Addresses

Probably the most important part of the browser window, besides the application window itself, is the **Address** or **Location box** shown in Figures 3.2a and 3.2b. This box is the place where you enter the **Uniform Resource Locator (URL)**—the Web address of the Internet site you want to visit. URLs are the Internet addressing scheme that defines the route to a site. The URL is used as the initial access to a resource.

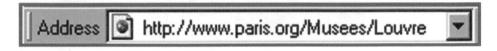

Figures 3.2a and 3.2b
The address (in Explorer) and location (in Navigator) boxes

The address box is your ticket to adventure, knowledge, and fun! Let's get to know how to use it right away.

1. Open your browser. If you need to connect to your Internet service provider, do so at this time.

2. Click once in the *Address* box. The URL already in the box is the address of your **home page**, which is a page of information on the Web that appears in your browser window. Often called a "Web page," the home page is usually the first page that users see when they go to a Web site. The home page address should be highlighted at this point. If it isn't, point at it and click once to highlight the URL. Press ⟨Delete⟩ to remove the address in the window.

3. Key in the following address: *www.yahoo.com*

4. Use the scroll bar to take a quick look at the list of topics available at Yahoo! We're going to come back to Yahoo! in a later lesson.

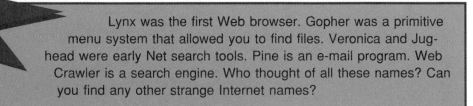

Lynx was the first Web browser. Gopher was a primitive menu system that allowed you to find files. Veronica and Jughead were early Net search tools. Pine is an e-mail program. Web Crawler is a search engine. Who thought of all these names? Can you find any other strange Internet names?

Another way to access the address window is through the File pull-down menu, as shown in Figure 3.3.

1. Click *File → Open* (in IE) or *Open Page* (in NN).

2. Key in the address:
   www.paris.org/Musees/Louvre/

3. When you are finished keying, press the ⟨Enter⟩ key or click the *OK* button. What do you see?

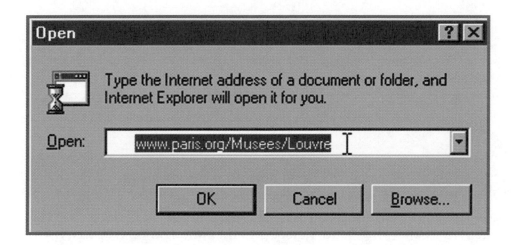

Figure 3.3
Accessing the address box in Internet Explorer

THINKING ABOUT TECHNOLOGY

Think about the address where you live. What information do the different parts of your home address supply? Why is this information needed? How is the information conveyed by your home address similar to the kind of information conveyed in a URL for a Web site?

ACTIVITY

3.3

Objective:
In this lesson, you will
learn to use the
toolbar buttons.

The Toolbar: One-Click Commands

The toolbar gives you one-click access to the tools you will use most. Although the organization is a little different between Navigator and Explorer, the most important buttons, including Back, Forward, Home, Stop, Refresh/Reload, Search/Find, and Print, are all easily accessible no matter which browser you use. (See Figures 3.4a and 3.4b.)

Figure 3.4a
Netscape Navigator's toolbar
Figure 3.4b
Internet Explorer's toolbar

Using the Back and Forward buttons is a good way to move quickly between a few of the most recent pages you've visited. If you've continued from Activity 3.2, then you can jump right into this activity. Otherwise, go to Yahoo! and then the Louvre (see Activity 3.2). Your browser window should look similar to Figure 3.5.

1 At the Musee du Louvre home page, click the hyperlink to the *Louvre Floor Plan*.

Figure 3.5
The Paris Musee du Louvre home page

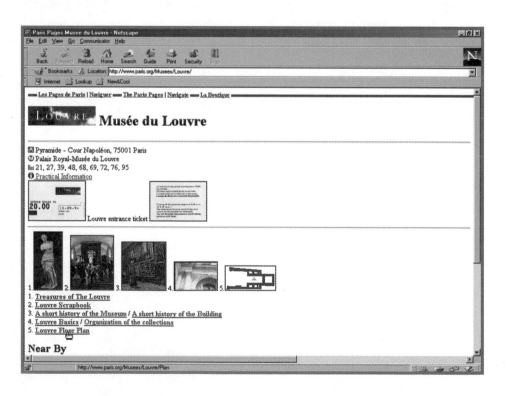

2 Click the *Back* button to take you back to the Musee du Louvre home page. (The Forward buttons and Back buttons for Navigator and Explorer are shown in Figures 3.6 and 3.7.)

3 Click the *Forward* button to move to the Louvre Floor Plan page.

4 Click the *Back* button twice, and you will move back to the Yahoo! home page.

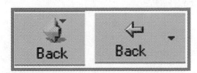

Figure 3.6
Back buttons

The Home button (pictured in Figure 3.8 for both browsers) is a good button to use when you want to jump quickly to your home page. While we go back to the home page, let's learn about the Refresh/Reload and Stop buttons.

The Stop button (Figure 3.9) is good to use when a page is loading too slowly or when you've changed your mind and want to follow a different link.

The Refresh/Reload button (Figure 3.10) can be used to reload a page if you stopped in the middle of loading it, or if you want to update it to see if any changes have been made since you last accessed it. Now follow steps 5–7.

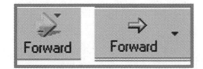

Figure 3.7
Forward buttons

5 Click the *Home* button.

6 As soon as your home page starts loading (but before it's finished), click the *Stop* button. Your page may have some text on it, but probably won't have many of the graphics completely loaded.

7 Click the *Refresh* (or *Reload*) button to reload the page.

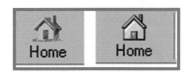

Figure 3.8
Home buttons

Figure 3.9
Stop buttons

Thinking About Technology

What do the Forward and Back buttons do for you? In what situations might they not be so useful? When you clicked the hyperlink to go to the Louvre Floor Plan, what happened to the URL in the Address box? Why?

Figure 3.10
Refresh/reload buttons

Log On, and On, and On

The Net has never been more popular than it is today. This popularity has led to traffic jams and tie-ups on the Information Superhighway interstate. In the old days, you were charged for every minute you were online. Today, for a monthly fee, you can stay online for an unlimited amount of time. This change in price structure has brought costs down and has made it easier and easier to get your Net work done. However, if you are finished for the day, take some pressure off your Internet service provider and log off. This will free up a line for another **netizen** (Net citizen, or fellow traveler on the Information Superhighway) who may have been trying to get connected. It is only polite to disconnect when you are truly finished for the day.

Help eliminate superhighway traffic jams, and log out when you are finished surfing.

ACTIVITY 3.4

Objective:
In this lesson, you will learn to use the History folder to return to a previously visited Internet page.

Using the History Folder

In Activity 3.3, you learned how to use the Back and Forward buttons. The Back button is good to use when the page you are looking for is only a few steps back, but not so great when the page is a few hundred steps back or three days ago. Fortunately, your browser keeps track of the most recent URLs you've visited in a **History folder**.

Although the History folders show different amounts of information, depending on which browser you use, both show the name of the page that appears in your Title Bar and the Internet address of the sites you visited. This should be enough to help you find what you're looking for, even when your history list starts numbering in the hundreds.

1. Click the *History* button in IE or click *Communicator → History* in NN.

2. Scroll through the list and find *Yahoo!* (See Figures 3.11 and 3.12.)

3. Double click the entry to jump to it in your browser.

Net Ethics   *Good Cookies, Bad Cookies*

Whenever you connect to a network of any kind, including the Internet, you are open to viruses and other "infections." A **virus** is a program written to alter the functioning of the infected computer. The virus code is buried within an existing program. When that program is executed, the virus code is activated and attaches copies of itself to other programs in the system. The virus may be a prank that causes a small annoyance, or it may be malicious vandalism that destroys programs and data. A hacker can plant a virus "bomb" that can destroy the programs on your hard drive.

You may be unaware that every time you visit a Web site, a "cookie" can be saved to your hard drive. A **cookie** is information created by some Web sites that enables the site to collect information about you. It provides a way for the Web server to keep track of your patterns and preferences and, with the cooperation of your Web browser, to store them on your own hard disk in a *cookies.txt* file. This data can add to the database of the company providing the cookie. This information can help the company adjust its advertising campaigns or even send you information or junk mail about things you might be interested in. Some cookie-like programs are powerful enough to read every file on your hard drive and scan every software program on your system.

Check the list of files on your hard drive. Do you have a *cookies.txt* file? Do companies have a right to put something on your hard drive without your knowledge? Do they have a right to scan your hard drive? Is this an invasion of privacy? If you request a file from a server on the Web, should you be obligated to provide some kind of information back to the sender? What rules govern this type of information gathering? Is your hard drive like your home and can only be invaded with a warrant from a court? Or is your hard drive just another part of the Internet, open for all who have the technology to scan and read? What benefits might cookies have for the receiver?

Discuss these issues with your team.

Figure 3.11
The History option in Internet Explorer

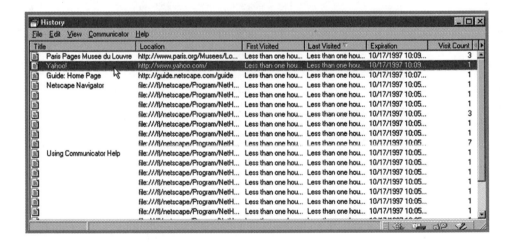

Figure 3.12
The History option in Netscape Navigator

THINKING ABOUT TECHNOLOGY

Check your History folder. (If you don't have much history yet, check a friend's history folder.) Do your travels show any patterns that reveal your (or your friend's) interests or habits? Why might such information be of interest to companies operating sites on the Web?

ACTIVITY

3.5

Objective:
In this lesson, you will learn to add URLs to a Favorites or Bookmarks list.

Adding to Favorites/Bookmarks

Throughout your Internet travels, you will want to return to many sites. Fortunately, there is an easy way to keep track of these URLs. Netscape Navigator uses the term "Bookmarks," whereas Internet Explorer uses "Favorites." They both do the same thing—keep track of the URLs you visit so you don't have to. In this activity, we'll bookmark a few search services that we'll be making good use of in Section 3. **Search services**, such as Yahoo! and AltaVista, are Web sites that maintain a directory database of other Web sites. You can look for information on the Web by entering a search criterion, such as a key word, where indicated on the search service Web site.

1 Open your browser.

2 In the Address box, key in *www.yahoo.com*. Your screen should look similar to Figure 3.13.

3 In IE, click the *Favorites* menu. In NN, click *Communicator → Bookmarks*.

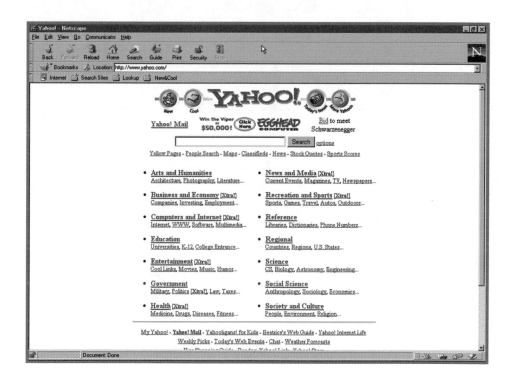

Figure 3.13
The Yahoo! home page

Internet Milestone

YAHOO!

The brainchild of David Filo and Jerry Yang, two Ph.D. candidates in Electrical Engineering at Stanford University in 1994, Yahoo! quickly became a model for other search engines on the Internet. David and Jerry wanted a way to keep track of their favorite sites on the Internet. They designed Yahoo! as a search tool that maintains a directory database of other Web sites. This easy-to-use search service has become a popular starting point for nearly everyone looking for information on the Internet.

④ Select *Add to Favorites* (IE) or *Add Bookmark* (NN). (See Figure 3.14.)

⑤ Click *OK* to add Yahoo!'s address to your Favorites list.

⑥ Let's add one more. Enter the address
www.altavista.digital.com

⑦ You are now at the AltaVista home page, which may look similar to Figure 3.15. (Remember, a Web site can change at any time—whenever

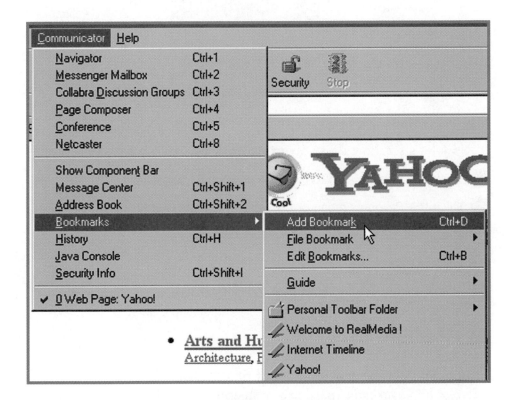

Figure 3.14
Add to bookmarks in NN

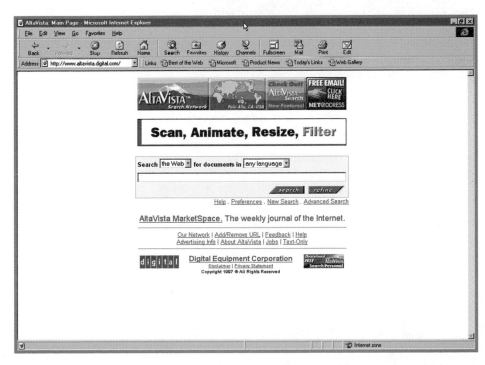

Figure 3.15
The AltaVista home page

the site operator wants to change it!) AltaVista is one of the most powerful search services on the Internet. It's also a site we'll frequently visit; so, add it to your favorites by repeating steps 3–5. (See Figure 3.16.)

Figure 3.16
Add to Favorites in IE

Now let's see how those favorites work when we want to go back.

1 Click the *Home* button to return to your home page.

2 Click the *Favorites* menu or click the *Bookmark* button.

3 Drag your pointer down until Yahoo! is highlighted.

4 Click on *Yahoo!*

5 Notice that in your address box, Yahoo!'s URL appears, and your browser whisks you back to Yahoo!, no questions asked.

6 Try again with *AltaVista.*

Bookmarks can save you a lot of time. Obviously, *www.yahoo.com* isn't that hard to keep track of, but wait until you find an address that won't fit in the address box!

THINKING ABOUT TECHNOLOGY

Think of something that interests you and that you might like to look up on the Web for more information. What one or two key words best describe what you are looking for? One way that search services work is by searching for key words supplied by the user. The more specific you can be in selecting your key words, the better!

Cleaning House—Organizing Your Favorites

ACTIVITY

3.6

Objective:
In this lesson, you will learn how to organize your Favorites folder.

The more Favorites you add, the more cluttered your Favorites list is going to become. (See Figure 3.17a.) You need a way to organize the Favorites list so that you can quickly find exactly what you need, when you need it.

Let's start with the first two bookmarks you added. Both of the bookmarks are links to search service Web sites; so, you have an obvious place to put both of these links—in a folder called *Search Sites*.

1 Click the *Favorites* or *Bookmarks* button.

2 Select *Organize Favorites* or *Edit Bookmarks*.

3 For IE, on the toolbar, click the *New Folder* button or right click (click with your right mouse button) in the window pane and select *New → Folder* from the pop-up menu. In NN, click *File* and then *New Folder,* as shown in Figure 3.17b.

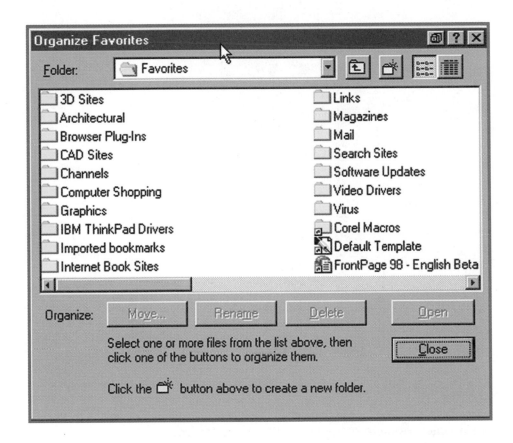

Figure 3.17a
Organizing favorites

④ Give the *New Folder* a name. *Search Sites* would be a good name for this folder.

⑤ Click and drag the *Yahoo!* URL to the *Search Sites* folder.

⑥ Click and drag the *AltaVista* URL to the *Search Sites* folder.

If you are doing research for a business class, you may want to bookmark sites into a folder called *Business.* For sites related to your favorite football team, a folder called *Sports* or *Football* will do nicely. The most important thing to remember is to organize your folder system so that it makes sense to you.

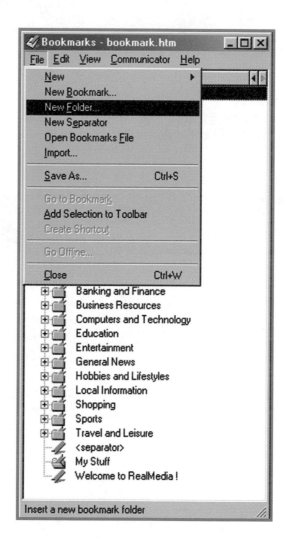

Figure 3.17b
Create a new bookmark folder

THINKING ABOUT TECHNOLOGY

A Favorites list sure makes it easy to organize your favorite sites. If you could go anywhere on vacation, where would you go? If you were to go on the Web to learn more about your fantasy vacation destination, what kinds of information might you find? What folders would you need to keep track of the sites, so you can find them when you can actually take that vacation?

CHAPTER REVIEW

NET VOCABULARY

Define the following terms:

1. *user-friendly*

2. *Mosaic*

3. *hypertext*

4. *Address/Location box*

5. *Uniform Resource Locator (URL)*

6. *home page*

7. *netizen*

8. *History folder*

9. *virus*

10. *cookie*

11. *search services*

Label the lettered parts of this browser:

A _____

B _____

C _____

D _____

E _____

F _____

G _____

H _____

I _____

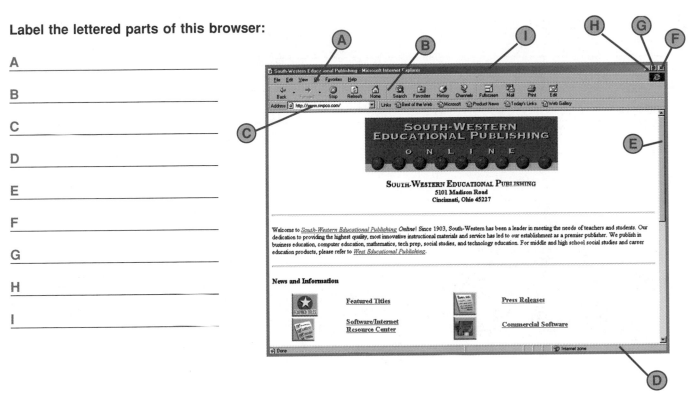

NET REVIEW

Give a short answer to the following questions:

1. *How do you locate a specific address or URL with a Web browser?*

_____

_____

_____

_____

2. What is the purpose of the Reload or Refresh button?

_____

_____

_____

_____

3. How can the history feature help you?

_____

_____

_____

_____

4. What do "bookmarks" or "favorites" do for you?

_____

_____

_____

_____

_____

Ever forget a Zip code? Forget the two-digit code for Guam? Is AL the abbreviation for Alabama or Alaska? Want to know how to address a letter to your brother in the Army? Check out the U.S. Postal Service Web page at *http://www.usps.gov.*

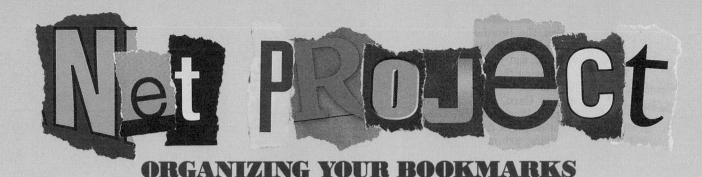

ORGANIZING YOUR BOOKMARKS

As you get settled into your job at *Great Applications, Inc.,* you learn that a good deal of your time on the job will be spent doing research on the Internet. Because you will be visiting so many sites, you know how important it will be to keep track of the sites you will want to return to. It is also important that you demonstrate your ability to be organized.

Starting at Yahoo!, find 25 Web sites of interest to you and bookmark them. However, it isn't as simple as clicking randomly on 25 links. You must organize your 25 Web pages into no more than 5 topics, as explained in Activity 3.6. You can only have five URLs or Web sites in each category. Here is an example:

Search Services

Title	URL
1. AltaVista	www.altavista.com
2. Excite	www.excite.com
3. Yahoo!	www.yahoo.com
4. WebCrawler	www.webcrawler.com
5. Northern Light	www.northernlight.com

Use what you have learned so far to organize your bookmarks. You may want to explore in depth some of the different options not covered in this book. Remember, you can always get help from the Help menu.

Use the following planning pages to organize your five subcategories. Then, transfer your work to your Web browser.

First Category

Title	URL
1.	
2.	
3.	
4.	
5.	

Second Category

Title	URL
1.	
2.	
3.	
4.	
5.	

Third Category

Title	URL
1.	
2.	
3.	
4.	
5.	

Fourth Category

Title	URL
1.	
2.	
3.	
4.	
5.	

Fifth Category

Title	URL
1.	
2.	
3.	
4.	
5.	

NET PROJECT TEAMWORK   Narrowing Down Your Lists

Sometimes when you work alone, you get stuck, fall into a cyber rut, and can't locate the best sites for each category you are researching. Teamwork can improve your selection of titles and Web addresses.

In teams of three or four, review the lists you just created individually. Compile a team list including only the best URLs or Web addresses in each category. (If someone in the group knows HTML, have him or her create a simple Web page that will display the group work.) If you have a common place to save information, place your list in this common folder on your local network. Make sure all team members have a backup copy of this combined data in their personal WebPages folders.

WRITING ABOUT TECHNOLOGY Browsers, Bookmarks, and the Net

With what you know about the Net and Web browsers, write a 100-word answer, on a separate piece of paper, to one of the following questions:

Option 1. How is the organization of your favorites or bookmarks like the organization of the files and folders on your computer's hard drive?

Option 2. In your opinion, which is the best Web browser? Why?

Option 3. Explain, step-by-step, the process of finding a Web site or a specific Web page on the World Wide Web.

Option 4. Try several Web search services. Which provides you with the best Information? What are the strengths and weaknesses of the search service you have selected?

Option 5. Many people say they can't live without the Net. However, most people on the planet have never seen or used the Net. How important do you think the Web is in the personal life of the average individual?

CHAPTER 4

WWWhat? Understanding Net Addresses

Chapter Objectives:

In this chapter, you'll learn how Internet addresses are put together. After reading Chapter 4, you will be able to

1. identify and use hyperlinks.

2. explain Internet addresses.

3. explain domain names.

4. find IP or Internet Protocol numbers.

Net Terms

hyperlink

HyperText Markup Language (HTML)

newbies

protocol

Web servers

HyperText Transport Protocol (HTTP)

InterNIC (Internet Network Information Center)

domain name

IP (Internet Protocol number)

Domain Naming System (DNS) computer

Hyper About Hyperlinks

The world seems to have gone hyper—hyperlinked, that is. A **hyperlink** is a link between one object and another. The link is displayed either as text or as an icon. On World Wide Web pages, a text hyperlink displays as underlined text, typically in a different color, and a graphical hyperlink is a small image or picture. Hyperlinks made the Web popular by giving it an easy point-and-click interface. Hyperlinks allow you to point your cursor over underlined text or a picture, click once, and before you know it, you've jumped or linked to another page.

In this chapter, we'll show you how hyperlinks actually

work. This is important, because you will probably be on the Web a great deal during your business career and in school.

Because of its popularity, the Internet is attracting big business. Indeed, Web addresses seem to be the hottest thing in advertising. You'll find them in ads in your favorite magazine, on TV, even on the radio. Unfortunately, a Web address is sometimes long and it isn't always the easiest thing in the world to remember. This is especially true if you don't understand the different parts that make up a Web address. Let's take apart a Web address and identify the different pieces.

Understanding Hyperlinks

Objective:
In this lesson, you will
learn how to
use hyperlinks.

Because the Internet is easy to use, it is popular with **newbies** (people who have never used the Internet). Hyperlinks have a lot to do with this.

In the old days, before GUI interfaces, information was only available through difficult-to-use text-based commands. Today, however, the Net is as simple as point and click—no need to key long strings of text.

1 Start your Internet browser by double clicking its icon on your desktop.

2 Revisit the Louvre at *www.paris.org/Musees/Louvre/*. You will see pictures, regular text, and text that is underlined and colored differently.

3 Move your pointer over the different elements of your browser window.

4 When your pointer turns into a pointing finger, as shown in Figure 4.1, you've found a hyperlink. Remember that pictures and words can be links.

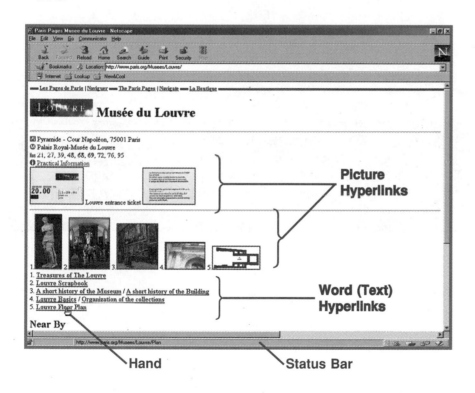

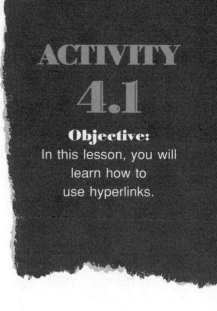

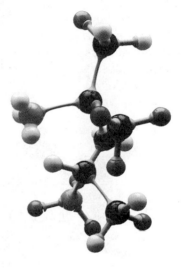

Figure 4.1
Pictures and text can all be links

NET FACT

How Hyperlinks Work

Hyperlinks work because of hidden **HTML (HyperText Markup Language)** commands that exist on Web pages. HTML is the standard document format used on the World Wide Web. The HTML commands define how the Web page will look, including text styles, graphic artwork, and hyperlinks to other documents on the Web. The commands you can't see that make a hyperlink work are similar to this:

⟨A HREF=“http://www.disney.com”)Click to go to the Disney Web site⟨/A⟩

This link appears on your screen like this:

Click to go to the Disney Web site

As you can see, the Web address (URL) *http://www.disney.com* is important in the command. Knowing how URLs work is essential to understanding how links work.

NET TIP
Web Addresses

Note that current links to most Web sites presented in this book can be found on the Internet Concepts and Activities *Home Page. Choose* Resources *at* **computered.swep.com**. *Remember that a Web address may change at any time. An address given in this book as an example may no longer be valid. If this is so, either access the Home Page for the current link or do a search to find a similar site (see Chapter 9 for a discussion of search methods).*

5 With the pointer over a hyperlink, look in the status bar on your browser. It will display the address of the hyperlink.

6 Move your pointer to another hyperlink. Notice the change in the status bar.

7 Pick a hyperlink on the page and click it once.

8 Your browser will take you to the new address.

THINKING ABOUT TECHNOLOGY

What do you think of the Internet's interface? Is it simple enough for anyone to use? Could it be improved? How?

Net Fun

Ever lose your top like Mount St. Helens or Dante's Peak? Which one is real? Mount St. Helens or Dante's Peak? Find out by visiting Volcano World at *http://volcano.und.nodak.edu/vw.html* or key *Volcanos, Mount St. Helens OR Dante's Peak* into a search engine.

Understanding Internet Addresses

A street address helps someone looking for a business or a residence by narrowing the search to a state, to a city, to a particular area of the city (using the Zip code), to a certain street, and, finally, to a specific location on the street.

A real address has at least five parts: ①a name, ②a street address, ③a city, ④a state, and ⑤a zip code.

①*John Doe*

②*1234 Anywhere Street*

③*Santa Clause,* ④*CA* ⑤*09876*

As you learned in Chapter 3, Internet addresses are called "URLs" (pronounced "Earls"), which stands for Uniform Resource Locator. URLs serve the same purpose as street addresses—they organize the computers on the Internet so that no two have the same address.

Here is a sample URL. The circled numbers are for reference.
①*http://*②*www.somewhere.edu/*③*thisis/apath/toa/*④*file.html*

① The first part of a URL identifies the **protocol** that the computers use to talk to each other. "Protocol" is a communications system used to transfer data over networks. It is like a language that both computers can speak and understand.

② The second part of a URL is the Web server or host computer where the page is located. **Web servers** are host computers on the Internet that allow others to access their drives, folders, and files. They accept requests from Web browsers to transmit HTML pages and other stored files.

③ The path name tells the server where the file is found. The slashes (/) represent folders, just like those on your computer. To get to the file, the Web server looks in several folders, like the mail carrier weaving through the streets to get from the post office to your house.

④ The last part of a URL is the actual file name you are trying to find. Most of the time it will be an HTML file.

❶ Analyze this address. Explain to a friend or another student the four parts of the URL.
http://www.disney.com/mickey/friends/pluto.html

THINKING ABOUT TECHNOLOGY

Think about the fantastic number of business URLs that must be on the Web now. What happens if two or three businesses want the same URL? What if *www.mcdonalds.com* would fit a large restaurant chain or a shoe repair business in Lubbock, Texas? Who resolves this conflict? Go on to Activity 4.3 and find out!

ACTIVITY 4.2

Objective:
In this lesson, you will learn to identify the different parts of an Internet address.

NET FACT

The Protocols of the Internet

The Internet uses many protocols to allow computers to share information. The most important of these is **HTTP**, which stands for **HyperText Transport Protocol**. HTTP is the communications protocol used to connect to servers on the World Wide Web. Its primary function is to establish a connection with a server and transmit HTML pages to the client browser. Addresses of Web sites begin with an http:// prefix. Other protocols are FTP for File Transfer Protocol, NEWS for Usenet news groups, and GOPHER (a transfer protocol used mainly when the Web was more text-based).

ACTIVITY

4.3

Objective:
In this lesson, you will
learn the meaning
of domain names.

Internet Domain Names

The "Thinking About Technology" section for Activity 4.2 asked you to think about what might happen if more than one company wanted the same Internet address. Who decides who gets what address? In this activity you will visit InterNIC, the people responsible for all Internet addresses.

InterNIC, or the ***INTER*net Network *Information Center***, is the organization that assigns and registers Internet domain names. InterNIC explains a **domain name** as follows:

> . . . a description of a computer's "location" on the Internet. It contains a few components, separated by a period ("dot"). Reading a simple domain name
>
> widget.example.com
>
> from left to right (most specific to least specific), the first item (*widget*) is the name of the host computer itself, or the hostname. The next item (*example*) is the second-level domain name, and is registered by an organization or entity with InterNIC Registration Services. The last item (*com*) is a top-level domain name, and describes the purpose of the organization or entity who owns the second-level name. A domain name may include other components between the hostname and the second-level domain name; these are called subdomains.
>
> In an e-mail address, the domain name follows the @ symbol, and often consists only of a second-level domain and top-level domain name (*example.com*).
>
> *Source:* From InterNIC Web site *http://rs.internic.net/faq/def_domain.html*, accessed 10/24/97.

Anyone can register with the InterNIC for a second-level domain name—businesses, organizations, or individuals. However, there is a fee for having one's own second-level domain name. In the address *www.mcdonalds.com,* "mcdonalds" is the second-level domain name registered by the McDonald's restaurant chain (not a shoe repair business in Lubbock). The "www" designates the World Wide Web as the host.

Understanding domain names will help you identify the type of information you are likely to receive from a certain site. For example, the top-level domain names tell you what kind of entity owns that domain. The traditional and most common top-level domain names are:

.com *Commercial institutions or businesses*

.edu *Educational institutions*

.gov *Government sites*

.mil *Military sites*

.net *Network gateways*

.org *Organizations*

Countries have top-level codes as well, but they aren't seen often.
Here are a few:

.us   United States   .fr   France

.ca   Canada   .ja   Japan

1 Let's see who owns what names on the Web. Enter the following URL:

   http://rs.internic.net/rs-internic.html

2 Scroll down and click on the *Whois* link, as shown in Figure 4.2.

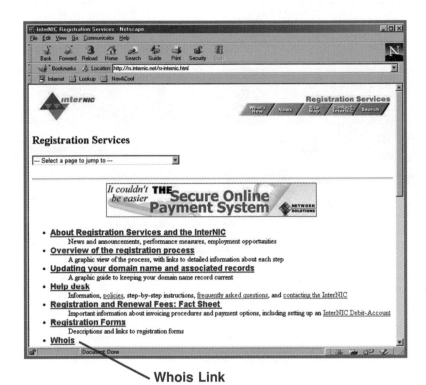

Whois Link

Figure 4.2
InterNIC registration service
Web page

New Top-Level Names

   InterNIC is considering other proposed top-level domain names. Can you guess what these domain names are? Match the following domain names and meanings.

.arts   ____   **A.**   *Businesses and firms*

.firm   ____   **B.**   *Businesses that sell goods*

.info   ____   **C.**   *Individuals*

.nom   ____   **D.**   *Arts and entertainment*

.rec   ____   **E.**   *Information provider*

.store ____   **F.**   *Recreation and entertainment*

.web   ____   **G.**   *Web activities*

3 Key the following domain names into the site's search box, as shown in Figure 4.3, and see who owns these names.

Domain name	Owner	IP number
disney.com		
nbc.com		
cbs.com		
fox.com		
espn.com		

Type domain name and press Enter or Return.

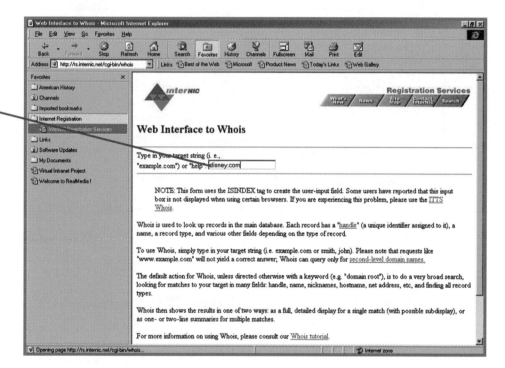

Figure 4.3
InterNIC page showing domain name owner

Net Ethics One Domain, Two Domains, Three Domains, More

Domain names must be unique. In other words, there can be only one *www.disney.com* on the Internet planet. Only one *www.abc.com* can exist in cyberspace. Only one *www.cbs.com* can be found.

But what if Mary Disney registers the domain name *www.disney.com*? Can she hold onto that name, even if The Walt Disney Company seems to be a more logical owner?

Many people have deliberately registered domain names that major companies are likely to want. The registration may have cost a few hundred dollars. They then sold the names to the companies at several thousand or even tens of thousands of dollars.

Is this ethical? For example, should Mary Disney be able to keep her domain name if she wants to—especially since she got it first? Who should argue copyright disputes regarding domain names on the Net? What if Mary Disney is a travel agent who specializes in tours to DisneyWorld? Should she be able to use the Disney name to promote her business? If she pays $100 for the name, can she sell the domain name *www.disney.com* to anyone she likes for $10,000, $100,000, or even $1,000,000?

Discuss this issue with your team.

Domain Names and Computer Numbers

A domain name is an address, not unlike the address used by the postal service to find your home among the millions of homes around the world. Web addresses locate specific computers from the millions and millions of Web servers on the Internet. Take this popular address: *www.disney.com.* But hold on a second! Computers use numbers to communicate. So, how does this work?

A domain name like *www.disney.com* points specifically to a computer whose number (called an **IP** or **Internet Protocol number**) may be something like 208.232.91.5. No other computer on the Internet can use that same number. When you want to visit the Disney Web site, you key in the domain name *www.disney.com.* A special **Domain Naming System (DNS) computer** looks up the name and matches it with its assigned number. Then, off you go, winging your way through numbered cyberspace to the correct computer, namely: 208.232.91.5.

4 When the answer appears, enter the owner and one IP number associated with the name, as shown in Figure 4.4.

Owner

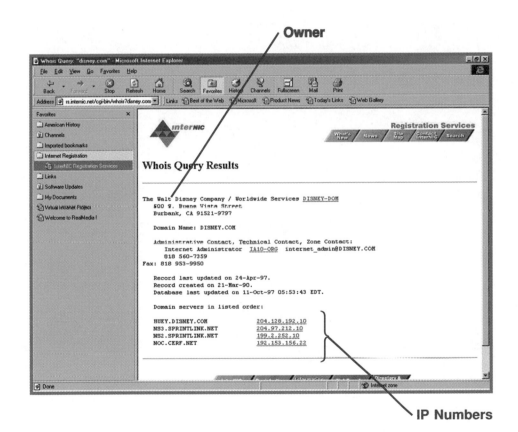

IP Numbers

Figure 4.4
Locate the owner and an IP number

THINKING ABOUT TECHNOLOGY

Some top-level domains, like *.com*, are beginning to fill up. Alternative domain names, like *.store*, are in the works. Think of some other domain names (or categories) that would help decongest the Internet. Remember, top-level domain names should describe the purpose of the organization.

CHAPTER Review

NET VOCABULARY

Define the following terms:

1. *hyperlink*

2. *HyperText Markup Language (HTML)*

3. *newbies*

4. *protocol*

5. *Web servers*

6. *HyperText Transport Protocol (HTTP)*

7. *InterNIC (Internet Network Information Center)*

8. *domain name*

9. *IP (Internet Protocol number)*

10. *Domain Naming System (DNS) computer*

NET REVIEW

Identify the different parts of the following URLs:

1. *http://www.thomson.com/swpco/*

2. *http://home.netscape.com/*

3. *http://www.paris.org/Musees/Louvre/*

4. *http://www.cs.indiana.edu/docproject/zen/zen-1.0_3.html*

5. *http://www.netlinks.net/netlinks/spot1.html*

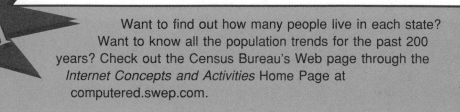

Want to find out how many people live in each state? Want to know all the population trends for the past 200 years? Check out the Census Bureau's Web page through the *Internet Concepts and Activities* Home Page at computered.swep.com.

START YOUR URL COLLECTION

Your first project at Great Applications, Inc. is to do a little homework on what other companies are doing on the Internet. To do that, you first need to collect some Web addresses. Using resources you have at home or in your library's periodical section, collect a list of URLs. You will need to find addresses in several different categories to get a broad view of the information available. Try to find URLs for companies in each area on the chart.

Source of address	URL	Company name	IP number (if available)
Automotive			
Technology/computers			
News/information			
Home shopping			
Food/beverage			
Entertainment			

Collecting URLs Together

Instead of finding all the URLs for the chart yourself, get together with your team and divide up the topics among team members. Team members should note the two most interesting sites they find for their assigned topic and view these sites with the team.

Top-Level Domain Names for Other Countries

The international office of Great Applications, Inc. has written you an e-mail asking for the top-level domain names of the following countries. You know the easy ones, like France = .fr and the United States = .us. But the following four are a problem. Search *http://rs.internic.net/rs-internic.html* for the following top-level domain names:

1. Kuwait   =
2. Kyrgzstan =
3. Nigeria   =
4. Zambia   =

The Impact of the Web

With what you know about business and the Internet, give a 100-word answer, on a separate piece of paper, to one of the following questions:

Option 1. How important is it for businesses to have an Internet site? Why do you think it is or isn't important?

Option 2. Is the Internet really a tool for business or is it just for entertainment? Give examples to support your answer.

Option 3. How do you think the Web is changing the way we work? Give examples.

Option 4. How has the Web changed the way we interact with one another? Is the change good or bad? Give examples.

CHAPTER 5

Beyond the Looking Glass: Your Dream Browser

Chapter Objectives:

In this chapter, you will learn how to customize your Internet browser. After reading Chapter 5, you will be able to

1. turn the toolbar and status bar on and off.

2. change font sizes and styles.

3. change colors of fonts, hyperlinks, and background.

4. turn multimedia options on and off.

Net Terms

interface

operating system (OS)

toggle

list box

Your Personal Interface

What if you were told that you could not have any pictures or decorations in your room or office? Your "space" wouldn't be personal, would it? Your work and living areas don't seem like your own until you turn them into your personal space.

Before graphical interfaces, programs were not easy to learn. To perform the simplest task, you had to memorize keyboard commands. There were no button bars or menus. However, as more and more people began using computers as a tool, they demanded simpler, more intuitive interfaces. User-friendly programs were born.

An **interface** is the way you interact with a computer program—how you tell it what to do. The interface includes toolbars, pull-down menus, title bars, and dialog boxes.

Since you are the one who is going to sit in front of your browser day after day, you might want to personalize it a little, make it "yours." Let's get started! ■

ACTIVITY
5.1

Objective:
In this lesson, you will learn to change toolbar settings.

Toggling the Toolbar and Status Bar

As you learned in Chapter 1, the graphical user interface allows you to surf the Net by pointing and clicking with a mouse. What could be easier?

With top-quality software, you can customize your interface to fit your needs and likes. For example, you can change the way your Web browser displays hypertext links, or you can turn off the toolbars and status bar to increase your browser window size. Try the optional settings listed below on your browser.

NOTE: *Windows and Macintosh browsers are becoming more and more alike. However, each version of the software will have slight differences. If you don't have the exact version pictured here, you can probably still figure out from the directions below how to accomplish these actions in your version.*

Internet Explorer toolbar settings for Windows:

1. Click the *Fullscreen* icon pictured in Figure 5.1. Presto! The toolbar shrinks, the menus disappear, and the address and links toolbars vanish, giving you maximum screen "real-estate" to view the Web.

2. Click the *Fullscreen* icon again to restore the previous settings.

Internet Explorer menu settings for Windows and Macintosh:

1. Click the *View* menu. Windows users should click the *Toolbars* option in the View menu to see a cascading menu, similar to the one in Figure 5.2a. Macintosh users may see the toolbar list immediately, as shown in Figure 5.2b. The options in the toolbars list are toggles. A **toggle** is a control that allows you to alternate between two options. In this case, the options are "on" or "off." A checkmark shows that the option is on. If no checkmark appears next to the option, then the option is off.

Figure 5.1
The Fullscreen icon in IE 4.0

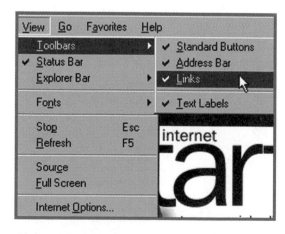

Figure 5.2a
Windows toolbar toggles in IE 4.0

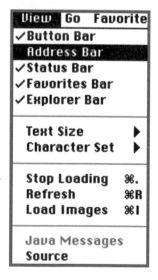

Figure 5.2b
Macintosh toolbar toggles in IE 4.0

The Windows maximize button that you learned about in Chapter 1 is also a toggle. When the window is full size, clicking the button makes the window smaller. Click the maximize button again, and the window returns to full size. So, the button is a toggle, because it allows you to alternate between two options, full size and reduced size.

2 Click each item on and off and see what effect the change has on the look of your browser.

Netscape Navigator collapse toolbar settings for Windows and Macintosh:

Figure 5.3
Collapsing toolbars in NN 4.02

1 You can collapse a toolbar by clicking the *arrow* button on the left side of the toolbar, as displayed in Figure 5.3. This doesn't turn the toolbar off; it puts it out of the way.

2 Click the *collapsed arrow* to expand the toolbar to full size, as shown in Figure 5.4.

Netscape Navigator menu settings for Windows and Macintosh:

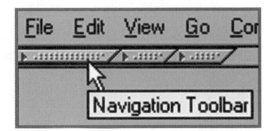

1 Click the *View* menu.

2 The toggles give you the option to hide or show the different toolbars. The menu updates itself to indicate the current status of each toolbar. Select *View → Hide Location Toolbar*, as shown in Figure 5.5, to turn off the location toolbar. Notice how your screen changes.

Figure 5.4
Expanding toolbars in NN 4.02

3 Select *View → Show Location Toolbar* to turn it on again.

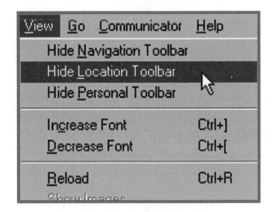

Figure 5.5
Hiding toolbars in NN 4.02

THiNKiNG ABOUT TECHNOLOGY

You just learned that a toggle allows you to alternate between two options. Think of other examples of "toggles" in your life. For example, the answers on a true-false exam are like toggles—each answer is either true or false. What other examples can you think of?

Objective:

In this lesson, you will learn how to change font sizes and styles.

Changing Font Options

Most Web pages use your browser's defaults to display fonts, background colors, and hyperlinks. However, you can personalize the settings on your browser to suit your taste. Remember that some Web pages will override your settings by specifying certain different fonts or color schemes.

NOTE: *Follow the directions for the browser you are using. Variations will occur for older and newer browsers. If these steps do not fit your unique browser, use the Help feature to learn how to accomplish these tasks.*

Changing font size in IE 4.0 (beginner):

1. In Windows, locate the *Font* button on your toolbar and choose *Medium*, or select *View → Fonts* and click the setting for *Medium* from the dialog box. (See Figure 5.6.) On a Macintosh, click the *Text Smaller* or *Text Larger* buttons on your toolbar, or select *View → Text Size* followed by *Medium*. (Flip back to Figure 5.2b, on page 58, to see the Macintosh View menu.)

2. Select *Largest* from the pop-up menu.

3. Select *View → Fonts → Medium* to restore the font size.

Changing font settings in IE 4.0 (advanced):

1. Select *View → Internet Options*. (Note: On a Macintosh, you can choose *Character Set* from the *View* menu and make your font selection.)

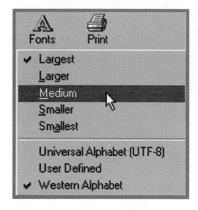

Figure 5.6
Changing font size in IE 4.0

2. On the *General* tab, click the *Fonts* button.

3. Click the *down arrow* next to the *Proportional font* box to display a list of font options. A list of options that you can scroll through to make a selection is called a **list box**.

4. Select a font from the list, as shown in Figure 5.7.

5. Click the *OK* button to close the Fonts dialog box.

6. Click the *OK* button to close the Internet Options dialog box. Notice how the type on your browser page changed.

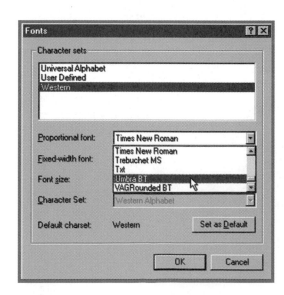

Figure 5.7
Changing font styles in IE 4.0

Changing font size in NN 4.02 for Windows and Macintosh (beginner):

1. Select *View → Increase Font* to view the Font options. (See Figure 5.8.)

2. Change the font and the size of the font and view the impact of the change on your Web browser display.

Changing font size in NN 4.02 for Windows and Macintosh (advanced):

1. Select *Edit → Preferences.*

2. Click the + or the triangle next to *Appearance* to branch out the appearance options.

3. Click the *Fonts* option, as shown in Figure 5.9.

4. In the *Variable Width Font* list box, select a font.

5. Select a font size from the *Size* list box.

6. Click the *OK* button to close the Preferences dialog box.

Figure 5.8
Changing font size in NN 4.02

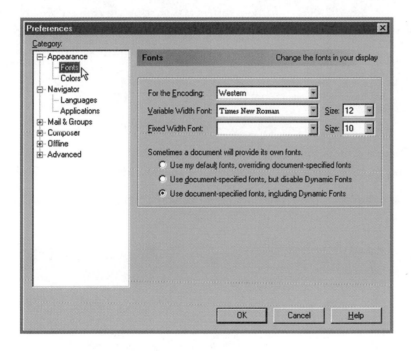

Figure 5.9
Changing font styles in NN 4.02

THINKING ABOUT TECHNOLOGY

Font sizes and styles affect the way a reader receives the message. For example, look at all the different font sizes and styles in this book. Why do you think some of these were selected? How does, say, bold type affect the message? If you were designing a Web page or overhead transparencies for a presentation, what would you consider in selecting font sizes and styles for different parts of your message?

ACTIVITY

5.3

Objective:
In this lesson, you will learn how to change colors of fonts, hyperlinks, and background.

Changing Colors

You can also change the color of many items in the browser window, including hyperlinks, fonts, and the background.

Changing colors in IE 4.0:

1 Select *View → Internet Options* in Windows. On a Macintosh, select *Edit → Preferences* and click on *Browser Display*.

2 Click the *Colors* button.

3 Click the *color swatch* button next to each option to select any color you like. (See Figure 5.10.)

NOTE: *In Windows you must uncheck* Use Windows colors *to change the text and background options. Also, if you have been to a site, a hyperlink to that page from any other page on the Web will be colored with the* Visited *color. Hyperlinks you haven't followed will display the* Unvisited *color. It's a good idea to keep these colors different. The* Hover *option will highlight a hyperlink when your cursor is over it.*

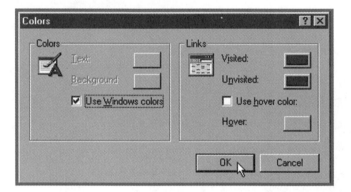

Figure 5.10
Changing color schemes in IE 4.0

Changing colors in NN 4.02:

1 Select *Edit → Preferences*.

2 Double click *Appearances* or click once on the + next to *Appearances*, and then click the *Colors* option, as shown in Figure 5.11.

3 Click the *color swatch* button next to each option to select any color you like.

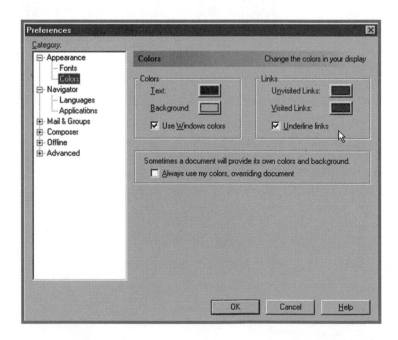

Figure 5.11
Changing color schemes in NN 4.02

An **operating system (OS)** is the master program that runs the computer. All applications must be able to "talk" to the operating system. Without an operating system, the computer hardware cannot interact with the software, so the computer won't work.

One of the earliest and longest lasting mainframe operating systems is called *UNIX*. In 1965, Bell Labs was working with MIT and

Internet Milestone

The UNIX Operating System

General Electric to write an operating system for their large mainframe computers, called Multics. When Bell Labs decided to leave the project, they still needed an operating system, so they continued to work on one.

As a sort of pun on Multics, the new Bell Labs operating system was named UNIX. Although it was slow to catch on outside of academic institutions, eventually businesses started using it. Written in a computer language called "C," UNIX went on to become the dominant network operating system for Internet computers, and remains a major force on the Net even today.

④ You must uncheck *Use Windows colors* to change the text and background options.

⑤ If you have been to a site, a hyperlink to that page from any other page on the Web will be colored with the *Visited* color. Sites you haven't been to will use the *Unvisited* color. It's a good idea to keep these colors different.

⑥ You can check the *Always use my colors* option to override individual page settings.

THINKING ABOUT TECHNOLOGY

As you can see, there are lots of options for customizing the way you see Web pages. What does this user flexibility mean to Web page designers? Will all Internet surfers see a page the same way? Could this be a problem for businesses operating Web sites?

Net Ethics   *Public or Private Funding*

In the early days of the Internet, most of the services were considered "free." They weren't really free. Many of the early Internet services were developed by government grants to universities. The National Science Foundation was a major force in the creation of the Net. Because of the grants, universities could provide students with free e-mail and other Internet services. The first Internet GUI Web browser (Mosaic) was free, for example.

In 1995, businesses started to discover the Web, and many corporations found ways to make money on the Internet. Do you think private companies have a right to make a profit on the Internet, since it was essentially started with taxpayer dollars? Where do businesses' rights to make money end and the needs of schools begin? What obligations, if any, should businesses have concerning the Internet?

Discuss this issue in teams. Two teams should take opposing views of this issue and may debate the issue aloud in class. Listen to the arguments on both sides before making up your mind on where you stand.

ACTIVITY

5.4

Objective:
In this lesson, you will learn
to toggle between
multimedia settings.

Toggling Multimedia Options

One drawback to the multimedia-rich Internet lies in the amount of information being transmitted. The majority of Internet surfers rely on slow modems and the limited capacity of *POTS* (Plain Old Telephone System) lines to carry the information. The aging phone system in service today was only intended to carry one type of data—voice calls. To make matters worse, the more popular the Internet becomes, the more it jams the phone lines. Some are lucky enough to have Internet access through dedicated data lines and improved fiber optic cables, which speed Internet content to your computer. Others have gone to wireless Net connections. However, if your connection runs slowly, you can give your browser a boost by turning off some of the media options. Here's how:

Figure 5.12
Changing multimedia settings in
IE 4.0

In IE 4.0:

1 Click *View → Internet Options* in Windows or *Edit Preferences → Web Content* on a Macintosh.

2 Click the *Advanced* tab and scroll down to the *Multimedia options.*

NOTE: *Uncheck any of the options you don't want to load while surfing, as shown in Figure 5.12. Try surfing for a couple of minutes with the* Show pictures *option off. Although the pages load quicker, you'll probably come running back to get pictures turned back on before long.*

In NN 4.02:

1 Click *Edit → Preferences.*

2 Choose the *Advanced* option.

3 Uncheck the *Automatically load images* check box, as shown in Figure 5.13.

4 With this setting off, you can still view images on a page by selecting *View → Show Images.*

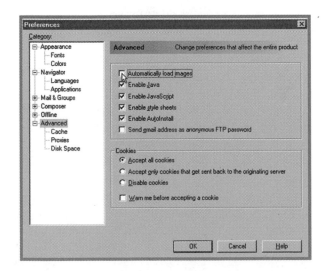

Figure 5.13
Disabling automatic image
loading in NN 4.02

THINKING ABOUT
TECHNOLOGY

Are there too many options? Do all the configuration options make it more confusing to use the program?

CHAPTER Review

Define the following terms:

1. *interface*
2. *operating system (OS)*

3. *toggle*
4. *list box*

NET REVIEW

Give a short answer to the following questions:

1. *If you started your browser one day and the navigation toolbar wasn't on your screen, what would you do to get it back?*

2. *Explain step-by-step how to change your browser's type to 11 pt. Arial in red on a blue background with black underlined hyperlinks.*

3. *Do you think the browser you are using is user-friendly? In what ways is it or isn't it? What would you change to make it more friendly for you?*

4. *How would you rate your browser's menu and toolbar organization? Is it easy to find the tool or option you are looking for? What could be done better?*

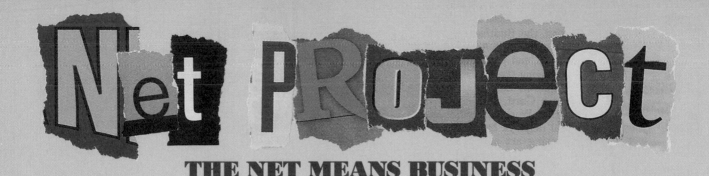

THE NET MEANS BUSINESS

GreatApplications, Inc., the company you just began working for, is a newcomer to the Internet. Your first real assignment involved gathering a list of advertised Web addresses. Noting your ability to gather and organize information, your boss has rewarded you with your first project: In next week's board meeting, you are to give an evaluation of how companies are using the Internet to enhance their business. Talk about pressure!

Surf the Net. Visit at least four business sites. Find out how top companies are using the Net. Explore as many pages on each site as possible. Try to avoid following links to other sites, since you will need time to properly evaluate the strengths and weaknesses of each site and write your summary for next week's meeting. Use the evaluation forms below to help you in your research.

Company Name _____
Address _____

Site Organization   Poor ❑   Fair ❑   Good ❑   Excellent ❑
    Are categories well-defined? _____
_____

Site Information   Poor ❑   Fair ❑   Good ❑   Excellent ❑
    Does the site (overall) provide relevant and pertinent information? _____
_____

Page Organization   Poor ❑   Fair ❑   Good ❑   Excellent ❑
    Do the pages (in general) contain too much or too little information? _____
_____

Visual Aspects   Poor ❑   Fair ❑   Good ❑   Excellent ❑
    Are the graphics on the page helpful or distracting? _____
_____

    Personal Impression—As a consumer, would this site help or hinder your purchasing decision? What other feelings did you have about the site? Would you visit the site again? Why or why not? _____
_____
_____

Company Name _____
Address _____

Site Organization   Poor ❑   Fair ❑   Good ❑   Excellent ❑
    Are categories well-defined? _____
_____

Site Information   Poor ❑   Fair ❑   Good ❑   Excellent ❑
    Does the site (overall) provide relevant and pertinent information? _____
_____

Page Organization   Poor ❑   Fair ❑   Good ❑   Excellent ❑
    Do the pages (in general) contain too much or too little information? _____
_____

Visual Aspects   Poor ❑   Fair ❑   Good ❑   Excellent ❑
    Are the graphics on the page helpful or distracting? _____
_____

    Personal Impression—As a consumer, would this site help or hinder your purchasing decision? What other feelings did you have about the site? Would you visit the site again? Why or why not? _____
_____
_____

Company Name _____
Address _____

Site Organization   Poor ❏   Fair ❏   Good ❏   Excellent ❏
   Are categories well-defined? _____
   _____

Site Information   Poor ❏   Fair ❏   Good ❏   Excellent ❏
   Does the site (overall) provide relevant and pertinent information? _____
   _____

Page Organization   Poor ❏   Fair ❏   Good ❏   Excellent ❏
   Do the pages (in general) contain too much or too little information? _____
   _____

Visual Aspects   Poor ❏   Fair ❏   Good ❏   Excellent ❏
   Are the graphics on the page helpful or distracting? _____
   _____

   Personal Impression—As a consumer, would this site help or hinder your purchasing decision? What other feelings did you have about the site? Would you visit the site again? Why or why not? _____
   _____
   _____

Company Name _____
Address _____

Site Organization   Poor ❏   Fair ❏   Good ❏   Excellent ❏
   Are categories well-defined? _____
   _____

Site Information   Poor ❏   Fair ❏   Good ❏   Excellent ❏
   Does the site (overall) provide relevant and pertinent information? _____
   _____

Page Organization   Poor ❏   Fair ❏   Good ❏   Excellent ❏
   Do the pages (in general) contain too much or too little information? _____
   _____

Visual Aspects   Poor ❏   Fair ❏   Good ❏   Excellent ❏
   Are the graphics on the page helpful or distracting? _____
   _____

   Personal Impression—As a consumer, would this site help or hinder your purchasing decision? What other feelings did you have about the site? Would you visit the site again? Why or why not? _____
   _____
   _____

NET PROJECT TEAMWORK   Present Your Top Sites

After you finish your individual analysis of business Web sites, meet with your team of three or four classmates. Nominate one person to act as the team leader to keep things organized. Nominate a presenter to summarize your research after your work is completed.

With an Internet browser running for all to see, review and analyze as a group the top company home
pages collected by each team member. Vote on the top three company sites your team found. Prepare to present your evaluations of these sites to GreatApplications, Inc., as examples of how the Net can be used effectively by a business.

WRITING ABOUT TECHNOLOGY   Summarize Your Findings

**Using your Web site evaluations, write a group summary of approximately 100 words, on a separate
piece of paper, for the board meeting next week. Your goal is not to say which site is the best or worst,
but rather to identify what worked and what didn't work (in general) for the sites you saw. Be specific.
Collaborate with your colleagues to gain more insight and perspectives on what makes a good Web
site. This is a perfect opportunity to prove to GreatApplications, Inc., that you can gather information
from multiple sources and present a cohesive, informative summary.**

Bringing It Home: Downloading Files

Chapter Objectives:

In this chapter, you will learn about downloading files, something you will need to do frequently. After reading Chapter 6, you will be able to

1. find shareware files.

2. explain why files are compressed on the Internet.

3. recognize common compression format extensions.

4. find information about decompressing files.

5. download and decompress files.

6. download and install FTP software.

Net Terms

download

shareware

patches

drivers

compressed files

extensions

self-extracting files

Get It, Try It, Buy It

The Internet has revolutionized transferring data from one place to another. Users can download many useful files from the Internet. **Download** means to transmit a file from one computer to another. Generally, "download" means "receive" and "upload" means "transmit."

The Internet has provided small software companies that otherwise couldn't afford to market their products through traditional retail channels a way to demonstrate their products to potential customers as shareware. **Shareware** is software that anyone can download for free, try it out for a certain period of time, and then purchase the product if they decide to continue using it.

Shareware benefits both user and software company. The user enjoys the insurance of "try before you buy" to determine if the product is really worthwhile. Also, the software company saves money in two ways:

1. It doesn't have to spend a lot on expensive packaging and documentation. Everything is transmitted electronically.
2. Most major software programs today allow you to click on a few browser buttons, access the company's

Web page, and have your software automatically updated. Again, the company saves money because the updates are provided electronically.

The ability to update the software on a customer's computer over the Net helps every user. Software code is very complex stuff. Often software has "bugs," or problems, that are not found until after the product is delivered. Software companies can provide patches on their Web sites for users to download. **Patches** are fixes for software bugs. Imagine the cost of mailing disks to every one of the registered Windows users in the world to patch a bug. Instead, companies can use their Web sites to supply new files and graphics

to update an interface, fix a problem, or update a program. Some virus protection companies will allow you to download new virus detection files for your protection software for up to a year after purchase, all through the World Wide Web.

Software companies can also electronically distribute updated drivers. **Drivers** are programs that allow hardware, like printers and sound cards, to communicate with your operating system. When you install a new hardware device on your computer, such as a scanner or CD-ROM drive, you must install its driver in order to run it. The operating system calls the driver, and the driver "drives" the device.

Nonsoftware businesses also benefit from the ability to

transfer data online. Architects can trade drawings across the Internet with their clients and the engineers working on the project. Salespeople on the road can dial into a company database and transmit the day's orders so they can be shipped the next day.

Consumers benefit as well. Virtual shopping malls have sprung up everywhere in cyberspace, allowing people to stay at home to do their shopping. You can compare as many different prices as you want, in the security and comfort of your own home. Then when you've made a decision, you can transmit your credit card information via encrypted (or secure) channels and have your item on its way to your door the very next day. ∎

Net Fun

If you have a relatively new copy of Internet Explorer or Netscape, you can enter a search word directly into the Location or Address box, and your browser will try to find the page you are looking for. Try this: Type Microsoft or Netscape in the window without all that "www" and "dot.com." If you have a new browser, you should jump right to the company's Web pages, no problem. Try other search word combinations this way.

ACTIVITY
6.1

Objective:

In this lesson, you will learn how to locate shareware, explain why file compression is necessary, and recognize common compression file name extensions.

Finding Shareware

Shareware can be found all over the Net. All you have to do is enter the word "shareware" in any search tool, and you will find a thousand possibilities. In fact, if you have trouble locating the software you want, try searching for it using a search service.

1 Start your browser.

2 Enter the address for *Shareware.com* maintained by C/Net, a very popular Net site:

www.shareware.com

3 In the search window, type in a *search word*, as shown in Figure 6.1. Here are three ideas:

games
business
compression

Figure 6.1
Search *Shareware.com* for shareware program

Enter search word.

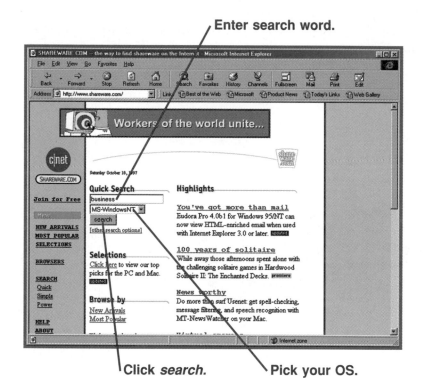

Click *search*.   **Pick your OS.**

Games open the doors of commerce

Downloading files and programs would be an obscure art were it not for the many games available on the Internet. Games like Doom and Descent became very popular in the early days of the Net. For many, the first real program they ever downloaded was a game.

4 In the operating system list box, choose your *operating system*. For example, Windows users select Windows 95, Windows 98, or WindowsNT, as shown in Figure 6.1. If you have an Apple, select Macintosh.

5 Click *search*.

6 View the files that appear and read the descriptions of the shareware. Scroll down the list so you can see the variety of the shareware offerings.

7 Try some other search words and find *new* categories of shareware.

Compressing Files

Compressed files are files that are compacted from their normal size to save space. File size is very important on the Internet, because the smaller a file is, the faster it can transfer. No one likes to sit around for hours, waiting for the newest shareware game to download. Text can generally be compressed to about 40 percent of its original size, and graphics files from 20 percent to 90 percent.

Extensions are file types, or file categories, that are added to the end of file names. The extension is separated from the file name with a dot (for example, *filename.doc*). An extension can have up to three letters or digits.

Compressed files are often called "archives," "zip files," "binhex files," or "exe files." The terms are used interchangeably, though they aren't exactly the same. You will notice that most of the files at *Shareware.com* end in extensions. In Figure 6.2a, you will see *.exe* and *.zip* extensions for the Windows list. In Figure 6.2b, you will see samples of Macintosh files that end in *.hqx*. (See the Net Fact on compression programs on page 73 for more details.)

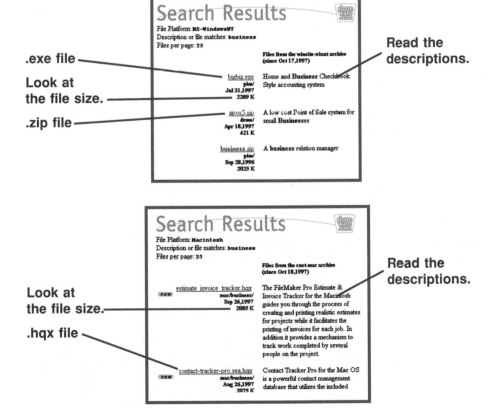

Figure 6.2a
Compressed file examples for Windows

Figure 6.2b
Compressed file examples for Macintosh

THINKING ABOUT TECHNOLOGY

Many Net users are unaware that files on the Net are compressed or made smaller by special compression software. What would happen if none of the files on the Net were compressed? What would the impact be on the worldwide transfer of data?

ACTIVITY 6.2

Objective:

In this lesson, you will learn how to decompress files.

Decompressing Files

As you learned in Activity 6.1, files are compressed to help them download quickly over the Net. Some file types, like *.exe* files, are easy to decompress. These are usually Windows files. If you click *Start → Run → Browse*, find your file, and then click *OK*, as depicted in Figure 6.3, your *.exe* file will launch an installation Wizard and install the program for you.

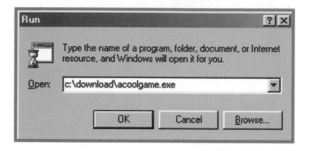

Figure 6.3
Use the *Run* option to open an *.exe* file

A Macintosh will allow you to open certain compressed files by double clicking on the downloaded file. If you have a decompression software, such as StuffIt Expander, that will handle the file type you are trying to download. Then after you download the file, the decompression software will expand the file back to full size.

1. Visit *www.aladdinsys.com* and read how *StuffIt Expander* works. (See Figure 6.4.) You can even download a version of the software and give it a try. Be sure to download the correct version for your computer, Macintosh or Windows.

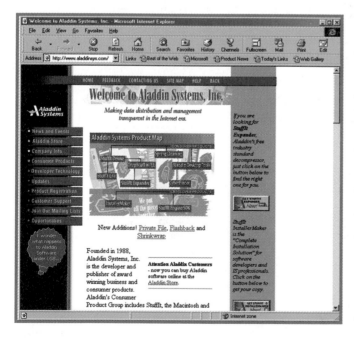

Figure 6.4
Visit Aladdin Systems, Inc., on the Web

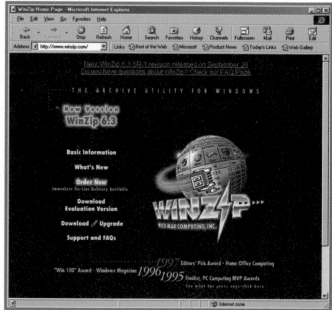

Figure 6.5
Visit WinZip on the Web

② If you are a Windows user, visit *www.winzip.com* and read the information about *WinZip* software. (See Figure 6.5 at the bottom of the preceding page.) Download an evaluation version and try it out!

THINKING ABOUT TECHNOLOGY

Do you think offering shareware is a good way for small companies to make money? What kinds of shareware do you think would be most popular with Net surfers? What are some possible pitfalls to shareware?

NET FACT

Compression Programs

There are many compression techniques and compression software programs on the Net. *PKZIP* is a very popular one for Windows users. Files that are "zipped" can be opened with *PKUNZIP* or *WinZip* software. On the Macintosh and in Windows, files can be decompressed with a free program called *StuffIt Expander*.

There are many other compression programs. Each of these uses different *algorithms*, which are complex mathematical formulas, to make files smaller. Although some programs can decompress several different compression styles, you may need to download a decompression program for each type.

It's good to be familiar with compression file types, so you will know which tool to use to expand them when you encounter these files. Here are some file extensions that identify a few of the more common compression types:

StuffIt = .sit	*GZIP = .gz*
Compact Pro = .cpt	*TAR = .tar*
Zip = .zip	*UnizCompress – .z*
ARC = .arc	*Uuencoded = .uu*
AppleLink = .pkg	*BinHex = hqx*

Windows *.exe* files are executable programs, not just files containing words and pictures. Executable programs will automatically expand when you run the file in Windows. Executable files use *.exe*, *.com*, and *.bat* extensions. Files that automatically decompress are called **self-extracting files**. StuffIt files on a Macintosh can also be self-extracting. To decompress an executable *.exe* self-extracting file, select *Start → Run → Browse* to locate the file, and then open it.

Net Ethics   *Shareware Dilemma*

How many "extra" or "pirated" copies of a program do you think exist for every copy that has been paid for? That is an interesting question. When you download a shareware program, you are given a certain length of time to try the product before you buy it. However, many people never pay. The developers of shareware often depend on user revenue to continue to improve the program. Discuss the following dilemma in class or with your team: What should you do if you're sure someone you know is using shareware without paying for it?

ACTIVITY 6.3

Objective:

In this lesson, you will learn how to download and install FTP software.

Downloading FTP Software

One of the primary methods for transferring files from one computer to another over the Internet is called *FTP*, which stands for *File Transfer Protocol*. Browsers can handle most FTP tasks "transparently," meaning that you don't have to know any more than ... you guessed it ... point and click. However, the FTP capability of a browser is often not efficient enough. Serious FTP users can download various FTP software programs from *www.tucows.com*.

1 Locate *www.tucows.com* with your Web browser, as shown in Figure 6.6.

NET TIP

If you have trouble with this activity, try using a search service and typing the letters FTP. *Surf until you find an FTP shareware program.*

Figure 6.6
Search for *www.tucows.com* with your browser

2 Scroll down to your state or country and click with your mouse.

3 Select the type of operating system you are using (see Figure 6.7).

4 Look for *FTP* on the menu. Scroll down and read the descriptions of the different FTP software, as shown in Figure 6.8.

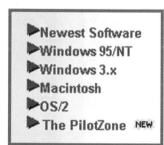

Figure 6.7
Select your computer operating system

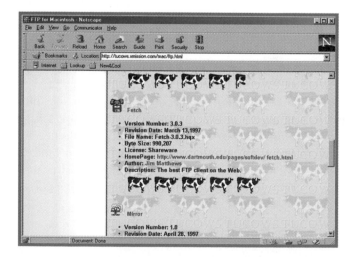

Figure 6.8
A Macintosh FTP software called *Fetch*

⑤ Get permission from your instructor to download an FTP shareware program. Create a download folder as you learned to do in Activity 2.2 on page 20.

NOTE: *Save the file in this folder, so you can find and then delete the .exe or .hqx file after you finish installing the software. (See Figure 6.9.)*

NET TIP
Web Addresses

Note that current links to most Web sites presented in this book can be found on the Internet Concepts and Activities *Home Page. Choose* Resources *at* **computered.swep.com**.

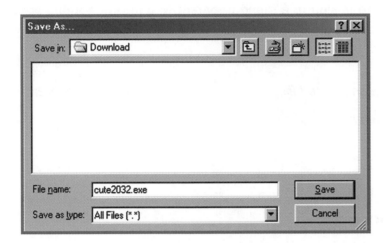

Figure 6.9
Downloading and saving FTP software

⑥ You can watch the progress of your download on the status bar, as shown in Figures 6.10a (Windows) and 6.10b (Macintosh). After your program downloads, run it from the *Start* menu or double click on it with your mouse. Follow the instructions as the program decompresses and installs.

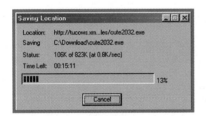
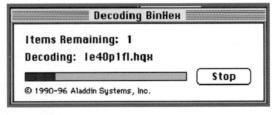

Figure 6.10a
Downloading status bar in Windows (left)
Figure 6.10b
Downloading status bar on a Macintosh

⑦ If you chose a file that needs special conversions, work with your instructor or other members of the class to learn how to convert and open your downloaded file.

⑧ Delete any unnecessary files after you have downloaded the FTP software.

THINKING ABOUT TECHNOLOGY

Tucows uses a cow rating system: five cows for the best programs and one cow for the worst programs. If you were a shareware provider and got four and a half cows, would you want your product listed? What if you only got a cow and a half? Would you still want to be listed? How could you make your shareware product the best five-cow program on the list?

CHAPTER Review

NET VOCABULARY

Explain each of these terms as if you were talking to a friend or parent who knows nothing about computers:

1. *download*

2. *shareware*

3. *patches*

4. *drivers*

5. *compressed files*

6. *extensions*

7. *self-extracting files*

NET REVIEW

Give a short answer to the following questions:

1. *Do you think the "try before you buy" philosophy is a good one? What are the advantages? What are the disadvantages?*

2. *What can software companies do to "encourage" people to pay for their shareware?*

3. *What is the advantage of compressing and decompressing files? Are compressing and decompressing more of a hassle than they are worth? Why or why not?*

TRAIN YOUR COLLEAGUES

GreatApplications, Inc., is a software company with a very open philosophy. They don't hire strictly from the ranks of computer science graduates and programming wizards. Many of the new people in your group have very little actual computer experience. This lack of experience is an important asset in the company's eyes, because they want to write software that anyone can use.

Since some of your colleagues have never used compression files before, you have been asked to conduct a training meeting on the things you have learned in this chapter. You may need to become a little more familiar with the various steps for finding, downloading, and decompressing files. Explore menus, help files, and Web sites for hints and help.

When you are comfortable with the process, write an outline to guide you through your presentation. Create a step-by-step guide you can hand out to your group. In your presentation, you will need to guide them through the process. Prepare any help files or folders you need for your presentation.

As usual, keep it short and to the point. Make your instructions clear and easy to follow. Teach the concept, and then follow it up with reinforcement. Remember, the better you teach your colleagues now, the fewer problems they will have in the future.

_____

_____

_____

_____

_____

_____

_____

_____

_____

_____

_____

_____

_____

_____

_____

_____

_____

_____

NET PROJECT TEAMWORK — Build a Training Program as a Team

Meet with your team of three or four classmates and combine your presentations into one training program for new employees. Create a multimedia presentation based on what your team has learned from each other about this important procedure.

_____

_____

_____

_____

_____

_____

_____

_____

_____

_____

_____

_____

_____

_____

_____

_____

_____

_____

_____

WRITING ABOUT TECHNOLOGY — The Advantages of Teams

Should Web site development be done by a group? What about software development? Should software programs be created by a team? What are the advantages and disadvantages of working in groups on these types of projects? When you were working with your team on various Net Projects, were people with different interests/skills able to contribute equally and usefully? Did you wish someone on the team had more specific knowledge about something?

Write a 100-word description, on a separate piece of paper, of your experience working with your team on the Net Projects.

PORTFOLIO · PROJECT ·

E-Communication: E-Mail and Newsgroups

E-mail is *the* communication protocol of choice for today's business world. As more and more computers head home and into schools, e-mail is becoming entrenched in our society. It's fast, easy, and—best of all—free for millions of Net users.

In this section, you will learn all about how e-mail works on the Internet. We'll show you the different parts of an e-mail message. You'll also understand the most important parts of an e-mail program.

E-mail, as the name suggests, is like a postal service for your computer. You can use it to send and receive letters, memorandums, announcements, and even junk mail. So throw out your printer, put your stamps in a collection, and stick your envelopes on the dog. In the digital world of e-mail, there are no dogs attacking letter carriers and no rain-soaked packages.

The other definitive source of communication on the Internet is *newsgroups*. Newsgroups can be formed whenever enough people have enough interest about *any* subject. These newsgroups can be formal or informal. Some are merely for entertainment or recreation; others are dedicated to furthering knowledge of a specific subject.

Chapter 7 will teach you the basics of sending, receiving, and sorting mail and using file attachments. Chapter 8 will take you into the world of newsgroups. You'll learn about posting, retrieving, spamming, and flaming.

Chapter 7   Goodbye Snail-Mail: An Intro to E-Mail   80
Chapter 8   What's New(s)? An Intro to Newsgroups   93

CHApTEr 7

Goodbye Snail-Mail: An Intro to E-Mail

Chapter Objectives:

In this chapter, you will learn how to use one of the most powerful Internet tools available: e-mail. After reading Chapter 7, you will be able to:

1 compose and send an e-mail message.

2 retrieve and read an e-mail message.

3 create folders and organize your mailbox.

4 send an attachment.

5 use the address book.

Net Terms

e-mail

proprietary software

spam

attachments

header

subject line

rich text format (RTF)

emoticons

E-Mail E-merges

E-mail means "electronic mail." It is memos, messages, and attachments transmitted over a network. Almost everyone on the Internet uses e-mail as the primary means of communication. With e-mail, you can communicate with anyone in the world within minutes. Even better, e-mail can be free.

Many businesses use e-mail as a primary means of communication both within and outside of the company. One advantage of e-mail is the ability to communicate the same message to one person or several hundred people at the same time.

E-mail used to be text only. But nowadays, thanks to improved transfer and file compression methods, almost any type of file can be attached to an e-mail message. You can send a sound clip of your band, your latest picture scanned into your computer, or a word processor document or spreadsheet.

You can receive e-mail service through a proprietary system, through an Internet service provider for a fee, or free over the Internet on an advertisement-based e-mail provider. ■

Proprietary E-Mail

Proprietary software is a program owned and controlled by a company or person. If your school or business maintains its own e-mail system, chances are it uses some proprietary e-mail software, such as Microsoft Exchange, Novell GroupWise, or LotusNotes. These e-mail systems allow a great deal of control for the system managers, but the trade-off is that they cost mega-bucks to purchase and maintain.

Your school or business may, however, use a less-expensive system built for the Internet. E-mail programs using the POP or "post office protocol" can be set up virtually for free. Most of these run on UNIX computers. Free or shareware e-mail programs, like *Pine*, *Pegasus*, and *Eudora*, offer all the user features found in e-mail systems costing thousands more. Still, these systems on an organization's network need to be maintained by someone in the organization.

E-Mail from an Internet Service Provider

Another alternative is to pay a small monthly fee to an Internet service provider (ISP) to provide e-mail service. America Online and the Microsoft Network are the largest of these ISPs, although there are lots of ISPs of all sizes to choose from. The ISP provides all the e-mail software you need and maintains the system for you. Purchasing e-mail service through an ISP is very popular, because it is inexpensive and mostly trouble-free.

Free Advertisement-Based E-Mail on the Web

Another alternative is very popular, particularly among students. Free e-mail can be obtained over the World Wide Web at any one of a hundred advertisement-based e-mail providers. You don't need any special software to use this kind of e-mail. At some of these free e-mail Web sites, you are also allowed to post a personal HTML Web page. To get all these goodies, all you need is a Web browser.

Advertising pays for this kind of e-mail service. Visit any one of the following sites and inquire about their free e-mail service. If you want to subscribe, you must provide certain personal information that is shared with advertisers. So, before you subscribe, read the information found in "Net Ethics: Subscription Ethics and Free E-Mail" on the next page.

Here is a short list of some of the better-known e-mail providers. We will leave it to you to determine their relative value. If you don't like any of them, you can find more providers by typing "free e-mail" in a search tool.

www.juno.com
www.hotmail.com
www.rocketmail.com
www.geocities.com
netaddress.usa.net

In 1972, e-mail was invented by Ray Tomlinson. Intended for communication among research scientists and military personnel over ARPANET, e-mail quickly gained popularity, but for a different reason. It was a great way for people to share common interests. The first newsgroup ever created was called SF-Lovers. No, it wasn't an online dating service. It was a forum for geeky scientists to talk about their one true love—science fiction books.

NET TIP
Web Addresses

Note that current links to most Web sites presented in this book can be found on the Internet Concepts and Activities *Home Page. Choose* Resources *at* **computered.swep.com**. *Remember that a Web address may change at any time. An address given in this book as an example may no longer be valid. If this is so, either access the Home Page for the current link or do a search to find a similar site (see Chapter 9 for a discussion of search methods).*

The value of advertisement-based e-mail systems is that you can access your e-mail account from anywhere in the world with any Web browser. If you change jobs, change ISPs, change schools, or just go home for the holidays, you can still get your mail by borrowing any Web browser that is nearby.

Net Ethics — *Subscription Ethics and Free E-Mail*

How much information should you provide to someone over the Internet? If you give out your name, address, and phone number to an advertisement-based e-mail system, chances are you will be "spammed" with junk mail, ads related to the interests you selected as you subscribed, and even phone calls. **Spam** is what netizens call unwanted and unsolicited advertising or other messages, such as political or social commentary.

The best free e-mail systems will not ask you for your personal phone number or home mailing address, but will only advertise to you via your e-mail account. As you visit the Web site, you will see active ads that you can choose to click on or ignore.

Some e-mail systems create personal profiles. This information is then shared with other users, who can then "look you up" in the address book. Do you want people to have this information about you?

The real scary option is to hook up with a free e-mail system that requires your credit card number. They may give you a reason like, "If you decide to buy something, you don't have to hassle entering in your number for the purchase." This is a lame reason. Your credit card number should be given only to reputable companies for specific services.

Given all these cautions, should you use a free e-mail system? Is anything ever really free? Do you give your real name or do you make one up? What are the rules that should guide your actions in this situation?

Debate these issues in class or with other students.

Net Fun

Go to any of the popular search service sites that host categories and start clicking down to your favorite topics—without using the search box tools. Which search engine has the best system of categories that lets you find what you want to know with the least effort?

Compose and Send a New Message

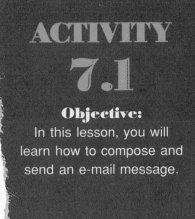

An e-mail message, like a regular letter, contains three or four main parts. A typical e-mail will contain header information, the body of the message, and a sign-off or signature line. Also, e-mail may contain one or more attachments. **Attachments** are files linked to an e-mail message, so that they travel to their destination together. Any type of file can be attached. However, attaching a file is usually a way to transmit a database, spreadsheet, graphics, or program file.

The **header** is the first part of an e-mail message, which gives controlling information, such as who sent the e-mail, who it was mailed to, who should receive copies, priority level, and the subject of the message. The **subject line** in the header is the place where the sender inserts a brief description of the message contents. This description is very important, because it gives the receiver a hint about the contents of the message. Also, as e-mail systems become more sophisticated and more automated, subject lines play another important role. They can be scanned by e-mail servers to automatically have you added to or removed from a mailing list, filter and route your message to different inboxes, or block your message from receipt.

Familiarize yourself with the parts of the e-mail message screen shown in Figure 7.1. Then let's compose an e-mail message.

1 Start your Internet browser.

2 Click the *Mailbox* icon in NN 4.02 (Figure 7.2a) or the *Mail* icon in IE 4.0 (Figure 7.2b), and choose *New Message.* Your screen should now look similar to Figure 7.1.

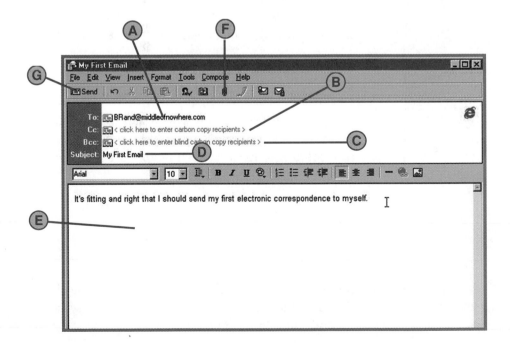

K E Y	
A	Receiver's Address
B	Carbon Copy Receiver's Address
C	Address Location for Receiver of "Blind" Copy
D	Subject Line
E	Body Text Area
F	Attachment Button
G	Send Button

Figure 7.1
An e-mail message screen

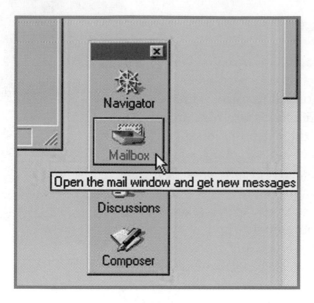

Figure 7.2a
The Mailbox icon in NN 4.02

Figure 7.2b
The Mail button in IE 4.0

③ In the *To* box, key in your e-mail address (your instructor should provide you with one). E-mail addresses are typically made up of the first initial and last name or first name and last initial of an individual, followed by the "at" (@) symbol, and then followed by the user's e-mail server name. For example, *jbrown@aol.com.*

④ In the *Subject* box, key in something like *"My First E-Mail."* The sender's name and the subject line are the first things people see in their inbox. Be sure the subject line is to the point.

⑤ In the body text area, key a short message to yourself. Remember to be concise in your communication. No one wants to or has time to read pages and pages of text.

⑥ You may want to close with a traditional *"Sincerely"* or a *"Thank You,"* or you may want to be more creative and use an ending that characterizes you, like *"Later."*

⑦ When you are ready to send your message, click the *Send* button, as shown in Figure 7.3. If you are not connected to the Internet, clicking the *Send* button will send your message to your *Outbox* for storage until it can be sent. You may need to click *Send* again to connect to your ISP and send any messages in your Outbox.

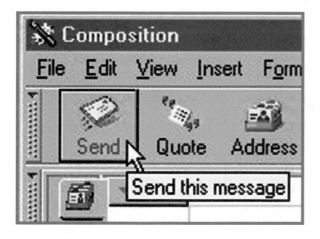

Figure 7.3
Click Send to speed the message on its way!

THINKING ABOUT TECHNOLOGY

Many professional people receive hundreds of e-mail messages a day. How do busy people handle that amount of e-mail? How can they quickly identify messages they may want to read first?

Read a Message

ACTIVITY

7.2

Objective:
In this lesson, you will learn how to retrieve and read a message.

Although e-mail messages are delivered quickly, don't assume your friend in Paris is going to receive and reply to your e-mail in half a second. It can take anywhere from several minutes to a few hours to deliver your message. It all depends on how much traffic is going through the servers that carry your message from you to your intended receiver.

When you send a message, it goes to the mail server of your ISP, where it gets in line behind all the messages that were posted first. Eventually, it will be sent to the recipient's mail server, where it will wait again until that person retrieves his or her mail.

And even though e-mail is pretty reliable, e-mail servers can crash and burn, leaving hundreds of people stuck without e-mail until the problem is corrected. Computers are only human, after all!

Let's retrieve the message you just wrote to yourself.

1. Start your browser and launch your e-mail application.

2. Click the *Send and Receive* button. This will send any messages lingering in your Outbox (Figure 7.4) and retrieve any new messages from your ISP's server, and bring them into your Inbox.

3. Unread messages in your Inbox will usually be bolded. Double click any new messages to read them.

4. Notice the header information. It will tell you who the information is from, when the message was sent, and other information about how the message was sent.

5. You can respond to a message by clicking the *Reply* or *Reply to Author* button. This will automatically fill in the *To* box and make a copy in your response of the message you received.

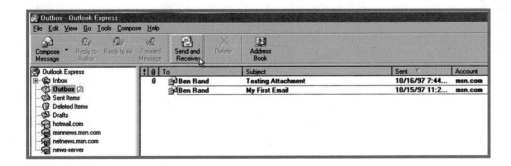

Figure 7.4
The Outbox with messages ready to be sent

THINKING ABOUT TECHNOLOGY

Did anyone ever hang an unwanted ad on your doorknob? Did your home mailbox ever fill up with junk mail that had nothing to do with you? Junk mail is an institution in our society, and with e-mail, it is now easier and cheaper to distribute to more people. What can be done about spam? Is there any benefit to you of receiving advertising by e-mail?

ACTIVITY

7.3

Objective:
In this lesson, you will
learn how to create
and use folders
to organize your mail.

Creating Folders to Organize Your Mail

In time, you will accumulate many messages. Multiply all the messages you send and receive by the number of other users on your network, and sooner or later your mail server is going to be very full. Be a thoughtful user and delete your mail when you are finished with it.

You may want to delete some messages after you have read and responded to them. Others, you will want to store. You can use multiple folders to store the important messages you need to keep. The *Sent Items* folder stores every message that you send, taking up room on the mail server. Go through this folder from time to time and delete the messages you don't want to keep.

Now let's create new folders for storing the important messages that you want to keep.

1 With your e-mail program open, click on your *Inbox*.

2 In NN 4.02, select *File → New Folder*. Your screen should look similar to Figure 7.5a. In IE 4.0, select *File → Folder → New Folder*. Your screen will look similar to Figure 7.5b.

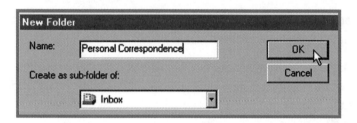

Figure 7.5a
Creating a new folder in
NN 4.02

3 You may need a folder for a specific project you are working on, or you may want a folder for a specific person you correspond with regularly. Create a folder called *Business Correspondence* by keying this label into the *Name* (NN 4.02) or *Folder name* (IE 4.0) field. Select *Inbox* as the location for your new folder, and then click *OK*.

4 Next, create a folder called *Personal Correspondence* in your *Inbox*.

5 You can create folders in your *Sent Items* box or any of the other boxes by simply selecting that location when you create the folder. You can drag and drop your messages between folders to organize them.

6 You can drag messages you no longer need to the *Deleted Items* folder, or select them and press ⟨*Delete*⟩.

Figure 7.5b
Creating a new folder in IE 4.0

THINKING ABOUT TECHNOLOGY

What impact has e-mail had on the postal system? Is there a future for snail-mail?

Send an Attachment

ACTIVITY

7.4

Objective:
In this lesson, you will learn how to send an e-mail with an attachment.

E-mail has definitely come a long way since its text-only days. Now you can send documents in rich text format. **Rich text format (RTF)** is a format that enables the use of enhancements, such as bold, italic, and different fonts and colors. You can also insert pictures, sound, and video clips or documents created in a variety of programs.

Using attachments makes sharing information one-click easy.

1. Start your e-mail program.

2. Click *Compose Message* to start a new e-mail.

3. Fill in the *To* box with the address of one of your colleagues.

4. In the *Subject* box, key in *"Attachment Exercise."*

5. Type a short note explaining the contents of your attachment or any questions you would like the receiver to answer about the attached file.

6. Click the *attachment button* (pictured in Figure 7.6).

Figure 7.6
The attachment button

7. In the file selection dialog box that appears, locate the file *Bubbles.bmp*, which generally comes with Windows and can be found in your *C:\Windows* folder. If you don't have this file, choose any file on your hard drive. If you have a Macintosh, try pasting a *Scrapbook* or *ClipArt* picture to a document and attaching it to your e-mail message.

 *Emoticons*

*In the early days of e-mail, people were constantly searching for ways to interject emotion into their messages. Shouting was accomplished by using ALL CAPS. Somewhere along the way, somebody discovered that you could make sideways faces with characters on the keyboard. A smiley face was made by keying a colon for eyes and a right parenthesis for a smile, like this: :)   A frowny face used the left parenthesis: : (
These creations became known as **emoticons**—icons that show emotion.*

Many others soon followed. Here are some of the common ones:

:-<	:-|	>:-(	:-o	:-{	;-)	:-Q	8-)
sad	so-so	mad	surprised	scared	wink	tongue hanging out (nausea)	smile (user wears glasses)

:-D	:-{}	:-{)}	*<|:{)}
wide smile	smile (user has mustache)	smile (user has mustache and beard)	Santa Claus

Emoticons have even gone to the next level. Sometime when you are surfing around, see if you can find the emoticon Macarena. Just when you thought you'd seen everything....

8 With the file selected, click *Attach*.

9 You should see an icon with the file name attached to your message, as shown in Figure 7.7a for IE 4.0 and Figure 7.7b for NN 4.02.

10 When you are finished with your message, click *Send*.

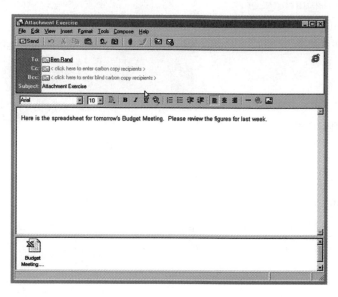

Figure 7.7a
Attached files in an e-mail message are displayed in the lower window in IE 4.0

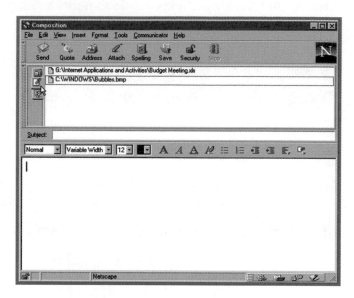

Figure 7.7b
Attached files are listed under the attachment tab in NN 4.02

THINKING ABOUT TECHNOLOGY

Why might you want to attach something to an e-mail? Assume that your best friend moved to another state. What would you like to send to him or her over the Internet?

NET FACT

Who is the ISP?

You can tell who is providing the e-mail service by looking at the first few letters after the @ sign. Guess who is providing the following services.

@aol.com _____

@msn.com _____

@pdgonline.com _____

@rocketmail.com _____

@usa.division5.mil _____

@yale.edu _____

Using Your Address Book

ACTIVITY

7.5

Objective:
In this lesson, you will learn to use the address book feature.

Your e-mail program has an address book feature to help you keep track of e-mail addresses. Using your address book, you can quickly select one or many recipients, and their addresses will automatically be inserted in the To, CC, or BC box, as you indicate. Some address books allow you to keep track of phone numbers, street addresses, and other important information besides e-mail addresses.

1. Start your e-mail program.

2. Begin a new message.

3. Next to the *To* box in IE 4.0, click on the *address card* icon. This will launch your address book. In NN 4.02, click *Communicator—Address Book* to launch the address book.

4. Click *New Contact* in IE or *New Card* in NN, and a dialog box will appear, as shown in Figures 7.8a (IE) and 7.8b (NN). Explore the different tabs in the dialog box. Notice the types of information the address book allows you to store. The IE address book can even keep track of multiple e-mail addresses for each contact.

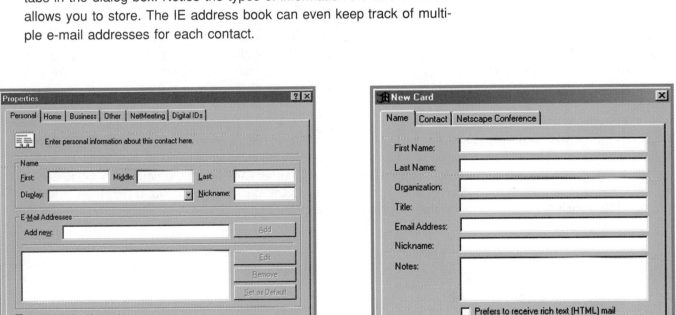

Figure 7.8a
Adding a contact to the address book in IE 4.0

Figure 7.8b
Adding a contact to the address book in NN 4.02

5. Using your *Personal Contact Cards* (remember those?), fill in the new contact information for each person you interviewed. When you finish filling in the information for a contact, click *OK* to store it in the address book.

POP *is short for* Post Office Protocol. *There have been many versions—POP1, POP2, and POP3 come to mind. POP was developed to communicate e-mail from UNIX computers to UNIX users over the early Internet. POP specifies how exchanges of information are made between e-mail servers and e-mail clients.*

6 Make entries for the people you worked with for your presentation in Chapter 6, so you can communicate with the group more easily about your current project.

7 Close the address book in NN to get back to your new message. Then click *Address* and select a recipient for your message. In IE, once you click *OK* to complete your last new contact card, the *Select Recipients* dialog box will appear. Select a recipient from the address list and click *To* and then *OK.* Your receiver will now appear in the *To* box in your new message.

THINKING ABOUT TECHNOLOGY

Do you think you could get used to an electronic address book? What are some of the advantages over the traditional handwritten book of addresses? Disadvantages?

Netiquette

Runaway E-Mail

In a major *Fortune* 500 company, an employee organized a group discussion via the company's proprietary e-mail system. As participants began to discuss company issues, many employees used the *Reply to All* feature, which means all the people on the company list received their response.

One employee returned home from a two-day business trip. When she opened her inbox, she found over 500 messages related to the discussion. Add to that the 160 e-mail messages she normally received in a two-day period. It took her hours on a Saturday to clean out the mess—all on her own time. Furthermore, this employee had no interest in the topic, which had nothing to do with her already busy job.

How do you control this kind of e-mail use? Should it be controlled? Shouldn't people be allowed to express their feelings, beliefs, and perceptions about the company? Should this kind of e-mail abuse become a big issue in this company?

Search an obscure topic like Kayaking in Costa Rica. Try to find a topic that brings back no results. Can you find one?

NET VOCABULARY

Define the following terms:

1. e-mail

2. proprietary software

3. spam

4. attachments

5. header

6. subject line

7. emoticons

8. rich text format (RTF)

NET REVIEW

Give a short answer to the following questions:

1. Describe the steps you would follow to write an e-mail message to a friend, with a copy to another friend. Assume that their addresses are already in your address book.

2. How would you go about attaching a file to your message?

3. Create two new emoticons of your own, and state what they mean.

4. What limitations should be placed on e-mail in a corporate environment and in a school environment?

PREP FOR YOUR BIG PRESENTATION

Your boss at GreatApplications, Inc., has asked you to send an e-mail to your team members, informing them that next Friday's meeting has been moved to this Monday. Panic! (Actually, just get used to it. Meeting times get changed all the time in business.) Remind all members that they must come prepared to share the three great corporate Web sites they found in the Net Project for Chapter 5. Anyone who is not prepared will be demoted, sent to a Siberian mink farm, and deleted from the e-mail address book.

Write an e-mail memo to your colleagues about the change in schedule. Inform them to be prepared to give a five-minute presentation on their Web site findings. They will need to have visual examples of good and bad Web sites. They also need to reply to you with a summary of their presentation, so that it can be previewed in the meeting agenda.

You need to prepare for your presentation, too. Return to sites or specific pages that you thought were well organized. In your browser, you can save a Web page to your hard drive by clicking *File → Save As*, selecting a location to save the page, and clicking *Save* to save it in html. Save your favorite Web pages in your *Research* folder that you created in the Chapter 2 Net Project. Also save examples of poorly organized pages in your *Web Pages* folder for future reference.

NET PROJECT TEAMWORK   Tag-Team E-Mail

E-mail systems vary in speed and efficiency. Some message systems take seconds to route messages. Other systems take hours, even days to clear the e-mail. How fast is your e-mail system?

Test the responsiveness of your e-mail system. Divide up into teams of four or five people. Teammate #1 starts the chain by sending an e-mail message to Teammate #2 with the message, "Hi, this is [name of Teammate #1]. Please forward this message to the next member of the team." Teammate #2 uses the *forward* feature to send the message to Teammate #3, and so on until the message reaches the last teammate. The last person must have the names of all the e-mail's previous senders to prove that the chain was complete. The first team to get the final forwarded message to the last teammate wins. This contest may take minutes, hours, or days.

WRITING ABOUT TECHNOLOGY   E-Mail's Impact on Writing

Write a 100-word essay, on a separate piece of paper, on how e-mail is impacting the way we write and communicate. Is it improving our writing or is it having a negative impact on the way people communicate?

PORTFOLIO · PROJECT

CHAPTER 8

What's New(s)? An Intro to Newsgroups

Chapter Objectives:

In this chapter, you will be introduced to the world of newsgroups. After reading Chapter 8, you will be able to:

1. find a newsgroup of interest to you.

2. subscribe to and unsubscribe from a newsgroup.

3. read a newsgroup post and mark for downloading.

4. post a response to a newsgroup.

Net Terms

newsgroups

Usenet

NetNews

thread

flaming

> **NET TIP**
> **Web Addresses**
>
> *Note that current links to most Web sites presented in this book can be found on the* Internet Concepts and Activities *Home Page. Choose* Resources *at* **computered.swep.com**. *Remember that a Web address may change. Either access the Home Page for the current link or do a search to find a similar site (see Activity 8.1 to learn how to search for a newsgroup).*

Newsgroups A-Plenty

Newsgroups, despite the name, are not electronic newspapers. They are collections of messages on the Internet about a particular subject. People subscribe to newsgroups on their favorite subjects, so they can meet and talk electronically with other people interested in the same subjects.

Chances are there is a newsgroup that fits your particular interest. Are you an *X-Files* fanatic? After you learn to use your newsreader, try *alt.tv.x-files*. Can the Chicago Bulls repeat? Look in *alt. sports.basketball.nba.chicago-bulls*. Are you into investing? Then *misc.invest.mutual-funds* or *misc.invest.stocks* might be for you. If, by some strange quirk in the universe, you can't find a newsgroup

about your special interest, you can start one up.

But newsgroups aren't just for entertainment. For example, users in the *comp.cad. autocad* newsgroup can post questions about their favorite drafting software, *AutoCAD*. More often than not, someone in the group has dealt with that problem and may know how to help or where the person can go to get help.

One warning: Though newsgroups can be a lot of fun, they are an open forum for all sorts of people. Anonymity when posting a message allows for freedom of speech that common courtesy might otherwise prevent. Exercise extreme caution when reading from and posting to a newsgroup. NEVER give out personal information about yourself. ■

What newsgroups are NOT

ACTIVITY
8.1

Objective:

In this lesson, you will learn how to filter a list of newsgroups and subscribe to newsgroups of interest to you. You will also learn how to unsubscribe.

Subscribing to and Unsubscribing from a Newsgroup

The first task is finding a newsgroup that interests you. Your network administrator will have to configure your browser to be able to access news servers. When you select a news server, a list of all available newsgroups will be downloaded to your browser. Select a newsgroup from the list to view or subscribe to.

If you subscribe to a newsgroup, your list of messages will automatically be updated when new messages are posted. Let's find a newsgroup to subscribe to.

1. Open your Internet browser.

2. In IE 4.0, click the *Mail* button, and then select *Read News*, as shown in Figure 8.1a. In NN 4.02, click on the *Discussion* button, as shown in Figure 8.1b.

NOTE: *If you don't see this Netscape toolbar on your screen at first, check the bottom of your screen. The toolbar may be "collapsed" so that it is out of the way. Click on the restore button on this collapsed toolbar to bring it back to full size.*

3. In IE 4.0, click the *Newsgroups* button. In NN 4.02, click the *Subscribe* button.

4. First, pick a news server. You may be limited to the news servers configured by your network administrator.

5. When you first select a news server, it will download a list of available newsgroups. This list can be rather long, so it may take a few minutes.

6. After you download the list, you can search for a newsgroup by keying a keyword into the "*Display newsgroups which contain*" box in IE 4.0. In NN 4.02, click the "*Search for a group*" tab to reveal the "*Search for*" box.

7. Key "*Simpsons*" into the "*Display newsgroups which contain*" box in IE 4.0 or in the "*Search for*" box in NN 4.02.

8. The keyword is used to filter the big list of newsgroups and display for you only the groups with your keyword in the name, as shown in Figure 8.2a (IE 4.0). Now you can pick one of the displayed groups and subscribe or read the posted messages. Figure 8.2b (NN 4.02) shows a list of news servers and the newsgroups that the user is currently subscribed to.

9. Select one or more of the newsgroups on the list and click the *Subscribe* button.

Figure 8.1a
Accessing newsgroups in IE 4.0

Figure 8.1b
Accessing newsgroups in NN 4.02

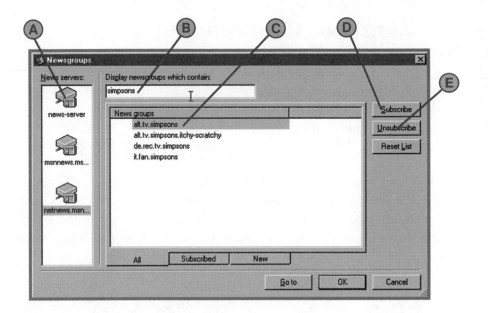

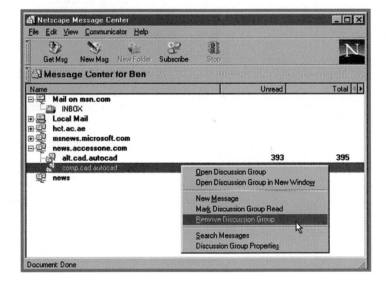

KEY

A News Servers
B Display Filter Box
C Subscription List
D Subscribe Button
E Unsubscribe Button

Figure 8.2a
Filtering a newsgroup list for the Simpsons in IE 4.0

10 To unsubscribe from a newsgroup, select the newsgroup and right-click.

11 Choose *Unsubscribe from this newsgroup* in IE 4.0 or *Remove Discussion Group* in NN 4.02, as shown in Figure 8.3.

Figure 8.2b
News servers and groups currently subscribed to (NN 4.02)

Figure 8.3
Unsubscribing in NN 4.02

Thinking About Technology

Recently in the news, some content providers decided to ban certain newsgroups whose content was patently offensive. However, many people felt that this was a violation of their First Amendment rights. Should there be censorship in newsgroups? Who should decide what gets through?

ACTIVITY

8.2

Objective:
In this lesson, you will learn how to read newsgroup posts and mark posts for downloading.

Reading and Downloading Newsgroup Posts

Newsgroups can be intimidating by the sheer number of posts made every day. Most users quickly browse through the list of postings, marking items of interest for download. When they have finished scanning the list, they download the postings for offline reading.

Sometimes, a user will post a question or a remark that encourages a lot of responses. When several users post responses to an earlier post, they have started a thread. A **thread** is several posts related to the same topic. Figure 8.4 shows a thread below the highlighted line.

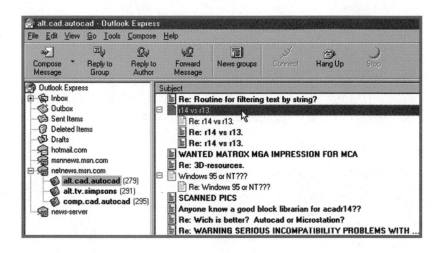

Figure 8.4
List of downloaded newsgroup messages. Notice the thread under the highlighted file.

Let's find some posts to read and download.

1. In your newsreader, click on a *news server.*

2. Click on the name of a newsgroup you subscribed to in the last activity.

3. Browse through the list. When you find something of interest, double-click it to open it in your newsreader.

Internet Milestone

USENET

Usenet comes from <u>USE</u>r <u>NET</u>work. It is a giant public-access network on the Internet, maintained by volunteers, that provides user news and e-mail. Newsgroups get their messages from the Usenet network. All the news that travels over the Internet is called **NetNews**, and a newsgroup is a running collection

of messages about a particular subject.

Usenet was invented in 1979 by students at Duke University and was originally used to exchange information with students at the Uni-

versity of North Carolina. In 1981, another college student, Mark Horton, and a high school student, Matt Glickman, improved Usenet's capabilities to handle larger volumes of postings. By 1995, the daily volume from all Usenet newsgroups and conferences exceeded 50MB of data. There are now tens of thousands of newsgroups.

Usenet Categories

Usenet has been divided into categories, or classes. Some of the more recognized classes are:

alt.	*Alternative topics or subjects*	*news.*	*Usenet news*
comp.	*Computer-related*	*rec.*	*Recreation*
biz.	*Business*	*sci.*	*Science and technology*
k12.	*Educational*	*soc.*	*Social issues*
misc.	*Miscellaneous*	*talk.*	*Debates about anything*

4 Your newsreader keeps track of what items you haven't read by bolding them. After you have read an item, it will be un-bolded.

5 Right-click on a posting and select *Mark Message for Download*, as shown in Figure 8.5.

6 You can mark as many postings as you like, but remember: the more your newsreader has to download, the longer it will take.

7 When you have finished marking the items you would like to read, click *Tools → Download All*. This will download all messages you have marked.

8 Click *View → Current View → Downloaded Messages* to view only those messages you downloaded.

9 Select a message and read its contents.

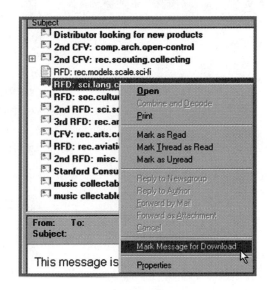

Figure 8.5
Marking messages for down-loading (IE 4.0)

THINKING ABOUT TECHNOLOGY

From browsing through the list of newsgroups, what kinds of groups did you see? What could you determine about the discussion topics from the group names?

Netiquette

Newsgroup Niceties

Here are some suggestions for new newsgroup users:

1. Read a new newsgroup for a few days before you start participating in the threads. This will help you get into the culture of the group before you jump in.
2. Stick to the topic of the group.
3. Be brief.
4. Be considerate. Remember that your postings may be read by thousands of group participants.
5. If you are responding to a message, quote the key point of the original message, so others can more easily follow along.
6. Sign your login name. This is a signal to the group members that you are willing to be responsible for what you write.
7. Don't repeat yourself.
8. Use descriptive titles for your postings.

ACTIVITY
8.3

Objective:

In this lesson, you will learn how to post a response to a newsgroup.

Posting a Response

Newsgroups have an etiquette all their own. You learned earlier about SHOUTING with all caps. Generally, people ARE NOT VERY HAPPY IF YOU DO A LOT OF THIS IN CYBERSPACE.

Usenet groups are also very opposed to any type of advertising in their newsgroups. It's kind of like an invasion of privacy. As you learned in Chapter 7, *spam* is unsolicited and unwanted advertising and other garbage on the Internet. Spamming can occur in newsgroups as well as through e-mail. The response to that sort of post is generally flaming. **Flaming** is emotional electronic communication where basically everyone in the newsgroup sends unkind messages to the message poster to discourage him or her from posting spam again.

Before posting a message, be sure to read through several of the posts. Get a feel for what kinds of discussion goes on in the newsgroup. If you decide to respond to a posting, think about whether your post will benefit the group or not. If not, you may want to e-mail the person whose message you are responding to rather than wasting valuable space.

Here is the process for posting to a newsgroup:

1 Click the *Compose Message* button. The name of the newsgroup is automatically filled in.

2 Fill in the *subject* of your message. Remember, it is important to be concise and specific in your subject line. Because of the number of postings in most newsgroups, most people never read more than a few messages. If you want someone to respond to your post, make the subject line count.

3 Be short and to the point in the body of your message.

4 When you are finished, click the *Post* button in IE 4.0, as shown in Figure 8.6a, or the *Send* button in NN 4.02, as shown in Figure 8.6b.

THINKING ABOUT TECHNOLOGY

Why are newsgroups so fussy about what gets posted? Although there don't seem to be many rules in cyberspace, there are definitely "do's" and "don'ts" in newsgroups. Why?

Visiting the Middle East can be a little dangerous at times. But you can get there safely on the Web. Here is a great URL to start with: *http://www.memst.edu/egypt/main.html,* or key *Egyptology* into your favorite Web browser.

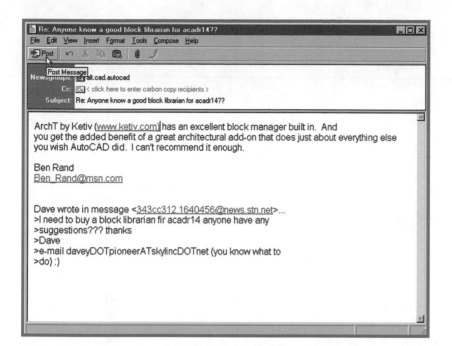

Figure 8.6a
Posting a message (IE 4.0)

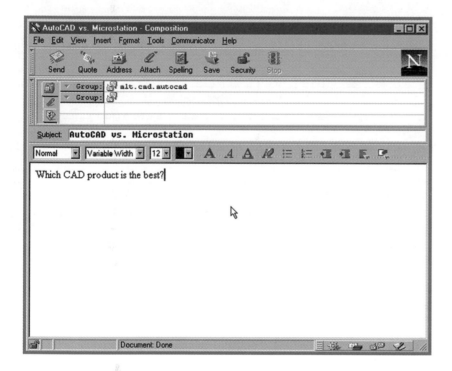

Figure 8.6b
Posting a message (NN 4.02)

Creating Newsgroups

What happens if you really can't find a newsgroup to fit your interests? You can create one! But before you try to form your newsgroup, take a look at *news.announce.newgroups*. You will see just what it takes to create a newsgroup.

To start a new group, you must submit a charter describing the goals of the newsgroup. Then, an *RFD*, or *Request For Discussion*, is issued. For a period of a few weeks, the new group can discuss any potential problems and try to garner support. This is kind of a trial period to see how popular the new group will be.

After the RFD period, a *CFV*, or *Call For Votes*, will be issued. Users vote on whether to continue the newsgroup or not. Generally, there are strict rules for what can and cannot be posted in newsgroups. Number one on the list, of course, is no spamming.

CHAPTER Review

NET VOCABULARY

Define the following terms:

1. newsgroups
2. Usenet
3. NetNews
4. thread
5. flaming

NET REVIEW

Give a short answer to the following questions:

1. List several "do's and don'ts" concerning newsgroups.

2. Choose a topic of interest to you and describe how you would go about finding a newsgroup on this topic.

3. How could you find help with a homework problem?

4. Why do you think newsgroups go through the RFD and CFV processes?

NEWSGROUPS AS SOURCES FOR
NEW PRODUCT IDEAS

GreatApplications, Inc., has just marketed a new product designed for the CAD (computer-aided drafting) market. It was a miserable failure. Evidently, there wasn't enough research done and there was little interest in the product. Still, the company is determined to establish itself in the CAD world with a useful product.

Thanks to your solid research abilities, your boss has asked you to find out what needs the next CAD product should address. Search through as many CAD newsgroups as you can find. Make a list of ten different questions or problems that seem to be asked frequently.

Often, users in newsgroups will have ideas about how companies could and should do things better. Of course, some of these "ideas" stem from frustration, but many of the ideas are good ones. And your company is going to learn from some of them. Try to identify five or six complaints that users have with the companies they deal with. List some ways that these problems could be overcome.

Commonly Asked Questions

1. _____
2. _____
3. _____
4. _____
5. _____
6. _____
7. _____
8. _____
9. _____
10. _____

List of Complaints

1. _____
2. _____
3. _____
4. _____
5. _____
6. _____

NET PROJECT TEAMWORK   Consensus and Recommendations

Bring your results together in your team. Prepare a team report that summarizes the findings of your team. Have a recorder keep track of the discussion. Have one team member report on the results and another team member keep the discussion moving. A final team member should provide snacks to keep the group motivated. Based on the information your team gathered from the CAD newsgroup discussions, what needs should your company's new product fulfill? What pitfalls should they watch out for in developing this new product?

WRITING ABOUT TECHNOLOGY   Newsgroups as a Business Resource

From your experience in completing the Net Project, write a 100-word report, on a separate piece of paper, that answers the following questions: Do you think newsgroups are a viable tool for business? What can businesses accomplish through newsgroups? What limitations or drawbacks do they have for business? Can a newsgroup help a business increase sales?

Net Fun

Seems like most high school and college students live on french fries, burgers, and cokes. They forget the dietary words of wisdom their mothers shared with them as children. Need a refresher course in good eating? Visit *http://www.dole5aday.com/* and listen to your mother.

Finding a Needle in the Global Haystack

By the time you have finished the activities in this section, you will be able to find almost anything on the Internet.

Locating the specific information you need was easier a few years ago than it is today, because the number of documents on the Web have multiplied exponentially. There is simply more information to search through before you find what you need.

Fortunately, search engines are improving every month, allowing you to narrow searches more expertly and with less effort than ever before.

Chapter 9 will introduce you to the world of search engines. You will learn how to use Boolean operators to give your searches real power. Chapter 10 will familiarize you with electronic versions of the more traditional sources of information: the library and the encyclopedia. Also, you'll see some of the world's greatest museums and search for a long-lost friend.

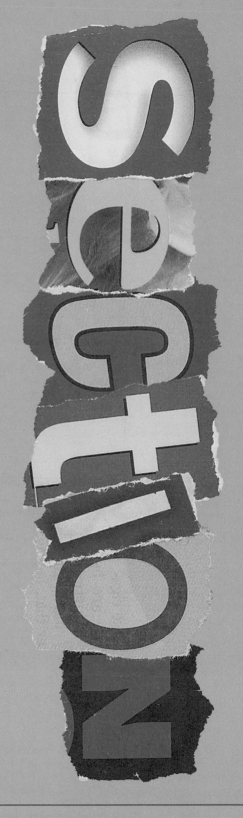

Chapter 9 "I Think I Can!" The Little Search Engine
That Could. 104
Chapter 10 Virtual Library: Using Online Resources 114

CHAPTER 9

"I Think I Can!" The Little Search Engine That Could

Chapter Objectives:

In this chapter, you will learn how to make the best use of Internet search engines. After reading Chapter 9, you will be able to:

1 use the *And/Or/+* operators.

2 use the *Not/-* operator.

3 use the *Near/Adj* operators.

4 use the parentheses operator in a search request.

5 use natural language and phrase searching.

Net Terms

search engines

hits

query

operators

Boolean logic

Boolean operators

Webmasters

phrase searching

natural language searching

Finding the Needle

In Chapter 3, you learned that you can search for information on the Internet using search services, such as Yahoo! and AltaVista. To make such a search possible, these services use software called **search engines** that allow you to look for information based on some criterion, such as a key word. Search engines catalogue the Web, organizing information so that it is easier to find. Some search engines offer indices, so that you can search by category. Often, the terms "search service" and "search engine" are used interchangeably.

The problem is the sheer amount of information avail-able. Often a search will produce a list of hundreds, if not thousands, of "hits." **Hits** can mean a couple of things. Every time someone goes to a Web page, it counts as a hit. Site owners often count the number of hits on their site to judge its effectiveness in attracting users. In this chapter, hits are the number of items found in response to a search query. For example, if your query results in a list of 25 items that meet your search criterion, then the query resulted in 25 hits.

A **query**, like a question, is a method of filtering data to find information that meets specific search criterion. If you

had to look at thousands of pages at random to find one or two containing useful information, then you wouldn't use the Internet much. Learning how to limit your search is essential to tapping the Internet's wealth. Search engines allow you to limit your search by using key words and **operators**—symbols or special words used to perform computer operations.

Search engines use **Boolean logic**, which is a system of logic invented by George Boole, a nineteenth century mathematician. This system uses operators to manipulate data, based on a simple yes or no ranking system. As add, subtract, multiply, and divide are the primary operators of arithmetic, AND, OR, and NOT are the primary **Boolean operators**.

The real benefit of using operators lies in combining them to refine your searches. As you learn more about each operator, try refining your searches by combining operators. Watch how your hit list shrinks to only the few most valuable pages. Remember to bookmark each search engine site. ∎

 *The Life of a Webmaster*

Webmasters are the guardians of cyberspace. **Webmasters** are people who create, organize, and manage Web sites. Most Webmasters got into the Webmaster business because it was fun. Since then, sites have become more and more complex. There are two kinds of Webmasters: those who focus on hardware, software, and protocols, and those who focus on the content of the site.

Every Webmaster must know the basics of the hardware that links computers to the Net, the soft-

ware the Internet uses, and the specialized languages and programming commands required to make the Web work. HTML, Java, JavaScript, CGI, and VRML are all familiar terms to Webmasters. Later in this book, you will be introduced to these terms.

Qualified Webmasters for major companies command large salaries, but the hours are long, and much of the work must be done at night when users are less likely to be on their computers.

ACTIVITY

9.1

Objective:
In this lesson, you will learn to use the *AND/OR/+* operators in a search.

And/Or/+

The *AND/OR* operators are among the easiest to use and understand. The *AND* operator instructs the search engine to search for all documents containing both key words you specify. For example, cats *AND* dogs. By default, all search engines search for documents containing all key words keyed into the search box. Some search engines use the + symbol as an operator. The + symbol acts just like the *AND* operator.

Most search engines do not require you to key the operator in all caps. However, it may be helpful for you to do this to keep your search words separated from the operators.

The *OR* operator instructs the search engine to search for documents containing either key word you specify. For example, cats *OR* dogs. Documents containing either word (or both) will appear.

Let's try out these operators.

1 Using your bookmarks (NN 4.02) or favorites (IE 4.0) in your browser, go to Yahoo!

Figure 9.1
Using the *AND* operator

2 You've had a chance to look through Yahoo! earlier. This time, let's let Yahoo! do the searching. Yahoo! searches for site categories first. Key *dogs* in the search box and click the *Search* button. Yahoo! will display all the categories with the word "dogs" in them.

3 Let's refine our search by adding an *AND* operator. Remember, search engines default to an *AND* search, so *dogs AND breeds* is the same as *dogs breeds.*

4 Click the *Back* button to return to the search box. Enter *dogs AND breeds*, as shown in Figure 9.1. Click the *Search* button, and view your results.

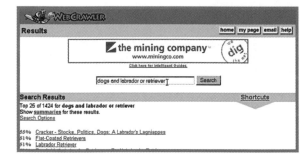

Figure 9.2
Combining the *AND* and *OR* operators in WebCrawler

5 Generally, the *OR* operator will expand a search to include more pages. It can be very helpful when used in combination with the *AND* operator. Go to *www.webcrawler.com* and key *dogs AND labrador OR retriever* in the search box. Click the search button to view your results, as illustrated in Figure 9.2.

6 To find out more about how using these operators changes the results, observe the different results you get from the following searches:

dogs   labrador
dogs AND labrador   retriever
dogs AND retriever   labrador OR retriever

THINKING ABOUT TECHNOLOGY

What did you learn about how the *AND/OR* operators affected your search results in Activity 9.1? Let's say you want to look up information about rattlesnake bites. How would you go about researching this topic?

Objective:
In this lesson, you will learn to use the *Not/-* operator in a search.

Sometimes it's easier to narrow a search by specifying what you are NOT looking for. The *NOT* operator excludes documents containing a key word you specify. Some search engines use the - symbol as the operator, which works the same way as the *NOT* operator. Be sure to check the instructions for using different operators on each search engine. Some, for example, require you to include *AND* with the *NOT* operator. For example: *simpsons AND NOT homer.*

1 Go to *www.hotbot.com.* In the *look for* list box, click the down arrow and choose *Boolean Phrase.*

2 In the *Search* box, enter *carbon monoxide poison AND symptoms*, and click the *Search* button. Note the number of hits returned.

3 This time, add *NOT com* and click the *Search* button. (See Figure 9.3.) This refinement will eliminate the *.com* domains, which are mainly businesses advertising carbon monoxide detectors. Notice that the number of hits is reduced significantly. Many of the remaining sites are educational or organizations that will (hopefully) contain useful information.

NET TIP
Web Addresses

Note that current links to most Web sites presented in this book can be found on the Internet Concepts and Activities *Home Page. Choose* Resources *at* **computered.swep.com.** *Remember that a Web address may change at any time. An address given in this book as an example may no longer be valid. If this is so, either access the Home Page for the current link or do a search to find a similar site (see Chapter 9 for a discussion of search methods).*

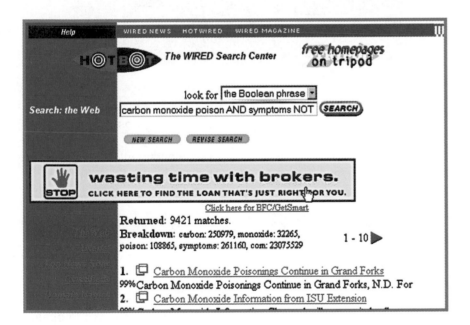

Figure 9.3
Combining the *AND* and *NOT* operators in HotBot

Searching is a process of trial and error. Entering different combinations can lead to drastically different results. It's better to spend a little extra time narrowing down your search than following every hit you get.

THINKING ABOUT TECHNOLOGY

The Net is a virtual library at your fingertips. The problem is too much information. You have to find ways to focus your searches. Why do you think the *NOT* operator works so well?

ACTIVITY
9.3

Objective:

In this lesson, you will learn to use the *NEAR/ADJ* operators in a search.

Near/Adj

The *NEAR/ADJ* operators are used by more advanced search engines. These operators look for key words in a certain proximity to another key word.

The *NEAR* operator looks for *tornadoes NEAR Texas* and usually defaults to within 25 words. You can change the proximity to within 5 words by using *NEAR/5*, where 5 can be any number. Most search engines don't check for word order, so *tornadoes* could be within 5 words before or after *Texas*.

The *ADJ* operator stands for *adjacent*. This operator will return only documents in which, say, *George* is adjacent to *Washington*. *ADJ* is more strict than *NEAR* and will return fewer hits. Let's try these operators.

1 In your browser, go to *www.lycos.com*.

2 Click the *Advanced Search* hyperlink, as shown in Figure 9.4.

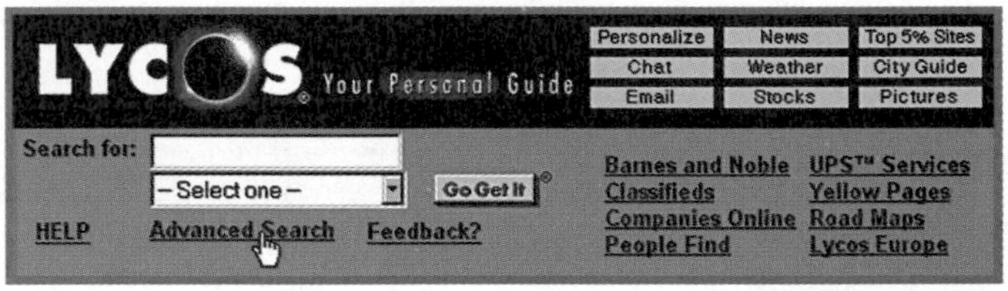

Figure 9.4
Use the *Advanced Search* option for more power in Lycos

Figure 9.5
Combining the *ADJ* and *NOT* operators in Lycos' Advanced Search

3 Key in *volleyball NEAR indoor* to find sites about indoor volleyball.

4 Look at the list of hits. Some contain information about outdoor volleyball. Add the *NOT* operator to eliminate those sites.

5 Enter *volleyball NEAR indoor NOT outdoor.* This trims your list even more.

6 Now try the search with the *ADJ* operator. Key in *volleyball ADJ indoor.* Note the number of hits.

7 Add the *NOT* operator to eliminate references to outdoor volleyball, as illustrated in Figure 9.5.

8 Practice using the *NEAR* and *ADJ* operators in combination with the other operators you've learned to find information about your favorite sport. The goal is to get a small list of sites containing very specific information.

THINKING ABOUT TECHNOLOGY

Now that you've been introduced to the most common Boolean operators, can you think of other ways you might want to filter information? Try to think of five useful ways to focus your hits.

Parentheses

ACTIVITY
9.4

Objective:
In this lesson, you will learn to use parentheses in a search.

Parentheses work in a similar fashion to parentheses in mathematics. In math applications, parentheses set up groups of operations that must be performed before other parts of the operation can be calculated.

Here are some math expressions using parentheses. Notice how different the results can be, depending on the placement of the parentheses.

$2*(4+8/2)=16$
$2*4+8/2=12$
$(2*4+8)/2=8$

Parentheses can be used to filter all sorts of lists and can be combined with most search operators.

1. In your browser, go to *www.excite.com.*

2. Key *cars* in the search box.

3. When your hit list is returned, click the *About Your Results* hyperlink. This will display how many hits your query returned as well as some information about how to refine your search.

4. Click the *Back* button.

5. Key in *cars AND NOT (truck OR rental)* in the search box and click *Search*, as shown in Figure 9.6.

6. Go to the *About Your Results* page and note the number of hits.

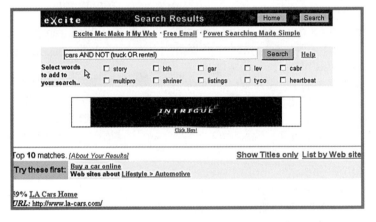

Figure 9.6
Using parentheses with the *NOT* and *OR* operators in Excite. Excite provides check boxes to further narrow your search, a nice feature.

THINKING ABOUT TECHNOLOGY

How important is math in developing Internet tools like search engines? What kinds of mathematical operations make complicated word searches possible? Remember that computers only speak in numbers. In fact, they only speak in 1's and 0's, yes or no.

Net Ethics — *What the Webmaster Knows*

Webmasters are in charge of Web computers for schools, businesses, and governmental organizations. As a result, they have access to all sorts of confidential files and sensitive information. On some sites, the Webmasters also maintain the e-mail system. If they want to, they can read all the mail sent to and from their Internet e-mail servers. What kind of a person do you want to be your Webmaster? What can organizations do to safeguard or at least increase the chances for maintaining confidentiality?

ACTIVITY 9.5

Objective:
In this lesson, you will learn to use natural language and phrase queries.

NET FACT

Boolean Operators and Binary Systems

Boolean operators can be combined to create very powerful queries. They operate on a simple system of binary numbers. Binary code uses only 1's and 0's (yes or no, on or off) to transmit information.

A search for *car AND NOT* (*trucks OR rental*) is turned into this set of questions: Does the page have the word *car* on it, yes or no? From the lists of yes answers, do any of the pages have the words *trucks or rental* on it, yes or no?

If the answer is yes to the first question and no to the second question, then that page is returned as a hit. Simple.

Figure 9.7
Using phrase searching in AltaVista

Natural Language and Phrase Searches

Phrase searching means searching for exact sequences of words in a query by enclosing the words in quotation marks. **Natural language searching** is a search method in which the query is expressed in English, French, or any other spoken language in a normal manner. Unfortunately, this is a technology still in its infancy.

In this activity, you'll use all the search engines we've visited (hope you bookmarked them) and perform the same search. Then we'll revise the search using only certain key words and compare the findings.

Phrase searching and natural language searching are among the easiest and most powerful techniques at your disposal. All search engines reviewed in this chapter support both methods.

Let's try phrase searching first.

1. Go to AltaVista and key in *food poisoning.*

2. Note the number of hits. By default, most search engines look for all pages containing the words you key in. Unfortunately, this method can identify many pages unrelated to the topic you are researching.

3. Try the search again, using the phrase operator (quotation marks). Key in "*food poisoning*".

4. Note the number of hits this time, as illustrated in Figure 9.7. Phrase searching is a good way to limit a search very quickly. It becomes even more powerful when used in conjunction with the operators *AND, NEAR,* and *parentheses.*

Let's try natural language searching. For this activity, you will use the same search on each search engine and compare the results.

1. In AltaVista, key in *Who won the Cy Young Award in 1996?* Before clicking *Search*, highlight the text and copy the question. Then you can paste it in the search box as you jump between search engines.

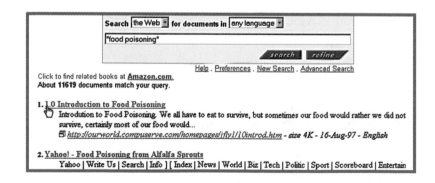

2. Note the number of hits, as illustrated in Figure 9.8. Skim through the displayed summaries to see if you can figure out who won the award in 1996.

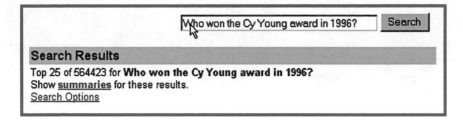

Figure 9.8
Natural language searching—a
good idea . . .

3 Repeat steps 1 and 2 in all the search engines you have bookmarked. Make a note of how many hits the query returned. Have you figured out who won yet?

THINKING ABOUT TECHNOLOGY

As computers get more powerful, scientists try to get them to emulate the most powerful computer on earth: the human brain. Natural language searching is one step in this process. Although it will one day be the best way to search for information, it isn't up to par yet. Try the search again, this time using only the words *Cy Young 1996*, as illustrated in Figure 9.9. How different are the results? Which method seems better at this time?

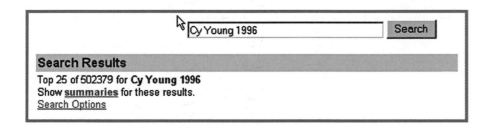

Figure 9.9
Key word searching

NET FACT

Search Engine Comparison

Not all search engines are created equal. Some search engines use categories to organize their information. All search engines permit the use of certain operators. This box gives you a quick overview of the capabilities of several of the more popular search engine sites. This list is not comprehensive, and new capabilities are added all the time. Many sites employ their own unique operators to make filtering lists easier. The best way to learn the search capabilities is to look for a Help hyperlink on the home page.

	Cat.	And/+	Or	Near	Adj	Paren.	Not/-	Nat. Lang.	Phrase
Yahoo	Y	Y	Y	Y	N	N	N	N	Y
AltaVista	N	Y	Y	Y	Y	Y	Y	Y	Y
Excite	Y	Y	Y	Y	N	N	Y	Y	Y
Lycos	Y	Y	Y	Y	Y	Y	Y	Y	Y
Infoseek	Y	Y	Y	N	N	Y	Y	Y	Y
WebCrawler	Y	Y	Y	Y	Y	Y	Y	Y	Y
HotBot	Y	Y	Y	Y	N	N	Y	Y	Y

NET VOCABULARY

Define the following terms:

1. search engines
2. hits
3. query
4. operators
5. Boolean logic
6. Boolean operators
7. Webmasters
8. phrase searching
9. natural language searching

NET REVIEW

Give an example of a search query using each of the following operators. Describe the limitations of searching with each operator and what can be done (how can the search be revised) to overcome those limitations.

1. AND

_____

_____

2. NOT

_____

_____

3. OR

_____

_____

4. NEAR

_____

_____

5. ADJ

_____

_____

6. ( )

_____

_____

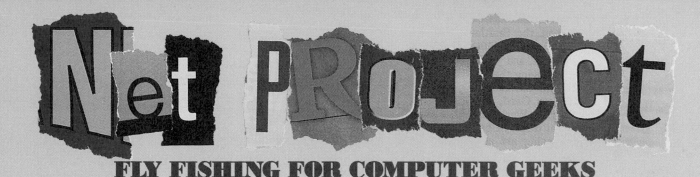

FLY FISHING FOR COMPUTER GEEKS

Since you have fast become the Internet guru at GreatApplications, Inc., the boss wants you to do some research for the company's forthcoming CD-ROM, "Fly Fishing for Computer Geeks." You need to find answers to the following questions:

1. How many Americans fish?
2. How many Americans fly fish?
3. How many women fly fish?
4. How fast is the sport of fly fishing growing?

Knowing what you know about search engines, what do you think is the most efficient way to go about accessing this information? Perform the search and find answers to the questions. Note the search queries that worked well and those that didn't work so well.

_____

_____

_____

_____

_____

NET PROJECT TEAMWORK   Fly Fishing as a Team Sport

After each member of your team has researched the four questions individually, work as a team to prepare an e-mail to your boss. In the e-mail, include the answers to the questions and the URLs of the five sites with the best information on fly fishing. Briefly describe to the boss the kinds of information on fly fishing each site contains.

_____

_____

_____

WRITING ABOUT TECHNOLOGY   Succeed with Search Engines

How useful would the Web be without search engines? Prepare a 100-word report, on a separate piece of paper, explaining various ways that small businesses can use search engines to help them succeed.

Virtual Library: Using Online Resources

Chapter Objectives:

In this chapter, you will learn about many of the online resources at your disposal. After reading Chapter 10, you will be able to:

1. locate online libraries and look up information in them.

2. locate and use encyclopedias online.

3. locate and look around online museums.

4. find people's e-mail and street addresses using search engines.

A Virtual World of Information

The Internet contains literally a world of information. You've just learned about using search engines to locate information. Did you know there are more traditional sources of information available on the Net as well?

Online (or on-line) encyclopedias are also valuable sources of information. The world is accumulating information at such a tremendous rate that printed materials can no longer stay up to date. Online versions can be updated with new information and statistics as soon as they are available.

As the world becomes digitized, libraries are making more of their content available online. You can "check out" a book at any time, since there are enough copies for everyone. And no books ever get lost.

The Louvre in France is one of the world's greatest museums. Millions of people visit it every year. But billions more have never had the opportunity—until now. You can take a virtual tour through many of the world's finest museums. You don't have to spend thousands of dollars getting there, or worry about finding a place to park.

Ever have a problem finding someone's phone number? How about someone who has moved away, but you don't remember where? A **people finder** is a search feature provided by search services on the Internet that helps you find addresses and phone numbers, and we'll show you how to use it in this chapter. ■

Virtual Libraries

ACTIVITY 10.1

Objective:
In this lesson, you will learn to locate online libraries and look up information in them.

One day, the world's books will all be available from virtual libraries via the Internet. But digitizing all that content takes time and money. Most organizations responsible for putting content online are nonprofit. They are working tirelessly with a lot of volunteer effort to accomplish a Herculean task.

The selection of titles at online libraries is growing steadily. But collections are far from complete. For example, one online library features 5,500 works, with authors as diverse as Shakespeare, Jane Austen, and Plato. However, the library has nothing by Ernest Hemingway or John Steinbeck.

Let's find a few online libraries and take a look at where the future of libraries is headed.

1 Go to your favorite search engine.

2 Key in *libraries AND (online OR on-line)*. You may need to be in the search engine's *Advanced Search* area to use Boolean operators.

3 Browse through the hits until you find a public library. Look for the bigger libraries, such as the Internet Public Library, The Library of Virginia, or the Houston Public Library.

4 Search the resources at the library you selected. For example, at the Internet Public Library lobby (Figure 10.1), you can visit the *Online Texts* link. Here you can search for an "e-book" by author or title, or browse by Dewey decimal categories. An **e-book** is a book that has been digitized and put into online libraries for public use.

5 Try looking up your favorite author. If he/she isn't there, look up a book you read for an English class. Find an e-book to read.

6 Go back to your search engine and locate the WWW Virtual Library or another major library. Perhaps you can even visit the Library of Congress!

7 Browse through your new library selection and compare it to the first library you visited.

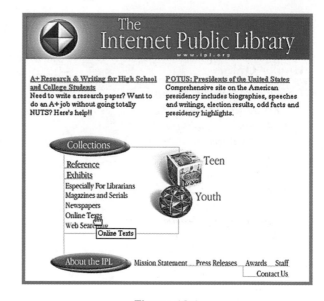

Figure 10.1
The Internet Public Library lobby

Thinking About Technology

The WWW Virtual Library seems to embody the very reason the Internet was invented. The articles and links found in the "library" are maintained by experts in each field from around the world. Truly, it is a collaborative effort. Does it work? How do you think it will evolve in the future?

Netiquette

Read Offline

If you intend to read an e-book, save the page to your computer. Then exit your browser and read the book offline, to avoid unnecessarily taking up valuable Internet access lines that your fellow Netizens could use.

Objective:

In this lesson, you will learn to locate online encyclopedias and compare content quality among different resources.

Virtual Encyclopedias

One of the biggest challenges in using the Internet as a research tool lies in the fact that anyone can post *anything*. It used to be difficult to get a book or article published. Facts had to be meticulously checked and cross-checked. Claims had to be supported.

But as more and more information becomes available, it becomes increasingly difficult to discern fact from fiction. There simply isn't enough time. In this lesson, you will locate several online encyclopedias, and then try and look up the same information in each of them. Evaluate the quality of the information you find at each site.

1. Start your browser and go to your favorite search engine.

2. Find a list of online encyclopedias. Try looking in Yahoo! under *Reference → Encyclopedia* or in other search engine sites under the *reference* or *education* sections.

3. Find articles about the country Yemen, located near Saudi Arabia. (See Figure 10.2.) See if the article lists the area of the country.

NET TIP
Books Online

Looking for books to buy on the Web is easy. The largest online bookseller is www.amazon.com. *But free e-books are harder to find. Use a search engine to find books you can read over the Web without having to buy them.*

Figure 10.2
A site with lots of information about Yemen. Hope you have your speakers on . . .

4. Your first search may be unsuccessful, or you may need multiple sources. Use a search engine to find more information. Key *Yemen* into your *Location* or *Address* window or into a search engine. Search until you find an article that tells you the area of the country.

5. Find an article about Yemen in a different encyclopedia. Does the information correspond? Never assume that your first find is the most accurate. Always double-check your sources.

THINKING ABOUT TECHNOLOGY

How would you rate the online encyclopedias you found? Are they better or worse than their text-based counterparts? How about CD-ROM based? Could you find the information faster if you just keyed *What is the area of Yemen?* in a search engine? Try it and see what you get.

Virtual Museums

**ACTIVITY
10.3**

Objective:
In this lesson, you will learn how to locate online museums and look around.

Virtual museums are popping up everywhere in cyberspace. Of all the reference sources, online museums seem to be the most numerous and offer the greatest variety. From the Louvre to the Smithsonian Institution, museums around the world are opening their electronic doors. People who would never be able to physically visit the world's greatest museums can now tour their collections all from the comfort of their own personal computer.

1. Let's visit the Smithsonian Museum of Natural History. Go to Yahoo! and key *Smithsonian Natural History* in the search box.

2. Follow a link from the list of hits to the museum.

3. From the home page, follow the links to *Exhibits and Programs*, and then to *Online Exhibits*.

4. Take the *Virtual Tour* (Figure 10.3) and choose the *First Floor*.

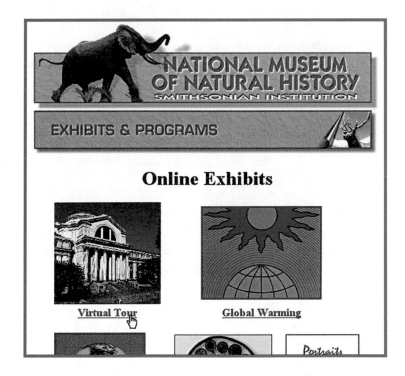

NET TIP:
Online Encyclopedias

Many of the well-known publishers of encyclopedias (both CD-ROM and text versions) have online versions as well. While many of these offer a free trial period, most require a fee to access their material. Some of these include Britannica, Microsoft (Encarta), Funk and Wagnall's, and Grolier's. Use a search engine to find one you can use.

Figure 10.3
Tour the National Museum of Natural History

Internet Milestone

Project Gutenberg

Want to read *Alice in Wonderland*, *War of the Worlds*, or one of Shakespeare's plays for free? Well you can, and you can thank Project Gutenberg for it.

In 1971, Michael Hart was given $100,000,000 worth of computer time on the mainframe computer at the University of Illinois. Wondering how to use the time effectively, he came up with "Project Gutenberg," which, among other things, replicates e-books and makes them available for free on the Net.

Project Gutenberg was the first major electronic publication and distribution project of its kind. Much of the philosophy of sharing found on the early Internet can be traced to this great project.

Try searching for schools that offer classes over the Internet. Can you find a school that will let you graduate without physically attending one class? Can you obtain your college degree entirely over the Internet? How would you like to sit home every day and take an e-class over the Web? What key words would you use to search for cyber-schools and universities?

Figure 10.4
Tour the Acropolis

⑤ How long ago did dinosaurs live? _____

⑥ Go to the *WWW Virtual Library*. Scroll through the list and click on the link to *Museums*.

⑦ Click the *World Museums* link. Scroll down to find different museums in Greece. Among these museums, locate the tour of the Acropolis (Figure 10.4). It may take some searching.

Virtual Tour of Acropolis

This is a photograph of the much-sung and much-praised Acropolis of Athens, taken from a plane. This imposing rock, 156.2 metres above sea level, measuring 330 metres in length at the base, 270 metres at the summit, rises at the sun-bathed plain of Athens, which extends in a semicircular sweep from Phaleron Bay to the foothills of the mountains in the hinterland of Attica.

Welcome to the tours of the *Acropolis*, the world famous monument of Athens, Greece.

For the time being you can entertain yourself with a historical guided tour with comments. Soon you will be able to walk around on your own. Enjoy !!!

⑧ Take the *historical guided tour* and find out what the Athenians call the Acropolis. _____

THINKING ABOUT TECHNOLOGY

Contrary to popular belief, most writers like to be paid for their work. Usually, they get a percentage of their book sales. If books are being made available on the Internet for free, how will writers have any incentive to write? What could be done to compensate them?

Use Local Mirror Sites

Sites that take a lot of hits (get a lot of visitors) will often set up mirror sites. A **mirror site** is a copy of the original site that resides in a computer in another location. Mirror sites contain the same information as the master host site, but are distributed to other computers to reduce network traffic to one host site. This strategy accommodates more people.

Another advantage of setting up mirror sites is to speed up transmission to various locales. If you are surfing the Internet in Florida, it is probably going to be faster for you to download the latest shareware from a mirror site in Washington, D.C., than from a host site located in Redmond, Washington, since Washington, D.C., is closer to where you are.

It is considered good netiquette to select the mirror site closest to your geographical location whenever possible. Another good strategy is to pick a site that is "in the dark." That is, if it is daytime in North America and 2 a.m. in Australia, download from a mirror site in Australia where netizens down under are probably asleep.

People Finders

ACTIVITY
10.4

Objective:
In this lesson, you will learn how to "find yourself" on the Internet.

People finders can help you locate long-lost friends, search for people who attended your high school, or even find the e-mail address of the president of the United States.

1 Many search engines offer a *people find* option. See if your favorite search site has one. If it doesn't, try Yahoo! or Lycos.

2 Click on the *people find* or *people search* option (whatever your search site calls it).

3 For your first search, fill in your own name and information about yourself. If the search doesn't find you at the city level, it may find you at the state level.

4 Search for yourself on more than one people finder. You may find yourself at any number of previous addresses, or you may not be listed at all, depending on which people finder you use.

5 For your second search, let's find the president of the United States. Enter in the people finder box *Bill Clinton* (or the name of the current president, if Clinton is out of office). (See Figure 10.5.)

6 Now search for *William Clinton*. Do you get different results?

NET TIP
Web Addresses

Note that current links to most Web sites presented in this book can be found on the Internet Concepts and Activities *Home Page. Choose* Resources *at* **computered.swep.com**. *Remember that a Web address may change at any time. An address given in this book as an example may no longer be valid. If this is so, either access the Home Page for the current link or do a search to find a similar site (see Chapter 9 for a discussion of search methods).*

Find People

○ E-mail addresses   ◉ Phone number & address

First Name: |Bill|

Last Name: |Clinton|

City: | |

State: |DC| [seek]

Provided by BigYellow.

Figure 10.5
Finding people on the Internet

What's shakin' in So. Cal? Find out at the Southern California Earthquake Center at *http://www.scec.org/* or key *Earthquakes Southern California* into a search engine to get to the rock-bottom of the earthquake scene.

Al Gore's Information Superhighway

Vice President Al Gore has been the national leader in the fight to improve the information superhighway and to make the Internet available to schools. In fact, he coined the phrase the "information superhighway." Visit Al Gore's Web page at the White House. Remember that this is a government site, so the address to the White House ends in *.gov.* Visit *www.whitehouse.gov* and click on the Al Gore links.

7. In Lycos, click on *PeopleFind* and then on *Federal Government.* Keep following the links until you find the president. In what domain category is his URL located? The logical place: *.gov.*

8. You can send an e-mail to the president at *president@whitehouse.gov.* An automatic reply system will answer your message.

9. Now search for someone you really want to find. Fill in as much information as you can about the person. If you only remember the last name, fill that in. Try to narrow your search to a state or city, if possible.

THINKING ABOUT TECHNOLOGY

Do you think most people would be happy to know that their name, address, and phone number is accessible to just about anyone in the world? How could you get yourself removed from those lists? How do you think the lists are generated?

Net Ethics   *Pretty Good Privacy's View*

Does anyone have the right to read your e-mail, your files, or your private publications? Phil Zimmermann, the creator of Pretty Good Privacy, Inc., doesn't think so. He made his now famous PGP (Pretty Good Privacy) encryption software available over the Net. In his view, every Net user has the right to electronic privacy.

However, the federal government had a different view. According to an official White House press release on November 15, 1996, "Encryption products, when used outside the United States, can jeopardize our foreign policy and national security interests. Moreover, such products, when used by international criminal organizations, can threaten the safety of U.S. citizens here and abroad, as well as the safety of the citizens of other countries."

In short, when PGP became available over the Net, anyone in any country could download and use it. Phil was charged with the crime of exporting encryption technology. The case stirred a great debate over personal privacy versus national security. Phil is now in the clear and has since started his own electronic security company, but the debate continues.

What do you think comes first, personal privacy or national security? Who is right: Phil, for protecting your personal communications, or the government, who knows that foreign agents and drug dealers can use encryption software to menace our lives?

CHAPTER REVIEW

NET VOCABULARY

Define the following terms:

1. *people finder*

2. *e-book*

3. *mirror site*

NET REVIEW

Give a short answer to the following questions:

1. *What are some of the issues surrounding online libraries?*

2. *What is Project Gutenberg and why is it important?*

3. *Describe how you would search the Web to find out what four countries last hosted the Winter Olympics.*

4. *You are going to Seattle on a business trip, and you would like to look up an old friend with whom you have lost touch. What steps would you follow to find this person?*

FREESTUFF

GreatApplications, Inc., needs a customized list of library, governmental, and other free research-oriented resources that employees can use when they are doing their business research. Compile a list of libraries, encyclopedias, and e-books that employees would find useful. Save this list of resources in an electronic file in your *Resources* folder. Include at least 25 resources on your list. Call this list *freestuff.*

NET PROJECT TEAMWORK   Teaming Up To Compile Useful Resources

As a team, combine *freestuff* resource lists together into a mega-list of over 100 resources that employees in a company like GreatApplications, Inc., would find beneficial. Save this list of resources in your common folder. If one team member knows HTML, that person can create an active hypertext version of your research.

Look back through previous Net Projects and find links that relate to this list. Consolidate and organize your list by topics, as Yahoo! and many other search services have done.

WRITING ABOUT TECHNOLOGY   Privacy versus National Security

With what you have learned about PGP and the national encryption security debate, prepare a 100-word essay, on a separate piece of paper, supporting one of the following opinions. Use your searching skills to find information that supports your point of view.

Option 1: Encryption technology should only be in the hands of the government.

Option 2: Encryption technology should be available to every Net user in the United States, but shouldn't be given to anyone in a foreign country.

Option 3: The Internet is an international tool, not subject to the laws of any one country. Therefore, encryption software should be available to all.

Option 4: Since the government funded the development of the Internet, it should control the use of encryption on the Net.

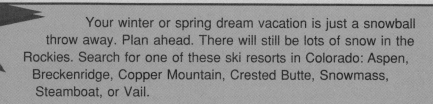

Your winter or spring dream vacation is just a snowball throw away. Plan ahead. There will still be lots of snow in the Rockies. Search for one of these ski resorts in Colorado: Aspen, Breckenridge, Copper Mountain, Crested Butte, Snowmass, Steamboat, or Vail.

Exploring the Net for Information and Fun

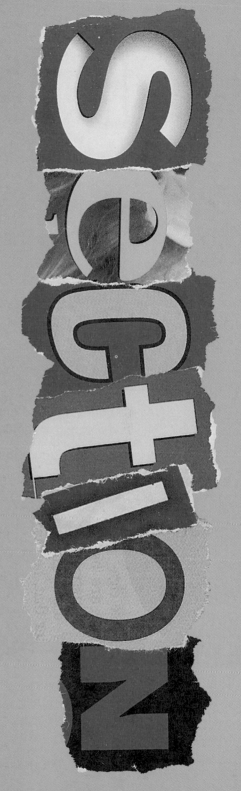

The Internet is becoming a major source of information for people around the world. The hardest part is finding what you need. You've already gained some of the tools to make you an effective Internet user.

In this section, we'll walk you through several subject areas. Along the way, you'll see many interesting and enlightening sites. You'll also have the chance to make your own reference list, so you can return to subject-related sites whenever you need them. You'll get plenty of practice using the skills you learned in the previous chapters—*plus, you'll have some fun!* So rev up your (search) engine and get ready to go!

Chapter 11 will introduce you to some of the amazing sites in the fields of science and math. Take a trip to Mars, look at the guts of a frog without any mess, and find out what the weather's going to be like next week.

In Chapter 12, you will visit sites that will help you become a better writer. You will also have a chance to walk through history and read historical documents. You'll also learn about the latest in news delivery and how the Internet is changing journalism.

Chapter 13 will show you some ways that business is using the Internet. You'll find out how much the U.S. government is in debt and where your tax dollars will be going in the next ten years. You'll also go shopping for computer equipment. After that, you will learn a little about the stock market's history, locate stock prices, and find out how you would do if you had $15,000 to invest.

Chapter 14 will help you be a more informed citizen. You'll learn about bills trying to become law. You'll get introduced to the Supreme Court justices. Finally, you'll learn about a couple of the issues concerning our country.

Chapter 15 gives you a chance to relax some. Kick back and surf to your favorite movie, TV, sports, or music CD sites. In the process you will experience some great technologies, like streaming, that allow continuous motion and sound on multimedia computers.

Chapter 11 Exploring Sciences and Math 124
Chapter 12 Exploring Writing, Journalism, and History 136
Chapter 13 Exploring Business 146
Chapter 14 Exploring Government 157
Chapter 15 Movies, TV, Music: The Web's Got You
Covered 167

Exploring Sciences and Math

Chapter Objectives:

In this chapter, you will explore the rich resources in science and mathematics. After reading Chapter 11, you will be able to

1 locate weather data for various locations and find other weather-related sites.

2 visit NASA's homepage and gather information about the Mars Surveyor mission and find other sites related to space and astronomy.

3 dissect a virtual frog and locate other biology-related sites.

4 find math puzzles and games, view geometric shapes, and find other math-related sites.

Net Terms

Black Thursday

Internet worm

VRML (Virtual Reality Modeling Language)

NET TIP
Web Addresses

Note that current links to most Web sites presented in this book can be found on the Internet Concepts and Activities *Home Page. Choose* Resources *at* **computered.swep. com**. *Remember that a Web address may change at any time. An address given in this book as an example may no longer be valid. If this is so, either access the Home Page for the current link or do a search to find a similar site (see Chapter 9 for a discussion of search methods).*

Space-Out on the Internet

Since the Internet was originally invented by and for scientists to share information, it makes sense that some of the richest content areas would be in the fields of math and science. You can explore everything from the most current subatomic particle tests being run at CERN in Switzerland to the latest pictures of far-off galaxies from the Hubble telescope.

The world was able to participate in the Shoemaker-Levy comet collision with Jupiter via the Internet. And now you can even drive your own virtual rover over the surface of Mars. ■

ACTIVITY
11.1

Objective:
In this lesson, you will learn to locate weather data for your area of the country and find other weather-related sites.

Planning a picnic? Hoping ski season will start early this year? Wanting more information about Hurricane Jane? The Internet definitely has the weather covered.

Most of the time, you won't have to search. Try looking on any of the search engines that use categories. Categories pool together the best resources, saving you the hassle of finding them individually. Cool! Look for a category called *Weather.* For this exercise, we'll use Excite. Yahoo! and Lycos have similar categories.

1 Go to Excite's home page and choose *Weather.* (Note: If Excite is unavailable, try looking for the weather on another of the super search sites on the Web by clicking your search button.)

2 Enter your Zip code or your city in the appropriate box (depicted in Figure 11.1), and click *Get local weather.* Tip: Your Zip code is generally better to use than your city. You may be disappointed if you live in Paris, Texas, and get the weather for Paris, France, instead.

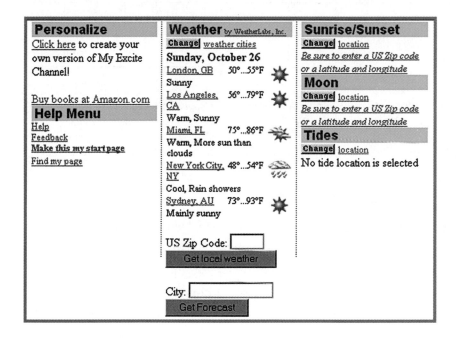

Figure 11.1
Excite's weather search page

Net Life *Zen and the Art of the Internet*

Zen and the Art of the Internet *was written by Brendan P. Kehoe in the earliest days of the popular Net. Zen remains today one of the best guides to some of the tricky aspects of Net science. It is also a great guide to the culture of the Net. You can find early copies on the Net by typing* Zen Art Internet *in a search engine. Consider it required reading.*

Kehoe introduces his book with the following very insightful quote: "One warning is perhaps in order— this territory we are entering can become a fantastic time-sink. Hours can slip by, people can come and go, and you'll be locked into Cyberspace. Remember to do your work. With that, I welcome you, the new user, to the Net."

This advice applies particularly to those netizens who enjoy science. There is so much to see and learn—you may take a virtually endless Net field trip and never return to that report that is due at the end of the term.

NET TIP

Web Addresses

Note that current links to most Web sites presented in this book can be found on the Internet Concepts and Activities *Home Page. Choose* Resources *at* **computered.swep.com**. *Remember that a Web address may change at any time. An address given in this book as an example may no longer be valid. If this is so, either access the Home Page for the current link or do a search to find a similar site (see Chapter 9 for a discussion of search methods).*

3 Now look up and record weather information for the following locations:

City, State	Cloud Cover	Precipitation	Temperature	Dew Point	Wind Velocity	Relative Humidity
New York, NY						
Atlanta, GA						
Dallas, TX						
Salt Lake City, UT						
Seattle, WA						
Los Angeles, CA						
Honolulu, HI						
Your Town						
Time						
Date						

4 Under the *Weather Links* section (illustrated in Figure 11.2), click on *The Weather Resource*.

5 From *The Weather Resource* home page, click on the link to *USA Weather*.

6 Follow the link to *Cloud Cover*.

7 Find the section titled *Earthwatch Data.* Use the following selections in the list boxes provided: *IR Satellite, Region you live in* (for example, *U.S. Southwest*), and *3D.* Then click *Submit Choices*.

8 You're as up-to-date as the weather person on TV. Many of the maps like the one illustrated in Figure 11.3 are updated every 15 minutes.

Weather Links

Change links

Discovery World   Monthly Astronomy Events

Nova Online   Sky and Telescope's Weekly News

Space Today   The Weather Resource

Today@NASA   WeatherLabs

Figure 11.2
Excite's weather links

Figure 11.3
A 3D view of the weather

Explore the other options or follow some of the links to find other weather-related information. The world is literally at your fingertips.

9 Locate five other weather-related sites and record your findings below.

Site Address   **Content Description**

1. _____   _____

2. _____   _____

3. _____   _____

4. _____   _____

5. _____   _____

THINKING ABOUT TECHNOLOGY

Thousands of people around the world are killed every year by weather. In many cases, people just weren't prepared. Can the Internet help save lives in weather-related incidents? How?

Internet Milestone

Black Thursday

The stock market has a pair of "Black Mondays." One occurred on October 19, 1987, when the market lost a gigantic 22 percent in a single day. The other was on October 27, 1997, when it lost over 550 points. The computer world also has a black day: November 3, 1988, **Black Thursday**, the day of the **Internet worm**.

The worm was a malicious computer program unleashed on the Internet by a hacker. The program exploited security holes to gain entrance to an Internet server. It then bogged down the host server by replicating itself and using the server's own connections to infect other computers.

The worm managed to infect over 6,000 computers, which was one-tenth of the computers on the Internet at that time. Eventually, all the systems infected by the worm had to be shut down. Some had to be shut down several times to purge themselves of all copies of the worm. Others were left without e-mail or access to important research projects for over a week. This devastating event did more to make netizens nervous about Internet usage than anything ever had before. It marked a sort of "loss of innocence" in Internet history.

Objective:

In this lesson, you will visit NASA's home page, find information about the Mars Surveyor mission, and locate other space- and astronomy-related sites.

Astronomy and Space Exploration

As a society, we are fascinated with the exploration of space. While sci-fi has infiltrated many TV shows, "hard science" has also become a mainstay on major news programs.

In the past few years we have witnessed the splendor of comets, explored a nearby planet, and considered the possibility of extraterrestrial life. The Internet has fueled this interest by providing up-to-date pictures as well as virtual-reality tours of other planets.

1 Go to NASA's home page located at *www.nasa.gov*.

2 Click on the image map (picture) link that leads to *Mars Global Surveyor*, as shown in Figure 11.4.

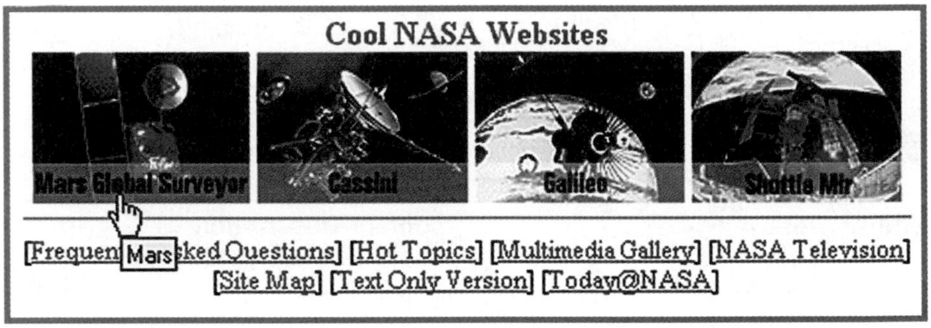

Figure 11.4
NASA's Cool Websites image map

3 Go to the *Mission Overview* page.

4 Fill out the table below with information you find at this site.

Date of surveyor launch

Date of arrival at Mars

Date to begin mapping phase

Date of end of mission

Amount of information surveyor will send back to earth

MOC (What does it do?)

USO (What does it do?)

MOLA (What is it?)

The Web Is the Net, Right?

Wrong. The Internet started in the 1960s, linking computers together with the TCP/IP protocol. The World Wide Web wasn't born until the late 1980s. The Web and the Internet are now symbiotic organisms, which live and grow together. But any technical geek, like the authors of this text, will tell you they are different and that there are many technical distinctions. Does it matter to the end user? Not really. But we thought we would mention the distinction here in the science section of this book, so that we can use a really intelligent-sounding word like *symbiotic*.

5 Locate five other space- or astronomy-related sites not directly sponsored by NASA.

Site Address	Content Description
1. _____	_____
2. _____	_____
3. _____	_____
4. _____	_____
5. _____	_____

THINKING ABOUT TECHNOLOGY

The Internet and science seem to be a perfect match. Does the Internet make it easier for young people to become more interested in science? How will it help scientists in the future?

Net Ethics   *How Much Can You Get Away With at Work?*

One of the big problems faced by corporations is that many computer-using employees use the Internet for personal reasons or to escape the dull routine of their job. When the author of *Zen and the Art of the Internet* suggested, "Don't forget to do your work!" he was addressing this concern. Nowadays, you can listen to thousands of radio stations around the world or even watch TV over your Net PC. Some companies have put in filters to block out any Internet site that isn't work-related. How do you resolve the conflict of giving Internet access to employees who spend more time on the Web than working for the company?

ACTIVITY
11.3

Objective:

In this lesson, you will learn how to dissect a virtual frog and locate other biology-related sites.

Biology

One thing's for certain: biology may never be the same. Forget the formaldehyde and the scalpel. Kermit can rest a little easier.

In this activity, we'll introduce you to Fluffy the Frog, one of the more interesting characters on the Internet. Fluffy was designed to give everyone the unforgettable experience of dissecting a frog—without the mess.

1 In a search engine, type in the phrase "*virtual frog dissection*" and click *Search*.

2 Find and click on the link to the *Virtual Frog Dissection Kit*.

3 This site allows you to see many different views of Fluffy the Frog. It also allows you to download movies of the frog. Read through the directions and then click the frog picture at the top of the page, as shown in Figure 11.5.

4 Describe the purpose of each of the following organs and systems:

Nervous System: _____

Liver: _____

Brain: _____

Kidneys: _____

Small Intestines: _____

Large Intestines: _____

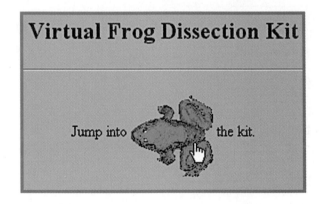

Figure 11.5
Meet Fluffy the Frog . . . and then dissect him

5 Locate five other biology-related sites and record your findings below.

Site Address	Content Description
1. _____	_____
2. _____	_____
3. _____	_____
4. _____	_____
5. _____	_____

THINKING ABOUT TECHNOLOGY

You can probably see many benefits of virtual dissection. Are there any drawbacks? See if you can find other animals available for virtual dissection.

Objective:
In this lesson, you will learn how to find math puzzles and games, view virtual-reality geometric objects, and locate other math-related sites.

Many of the math sites on the Internet are set up to let users ask questions in a Usenet-style discussion. Other users can then post answers or questions.

Other sites provide formulas, games, and story problems to help you brush up on math concepts. Some even provide virtual-reality objects to help you visualize volume and other concepts that are hard to grasp from a drawing in a book. Just as HTML uses simple tags to instruct a browser how to format a Web page, **VRML (Virtual Reality Modeling Language)** is a simple language that simulates 3D objects, lights, and textures, viewable using a VRML viewer within a Web browser. This language can create 3D "worlds," where users can interact with objects and other netizens in a virtual setting. After downloading a VRML page, its contents can be viewed, rotated, and manipulated, and simulated rooms can be "walked into."

1. Go to Yahoo! and search for *math games.*

2. Find a link that interests you and go to the site.

3. On a separate piece of paper, construct a table like the one below. Write down a math puzzle from two different sites and see if you can get the solution. Team up with a friend if you need help solving it.

Site Address	Puzzle	Solution
1.		
2.		

4. Pay attention to what each site offers. Some give prizes to people who can solve the puzzles.

5. Go back to Yahoo! and search for *Geometry and 3D.*

6. Follow the link to *VRML Geometry Teacher.* If you can't locate this site, try another in the list of hits. Then check out the three-dimensional geometric shapes, such as shown in Figure 11.6.

7. If your browser has a VRML viewer, download one of the 3D objects and try rotating it. Even if you don't have the necessary software, 3D geometry sites still offer good information, like formulas to calculate the areas of everything from a sphere to a trapezoid.

8. Locate five other sites related to math. Try to find at least one for algebra, calculus, and trigonometry.

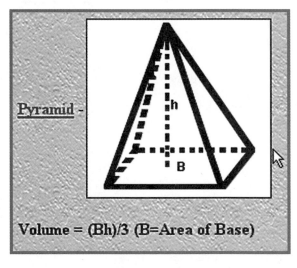

$$\text{Volume} = (Bh)/3 \quad (B = \text{Area of Base})$$

Figure 11.6
Pyramid in 3D

Site Address	Content Description
1. _____	_____
2. _____	_____
3. _____	_____
4. _____	_____
5. _____	_____

THINKING ABOUT TECHNOLOGY

Find a resource that allows you to post questions in whatever math course you are struggling with now or that has bedeviled you in the past. Try posting a question. How long did it take to get an answer? Was it helpful? Would you use this source again?

Net Fun

The Virtual Frog Dissection Web site in Activity 11.3 was one of the first really cool science sites on the Web, appearing long before most people had ever heard of the Web. We thought you would enjoy finding and using this classic milestone site. Good luck in your quest for frog enlightenment. There are lots of good frog science sites.

NET VOCABULARY

Define and explain the significance of the following terms:

1   *Black Thursday*

2.   *Internet worm*

3.   *VRML (Virtual Reality Modeling Language)*

NET REVIEWS

Give short answers to the following questions:

1.   *What are some benefits of getting a weather report from the Web versus getting the report from your local TV news program?*

2.   *How does VRML enhance an educational Web site, such as one on geometry? How does VRML enhance a computer game?*

3.   *What is* Zen and the Art of the Internet *and why is it considered an Internet milestone?*

4.   *What are some pros and cons of using the Internet at work?*

PLAN AN EDUCATIONAL CD-ROM

GreatApplications, Inc., is very interested in creating an educational science CD-ROM in the next year. You've explored some of the related sites available on the Internet. Write a memo to your boss describing the information you found. Spend some time evaluating the sites you visited, particularly the five sites you located under each content area. What information was difficult to find? What could be put on a CD that isn't readily available or accessible on the Internet? Include a list of sites that were interesting to visit, as well as a list of sites that didn't impress you. Explain why you included each site on the list you put it on.

_____

_____

_____

_____

_____

_____

_____

_____

_____

_____

_____

_____

Fractals are fun to view on the Web. A *fractal* is a complex mathematical model of a shape. The shapes can take on some beautiful and strange forms. Key the word *fractals* into a search engine and see what you get.

The Space Race

Time for a race. Okay, so the management of GreatApplications, Inc., may raise some eyebrows about employees having fun and getting their work done at the same time... whoever heard of such a thing.

To expand your list of science-related sites for your CD-ROM, have a race to find scientific URLs about the following topics. Every team member has the same list. See who can find the most resources about these topics in half an hour. Ready, set, here is the list:

Craters of the moon:

_____

_____

Mars exploration:

_____

_____

Galaxies:

_____

_____

Black holes:

_____

_____

Star Trek:

_____

_____

The space-time continuum:

_____

_____

WRITING ABOUT TECHNOLOGY   **The Internet's Role in Science Education**

Write a 100-word response, on a separate piece of paper, to one of the following questions:

Option 1. How will "virtual science," like Fluffy the Frog, change traditional science classes?

Option 2. How will the Internet change the way high school students do science reports?

Option 3. How will the Internet affect science books in the school library?

CHAPTER 12

Exploring Writing, Journalism, and History

Chapter Objectives:

After reading Chapter 12, you will be able to:

1 locate sources to help you improve your writing skills.

2 locate historical documents and other history-related sites.

3 find news sources.

A Tool for Then and Now

The Internet is a playground for surfers, a resource for academics, and a workhorse for the news media. It's also a virtual library of the past, an important tool for writers and historians.

As we've suggested earlier, the Internet started as a tool of science and technology. And it still is. However, now it is much more. It has quickly become the world's best tool for *then* and *now*, rivaling even TV in its ability to distribute information to many people at once.

It's certainly the best source for late-breaking news. You can find out what happened two seconds ago half way around the world. But it is more than that. The Internet

is also the world's largest repository for historical documents. You can just as easily discover what happened two hundred years ago or two thousand years ago.

Forget your copy of *King Lear*? No problem. Just visit one of the many Shakespeare sites on the Internet and download another copy. You may find an online glossary so useful that you'll never bring home a book again.

Besides offering books and research data, the Internet can help you become a better writer. **Online writing labs (OWLs)** are springing up at many college Web sites to answer your writing questions and evaluate your writing skills. ■

Net Terms

online writing labs (OWLs)

BITNET

FidoNet

bulletin board system (BBS)

Gopher

pull media

push media

BTW

IMHO

LOL

ROTFL

We've already visited some of the sources associated with literature on the Internet. But can the Web help you become a better writer? Let's find out.

1 Start at the Internet Public Library (IPL at *http://www.ipl.org*). Click on the *Teen* section and browse through *A+ Research & Writing for High School and College Students.* Check out this site's *Step by Step* approach to writing, illustrated in Figure 12.1.

Objective:
In this lesson, you will learn to locate sources that can help you improve your writing.

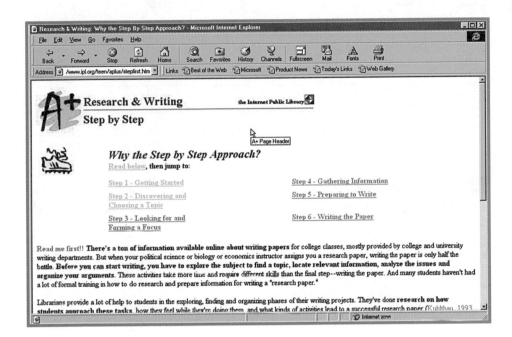

Figure 12.1
OWL at the Internet Public Library

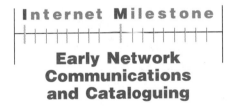

Internet Milestone

Early Network Communications and Cataloguing

Two of the earliest network communication systems serving educational users were BITNET and FidoNet. **BITNET** is short for "Because It's Time Network." It is a worldwide communications network created in 1981 by academic researchers who were tired of waiting around for electronic mail and file transfer capabilities. Not technically part of the Internet, BITNET pioneered and popularized e-mail among college professors and students. BITNET existed mainly on IBM mainframe computers and never achieved the popularity of the Internet.

FidoNet was a 1980s e-mail protocol that was most used for its bulletin board capabilities. A **bulletin board system (BBS)** is a computer system used as an information source and message system for a particular interest group. Users dial into the BBS, read and leave messages for other users, and communicate with other users who are on the system at the same time. BBSs are often used to distribute shareware.

Gopher was the most popular document cataloguing system in use on the Net during the late 1980s. At one time there were four Gopher servers to every Web server. Still around today, Gopher uses long descriptive file names and a hierarchical menu to catalogue millions and millions of documents. Gopher was mortally wounded by Mosaic and the popularization of the World Wide Web. Netscape built Gopher capabilities into its early browser, but the system had already lost momentum to the Web and began an abrupt decline.

2 But what happens if IPL isn't there or you don't find the resources you need? Try searching for additional OWLs. These online writing labs move around a lot, so it is best to use a search engine. In the search engine, try *National Writing Center OWL* or *Online Writing Labs* or even *University OWL*.

3 Search IPL and record below the six steps to writing a good research paper. If you can't locate IPL, try another OWL and record that site's suggestions.

Six Steps to a Good Research Paper	Sub-Step You Learned in this Exercise
1.	
2.	
3.	
4.	
5.	
6.	

4 Browse through each step. Find one sub-step under each step that you didn't know about or could do better. Write what you learned about that step.

5 Locate and describe five other sites that can help you improve your writing skills.

Site Address	Content Description
1.	
2.	
3.	
4.	
5.	

6 OWLs are appearing everywhere. Many OWLs post informative documents for you to read, download, or print for later reference. Using a search engine, locate five additional OWLs. Visit the five sites and browse through the documents they have posted. Read at least one article at each site and write what you learned.

College or University	Address	What You Learned
1.		
2.		
3.		
4.		
5.		

With the mass of information now available on the Internet, why is it more important than ever that the information presented be clearly written?

NET FACT

Citing Internet Sources

As the Internet becomes a regular source of information like an encyclopedia or magazine, it is necessary to set standards for citing Internet-based documents as sources. Citing Internet resources follows the same general pattern as other sources, though punctuation and location of elements vary, depending on the reference guide you use. Here is a general form: [Author. *Title of Article.* Medium. Available: e-mail address or URL of source. Access date.]

- E-mail example:
  Doe, John. *Amazon River Pollution Tests.* Online. Available: e-mail: *MyName@user.edu* from *JohnDoe@biz.com*, Sept. 23, 1997.
- WWW example:
  Coyote, Wiley. *How to Catch a Roadrunner.* Online. Available: *www.acme.com/catch/road@$#!.htm*, December 25, 1996.
- Online images example:
  CoyoteSplat.jpg. Online Image. Available: *http://www.acme.com/meepmeep/coyotesplat.jpg*, December 26, 1996.

Be sure to check the *MLA Handbook* for more information: *http://www.cas.usf.edu/english/walker/mla.html*

- Citing Online Addresses:
  http://www.pitsco.inter.net/p/cite.html
- Williams College Web Library:
  http://www.williams.edu:803/library/library.www/cite.html

Netiquette

Capital Ideas

YOU ALREADY KNOW THAT CAPITAL LETTERS ON THE NET IMPLY SHOUTING AND ANGER. So don't use capital letters unless you mean business. Many people mistakenly believe that good ideas and important points on the Net should be capitalized. Unnecessary capitalization may send the wrong impression.

because of the informality of the Net, many users forget to use capital letters at the beginning of sentences . . . they also leave off periods and use ellipses to excess. . . this is okay with informal messages between friends . . . but you don't want to write this way to your professor, your boss, or your parents. . . who will wonder what in the world you are NOT learning at school . . . not using capitalization is a bad idea when your audience expects a more formal use of proper grammar

ACTIVITY 12.2

Objective:
In this lesson, you will learn to locate historical documents and other history-related sites.

History

The Internet has become a repository for the world's greatest speeches and historical documents. Use what you have learned to locate a few of these sites.

1. Start your search by keying *historical documents* in your favorite search engine.
2. Narrow your search down to the *Declaration of Independence.*
3. Read the document (illustrated in Figure 12.2) and answer the following questions:

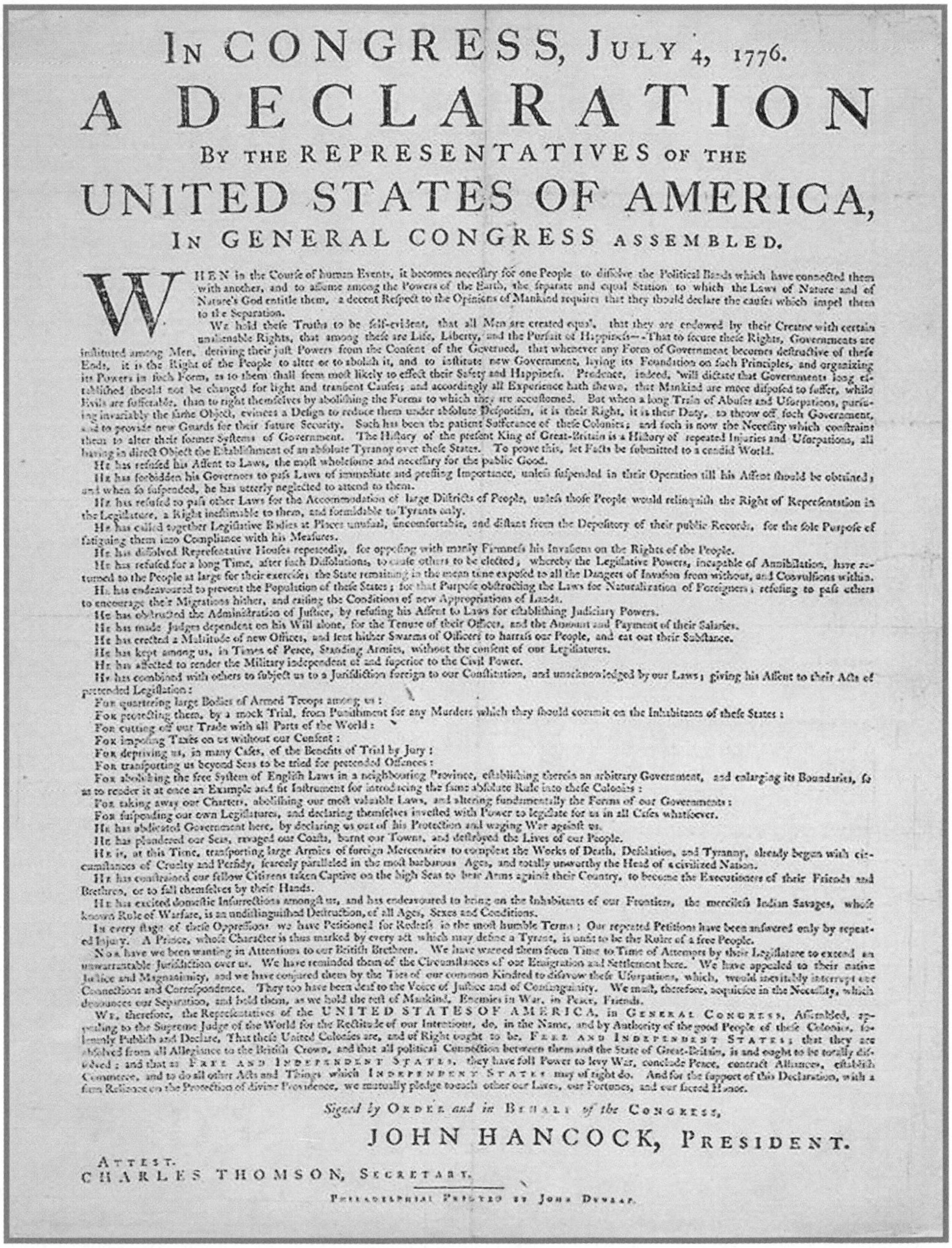

IN CONGRESS, JULY 4, 1776.

A DECLARATION

BY THE REPRESENTATIVES OF THE

UNITED STATES OF AMERICA,

IN GENERAL CONGRESS ASSEMBLED.

WHEN in the Course of human Events, it becomes necessary for one People to dissolve the Political Bands which have connected them with another, and to assume among the Powers of the Earth, the separate and equal Station to which the Laws of Nature and of Nature's God entitle them, a decent Respect to the Opinions of Mankind requires that they should declare the causes which impel them to the Separation.

We hold these Truths to be self-evident, that all Men are created equal, that they are endowed by their Creator with certain unalienable Rights, that among these are Life, Liberty, and the Pursuit of Happiness—That to secure these Rights, Governments are instituted among Men, deriving their just Powers from the Consent of the Governed, that whenever any Form of Government becomes destructive of these Ends, it is the Right of the People to alter or to abolish it, and to institute new Government, laying its Foundation on such Principles, and organizing its Powers in such Form, as to them shall seem most likely to effect their Safety and Happiness. Prudence, indeed, will dictate that Governments long established should not be changed for light and transient Causes; and accordingly all Experience hath shewn, that Mankind are more disposed to suffer, while Evils are sufferable, than to right themselves by abolishing the Forms to which they are accustomed. But when a long Train of Abuses and Usurpations, pursuing invariably the same Object, evinces a Design to reduce them under absolute Despotism, it is their Right, it is their Duty, to throw off such Government, and to provide new Guards for their future Security. Such has been the patient Sufferance of these Colonies; and such is now the Necessity which constrains them to alter their former Systems of Government. The History of the present King of Great-Britain is a History of repeated Injuries and Usurpations, all having in direct Object the Establishment of an absolute Tyranny over these States. To prove this, let Facts be submitted to a candid World.

He has refused his Assent to Laws, the most wholesome and necessary for the public Good.

He has forbidden his Governors to pass Laws of immediate and pressing Importance, unless suspended in their Operation till his Assent should be obtained; and when so suspended, he has utterly neglected to attend to them.

He has refused to pass other Laws for the Accommodation of large Districts of People, unless those People would relinquish the Right of Representation in the Legislature, a Right inestimable to them, and formidable to Tyrants only.

He has called together Legislative Bodies at Places unusual, uncomfortable, and distant from the Depository of their public Records, for the sole Purpose of fatiguing them into Compliance with his Measures.

He has dissolved Representative Houses repeatedly, for opposing with manly Firmness his Invasions on the Rights of the People.

He has refused for a long Time, after such Dissolutions, to cause others to be elected; whereby the Legislative Powers, incapable of Annihilation, have returned to the People at large for their exercise; the State remaining in the mean time exposed to all the Dangers of Invasion from without, and Convulsions within.

He has endeavoured to prevent the Population of these States; for that Purpose obstructing the Laws for Naturalization of Foreigners; refusing to pass others to encourage their Migrations hither, and raising the Conditions of new Appropriations of Lands.

He has obstructed the Administration of Justice, by refusing his Assent to Laws for establishing Judiciary Powers.

He has made Judges dependent on his Will alone, for the Tenure of their Offices, and the Amount and Payment of their Salaries.

He has erected a Multitude of new Offices, and sent hither Swarms of Officers to harrass our People, and eat out their Substance.

He has kept among us, in Times of Peace, Standing Armies, without the consent of our Legislatures.

He has affected to render the Military independent of and superior to the Civil Power.

He has combined with others to subject us to a Jurisdiction foreign to our Constitution, and unacknowledged by our Laws; giving his Assent to their Acts of pretended Legislation:

For quartering large Bodies of Armed Troops among us:

For protecting them, by a mock Trial, from Punishment for any Murders which they should commit on the Inhabitants of these States:

For cutting off our Trade with all Parts of the World:

For imposing Taxes on us without our Consent:

For depriving us, in many Cases, of the Benefits of Trial by Jury:

For transporting us beyond Seas to be tried for pretended Offences:

For abolishing the free System of English Laws in a neighbouring Province, establishing therein an arbitrary Government, and enlarging its Boundaries, so as to render it at once an Example and fit Instrument for introducing the same absolute Rule into these Colonies:

For taking away our Charters, abolishing our most valuable Laws, and altering fundamentally the Forms of our Governments:

For suspending our own Legislatures, and declaring themselves invested with Power to legislate for us in all Cases whatsoever.

He has abdicated Government here, by declaring us out of his Protection and waging War against us.

He has plundered our Seas, ravaged our Coasts, burnt our Towns, and destroyed the Lives of our People.

He is, at this Time, transporting large Armies of foreign Mercenaries to compleat the Works of Death, Desolation, and Tyranny, already begun with circumstances of Cruelty and Perfidy, scarcely paralleled in the most barbarous Ages, and totally unworthy the Head of a civilized Nation.

He has constrained our fellow Citizens taken Captive on the high Seas to bear Arms against their Country, to become the Executioners of their Friends and Brethren, or to fall themselves by their Hands.

He has excited domestic Insurrections amongst us, and has endeavoured to bring on the Inhabitants of our Frontiers, the merciless Indian Savages, whose known Rule of Warfare, is an undistinguished Destruction, of all Ages, Sexes and Conditions.

In every stage of these Oppressions we have Petitioned for Redress in the most humble Terms: Our repeated Petitions have been answered only by repeated Injury. A Prince, whose Character is thus marked by every act which may define a Tyrant, is unfit to be the Ruler of a free People.

Nor have we been wanting in Attentions to our British Brethren. We have warned them from Time to Time of Attempts by their Legislature to extend an unwarrantable Jurisdiction over us. We have reminded them of the Circumstances of our Emigration and Settlement here. We have appealed to their native Justice and Magnanimity, and we have conjured them by the Ties of our common Kindred to disavow these Usurpations, which, would inevitably interrupt our Connections and Correspondence. They too have been deaf to the Voice of Justice and of Consanguinity. We must, therefore, acquiesce in the Necessity, which denounces our Separation, and hold them, as we hold the rest of Mankind, Enemies in War, in Peace, Friends.

We, therefore, the Representatives of the UNITED STATES OF AMERICA, in GENERAL CONGRESS, Assembled, appealing to the Supreme Judge of the World for the Rectitude of our Intentions, do, in the Name, and by Authority of the good People of these Colonies, solemnly Publish and Declare, That these United Colonies are, and of Right ought to be, FREE AND INDEPENDENT STATES; that they are absolved from all Allegiance to the British Crown, and that all political Connection between them and the State of Great-Britain, is and ought to be totally dissolved; and that as FREE AND INDEPENDENT STATES, they have full Power to levy War, conclude Peace, contract Alliances, establish Commerce, and to do all other Acts and Things which INDEPENDENT STATES may of right do. And for the support of this Declaration, with a firm Reliance on the Protection of divine Providence, we mutually pledge to each other our Lives, our Fortunes, and our sacred Honor.

Signed by ORDER *and in* BEHALF *of the* CONGRESS,

JOHN HANCOCK, PRESIDENT.

ATTEST.
CHARLES THOMSON, SECRETARY.

PHILADELPHIA: PRINTED BY JOHN DUNLAP.

Figure 12.2
Declaration of Independence

What were five reasons for separation from England cited in the document?

1. _____

_____

2. _____

_____

3. _____

_____

4. _____

_____

5. _____

_____

How many future presidents of the United States signed the Declaration of Independence? Who were they?

_____

_____

_____

4 Locate five other sites related to history and write a description of their content.

Site Address	Content Description
1. _____	_____
2. _____	_____
3. _____	_____
4. _____	_____
5. _____	_____

THINKING ABOUT TECHNOLOGY

Will there come a day when the "traditional history textbook" will be outmoded? Could an entire history class be taught using sources currently available on the Internet?

This writing, history, and journalism section is a good place to mention spelling. The Net offers an unparalleled opportunity to write and share your thoughts. But don't try presenting a great argument in any Internet forum with misspelled words in the text. You will be torn apart. If you misspell a key word in the middle of your argument, you will be flamed into extinction. This is a common reply to Net spelling errors.

"If you can't spell DEMMOCRITIC, then get out of the thread and let someone with an education contribute."

Businesses that misspell words on their Web pages are also flamed and laughed at. A Web page becomes a liability, not an advertising coup, when spelling errors abound.

Thankfully, there are spell checkers for the spelling impaired. If you have a good argument going, use a spell checker before you share your writing. Let someone proofread your Web pages before you post them.

ACTIVITY 12.3

Objective:

In this lesson, you will learn to locate news-related sites and find information about careers in journalism.

Journalism and News

News is everywhere on the Internet. Although TV has a slight advantage in its ability to broadcast pictures worldwide instantly, the Internet has the unique capability of linking related information from numerous sources quickly and reliably.

New technology called "push" allows users to have news delivered right to their desktops. Most Internet surfing has been done by accessing one site at a time. Users click a link or enter a URL to select a particular site. This content delivery system is called **pull media**, because the user selects the content to "pull" into the computer. In contrast, **push media** is a content delivery system that automatically sends or "pushes" content to the user's computer. You don't have to go find the news; it comes to you! Using push technology, users can specify what information will be delivered and how often. Then push software does the searching and downloads the information to the user's computer. PointCast was the first popular push system on the Net (see Figure 12.3).

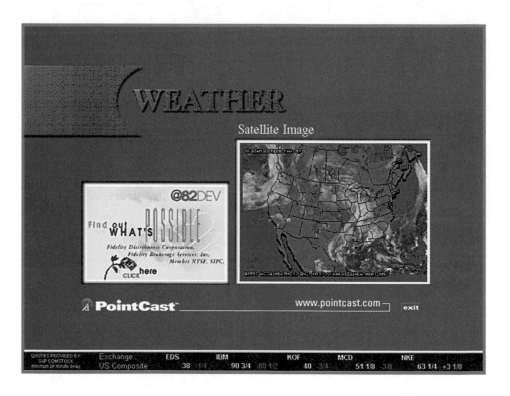

Figure 12.3
PointCast push system

There are also many traditional forms of news on the Web, including newspapers, magazines, and television-based news. In this activity you will explore various kinds of "new media" to disseminate the news.

The Net is a great resource for students in journalism. For example, *NewsWeb* is a site dedicated to high school newspapers. And there are many other sites as well. Use your search engine to locate *online newspapers*, *online magazines*, and *online publications* in different categories. Can you find any high school newspapers from your state? College newspapers? Professional newspapers?

1 Locate five college newspapers and complete the following table:

College	Name of Paper	Web Address
1.		
2.		
3.		
4.		
5.		

2 Locate five well-known newspapers and complete the following table:

City	Name of Paper	Web Address
1.		
2.		
3.		
4.		
5.		

3 Locate five TV stations and complete the following table:

Station	Web Address
1.	
2.	
3.	
4.	
5.	

THINKING ABOUT TECHNOLOGY

How can the mass of information on the Internet speed up a journalist's job? What are some cautions about using the Internet for news?

Net **Life**   *CyberWords Were CyberRific—for a CyberMoment*

In the early days of the Net, everything was cyber-this and virtual-that. It all started with William Gibson's term CyberSpace. Soon, a conversational thread on the Net or a chat group became known as a CyberChat. The Net's strange new vocabulary was called CyberSpeak or CyberEse. People even began to go on CyberDates. Virtual Universities and Cyber-Schools were started. The Net was called the Virtual- or CyberFrontier. Everything was Cyberized.

The overuse of "cyber" and "virtual" soon became apparent. It was no longer clever or cute to put the cyber prefix before every possible noun. Thankfully, this CyberTrend is beginning to die out.

CHAPTER Review

NET VOCABULARY

Define the following terms to your boss at GreatApplications, Inc., and explain how each term is used or applied. Remember, your boss has no clue about the Internet or what the Internet can do for the company. Be kind to the person who signs your check. Don't use big words and don't CAPITALIZE your frustrations!

1. online writing labs (OWLs)
2. BITNET
3. FidoNet
4. bulletin board system (BBS)

5. Gopher
6. pull media
7. push media
8. BTW

9. IMHO
10. LOL
11. ROTFL

NET REVIEW

Give a short answer to the following questions:

1. How is a BBS different from e-mail?

2. How would you go about finding writing advice on the Internet?

3. What is the value of the Web from a historian's viewpoint?

4. What are some advantages of push media over pull media? Disadvantages?

NEWS ON THE RUN

You have been asked to look into push technology for GreatApplications, Inc. The president of the company is interested in knowing how up-to-date information can be automatically sent to employees who need to follow economic and social trends that may impact business. Visit major news sources on the Web. Test each site. Learn about their push capabilities and report back on what you think are the top two news organizations that use push.

Start by finding and visiting the major sources of news and information. We won't give you the URLs. You need to figure that out yourself, but good starting points include: ABC, CBS, NBC, FOX, CNN, CNNFN, NPR, MSNBC. Save your report in your *Research* folder. Good luck!

NET PROJECT TEAMWORK   Team Up for the Big Push

Get together with your team and research the following Net technologies for use in your company: push, VRML, HTML, FTP, Telnet, BBS, Gopher, BITNET, FidoNet. Divide up the list. Look up information about each on the Web with your favorite search engine. As a team, rank the technologies from top to bottom as to their value to the company. Give reasons why the company should or shouldn't use each of these technologies. Save the results in your common team and in your individual *Research* folders.

WRITING ABOUT TECHNOLOGY   Is the Internet the End of Traditional News Media?

Do you think the Internet will be the end of newspapers and magazines as media for information delivery? What about TV? Take a stand on this issue (will it or won't it). Write a 100-word essay, on a separate piece of paper, describing why you have taken the stand you have. Feel free to use other sources to support your position.

· PORTFOLIO · PROJECT

CHapTer 13

Exploring Business

Chapter Objectives:

In this chapter, you will locate and work with information used in the business world. After reading Chapter 13, you will be able to:

1 locate economic information at the Congressional Budget Office.

2 go window-shopping online for computer equipment.

3 locate historical and current stock market information.

Net Terms

freeware

Dow Jones Industrial Average

ticker symbol

Internet and Business: Partners for the Future

The Internet has changed the way we do many things. Nowhere has this impact been felt more than in business. Businesses are scrambling to make the Web profitable. Nevertheless, traditional methods of advertising and distribution often aren't effective through the Web.

To attract visitors, Web sites have to be clearly organized, informative, and visually attractive. Also, visitors will not wait if it takes too long for pages to load.

Despite the growing pains, the future of business is on the Internet. Customers from around the world can access information and products quickly and easily. Orders can be placed and automatically processed for shipping without human intervention. Inventories can be instantly adjusted and orders placed to replenish stock on hand. Databases can be scanned to provide customers with lists of other items they might like to buy, based on previous purchases or the buying habits of other customers.

Investors can access important information, like financial reports, historical stock information, and corporate press releases. They can also see up-to-the-minute stock reports to help them make decisions to buy or sell stock.

The Internet as we know it is only a few years old. Yet in that time, it has experienced many fundamental changes, thanks mostly to big business interests. Perhaps the future of the Internet depends as much on business as the future of business depends on the Internet. ■

Economics

ACTIVITY

13.1

Objective:
In this lesson, you will learn to locate information about the U.S. public debt and find information at the Congressional Budget Office.

Although our economy is in one of the most phenomenal growth trends in history, the U.S. government is sinking further into debt. Want to find out just how much? To the penny? And where your tax dollars will go for the next ten years? Complete these activities to find the answers to these questions—plus a lot of other information.

1 First let's find some information about the public debt. Search for "*U.S. public debt*" and check out some sites that sound interesting.

2 Now let's find out exactly how big the debt is. Look for a link among your hits for "*public debt to the penny*" or key this phrase into a search engine to find it. (See Figure 13.1.)

The Public Debt

To the Penny

| HOME | NEWS | E-MAIL | INDEX | FORMS | FTP | FIND |

11/03/1997 $5,427,078,768,247.28

Figure 13.1
Public debt: Where your tax dollars go

3 Find and record the following information about the U.S. public debt:

Today's amount: _____

Yesterday's amount: _____

How much did the debt
increase from yesterday? _____

Amount 1 week ago: _____

Amount 1 year ago: _____

Amount 10 years ago: _____

How much has the debt
increased in 10 years? _____

4 Search for the "*Congressional Budget Office*" and follow the link to the CBO home page.

NET TIP
Web Addresses

Note that current links to most Web sites presented in this book can be found on the Internet Concepts and Activities *Home Page. Choose* Resources *at* **computered.swep.com**. *Remember that a Web address may change at any time. An address given in this book as an example may no longer be valid. If this is so, either access the Home Page for the current link or do a search to find a similar site (see Chapter 9 for a discussion of search methods).*

NET FACT

IRS Forms

You can find all kinds of tax help on the Web. The Internal Revenue Service (IRS) is required to post its tax forms and publications on the World Wide Web. Visit *www.irs.gov*. Many people don't realize that the IRS is a part of a larger Department of the Treasury. The IRS can be found there also at *www.irs.ustreas.gov*.

Figure 13.2
Economic forecasts by the CBO

5 The CBO is responsible for supplying Congress with figures and estimates for the budget and the economy. Look for a link to a report called *"The Economic and Budget Outlook: An Update."* (See Figure 13.2.)

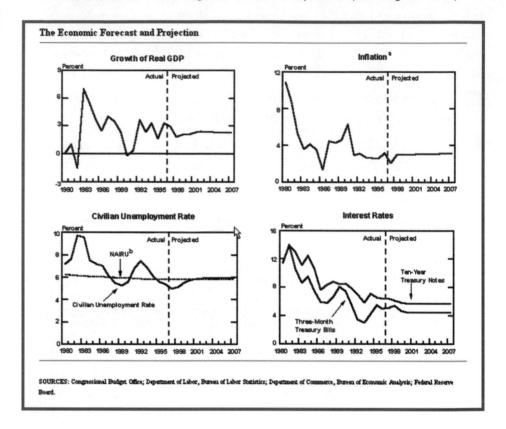

6 This report is revised every six months by the CBO to reflect what has happened. Scan through the report and look for the following information:

	1998	*1999	*2000	*2004	*2008
Current Deficit (−) or Surplus					
Gross Domestic Product (GDP)					
Wage and Salary Disbursements ($)					
Unemployment Rate (%)					
*These figures are projections					

THINKING ABOUT TECHNOLOGY

The national debt is a major issue in every national political race. Will the accessibility of this information via the Internet make any difference? Will it influence who we vote for?

Online Shopping

ACTIVITY
13.2

Objective:
In this lesson, you will learn to locate and compare prices online.

The Internet offers a unique shopping environment. While home shopping is nothing new, the Internet allows quick access to numerous sources. Also, users have the added benefit of being able to research background information about the store in ways not always possible at the store.

1 Use your search engine to locate information to fill in the following chart:

Product and Features	Vendor or Company Name	Price per Unit/Date
Computer: Find systems with the following specifications: 266 MHz Pentium II, 32 MB RAM, 24X CD-ROM, and 3 gig hard drive.		
Monitor: Find monitors with the following specifications: 17" screen, .28 dot pitch, 1024 × 768 resolution (at least).		
Modem: Find modems with the following specifications: 56K, internal.		

Internet Milestone

Amazon.com

While many large book companies stayed away from the Web, Amazon.com began to sell books exclusively over the Web. This company has no physical "store"! Within a few years, sales skyrocketed. Amazon.com proved that the Web can be a very lucrative medium for selling books... and maybe other products.

Continued

Product and Features	Vendor or Company Name	Price per Unit/Date
Multimedia kit: Find multi-media kits with the following specifications: 24x CD-ROM, 32-bit Wavetable sound card, amplified speakers.		
Software Applications: Compare office suites from Corel, Microsoft, and Lotus.		
Software Applications: Find a price for a new game from four different online vendors.		

THINKING ABOUT TECHNOLOGY

How would you rate your online "window shopping" experience? Was it easy to find the information you needed? Would you rather talk to a salesperson than look at a computer screen? Why or why not?

Net Ethics — *Fraud on the Web*

Web fraud is a big business. There are as many scam artists on the Web as anywhere else.

How can you protect yourself from Web fraud? Do your research. Use Usenet to ask questions about any company with which you are thinking about doing business. Pay attention to the rumors about Web fraud. There are some really scary stories. One scam had users download a new, free Web viewer. Once installed, the program routed the Web users' local phone Internet access to a long-distance line in an Eastern European country. The unwitting users had to pay the long-distance charges, which in some cases reached thousands of dollars. AT&T uncovered the fraud and reported it to the government, saving some individuals a great amount of real (not virtual) cash.

What should be done to stop Web fraud? The U.S. Postal Service looks for mail fraud, and the Secret Service patrols bank fraud. What agency should patrol Web fraud?

Look Up Stock Prices

ACTIVITY 13.3

Objective:
In this lesson, you will learn to locate historical charts of the Dow Jones Industrial Average and look up stock prices for your favorite companies.

The recent status of the economy has generated more interest in the stock market than ever before. Billions of dollars are invested every month. Thanks to the Internet, investors have quick, easy access to all sorts of economic information. This allows them to make smart, educated decisions about their investments.

The **Dow Jones Industrial Average** is a measure of stock performance of 30 large U.S. companies. The Dow serves as a benchmark, or standard, against which to judge performance of individual stocks. By watching the DJIA, you can get a general sense of how large established company stocks did on that particular day. If your stock did better, then you had a good day.

1 Go to *Yahoo!* and look for a link to *Stock Quotes*, as illustrated in Figure 13.3. (Most major search engine services offer stock quotes. As an alternative, try *Excite*. Click *Business and Investing*, enter the abbreviation for a company in the *Stock Search*, and get the quotes.)

Figure 13.3
Stock quotes category in *Yahoo!*

2 Locate the link to the *Dow* information. This leads to a table, similar to the one shown in Figure 13.4. This table is updated every twenty minutes. You will also see a graph of historical information, which is what we are interested in.

3 Click on the *max* link, as shown in Figure 13.4.

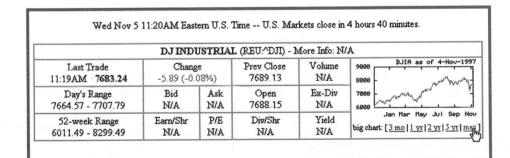

Figure 13.4
Dow Jones information, updated every twenty minutes

④ From the chart, try to determine what year the Dow passed the following marks:

	Mark	Year
a.	1000	
b.	2000	
c.	3000	
d.	4000	
e.	5000	
f.	6000	
g.	7000	
h.	8000	

⑤ At the top of the page, you will see a *Get Quotes* box. Every company with publicly traded stock is issued a **ticker symbol**, which is a two-to-five letter abbreviation for the company. For example, Microsoft's symbol is MSFT and Apple Computer's is AAPL. As illustrated in Figure 13.5, you can enter a company's ticker symbol in the box to find that company's stock quote.

Enter ticker symbol in this box.　　　　**Select detail level of quote.**

Figure 13.5
Get quotes for individual stocks

Don't know the ticker symbol? Click here.

Net Life *Free Fun*

Games are given credit for first attracting large numbers of customers to the Net. Some games you must pay for before you download. Shareware games can be downloaded and paid for later if you like them. But there are also free software games on the Net. Any software on the Net that you can download and never have to pay for is called **freeware**.

Type "free software" in a search engine, and find some good games. Be careful, however. Some freeware may contain viruses that can cause damage to your computer system. Use at your own risk. Get permission before you download anything to the network.

6 Pick five companies whose products you use on a regular basis. They can be computer, soft drink, fast food, clothing, automobile, or any other type of company you can think of. Find and record the following information for each company.

Company Name	Ticker Symbol	Most Recent Price	52-Week High	52-Week Low	Average Recommendation (Buy or Sell)

THINKING ABOUT TECHNOLOGY

In the past, investors were dependent upon investment houses and after-the-fact newspaper reports for current stock information. How will up-to-date information affect the average stock buyer?

As more and more businesses think of ways to entice you to spend your money on the Web, it is only natural that banks have found their way to cyberland. However, rumors about insecure transactions kept banks away from the Web for many years. The conditions before 1995 weren't right for Internet banking. Transactions were not secure, and many experts thought that customers would not use an online bank.

Then Netscape paved the way for banking by adding security fea-

Internet Milestone

Security First Network Bank

tures to its browser. (You can tell that you have a secure transaction by noticing the solid key or closed lock in the corner of your Browser's status bar.)

Finally, taking the risk, a lone bank opened up its Internet doors. Security First Network Bank (*www.sfnb.com*) went online, and everything changed overnight.

Soon, the major banks took on Web banking. Wells Fargo, the Toronto Dominion Bank, and the Bank of America were among the first to offer online accounts. Now it is hard to find a bank that doesn't have an online presence.

Once banks believed the Net was secure enough for their clients, other companies and consumers gained confidence in the security of Web transactions.

Net Fun

Visit one of the first online banks and see how it is doing after all these years. Try *www.sfnb.com, www.wellsfargo.com,* or *www.bankamerica.com.*

CHAPTER REVIEW

NET VOCABULARY

Define the following terms:

1. freeware

2. Dow Jones Industrial Average

3. ticker symbol

NET REVIEW

Give a short answer to each of the following questions:

1. Describe how you could locate the ticker symbol for a particular company and locate information about that company's stock performance online.

2. Explain to a friend how to locate information about top-quality, yet inexpensive, computer systems online. Also explain how your friend could pay for an online computer purchase.

3. Give your opinion about the benefits and drawbacks of banking online.

4. Do you think it is in the public interest to distribute tax forms and tax information without cost over the Web?

5. Explain how a taxpayer can locate critical tax information over the Web.

ONLINE INVESTING

Several promotions at GreatApplications, Inc., have resulted in a healthy bankroll for you. You managed to save $15,000, and you want to invest in the stock market. Most investment firms research companies by looking at financial reports to determine if the company is in good financial condition. Many companies post their financial reports on the Internet for potential investors to review.

Your job is to find the financial reports of five companies you are interested in. Save the financial reports to your personal folder so that you can read through them later. You will make an "investment" in these companies, and then track your holdings to see how your picks perform.

You will invest $3,000 in each company. On the day you start, divide the amount invested in each company ($3,000) by the price of the stock that day to determine the number of shares you now own. For example, if the price of one share is $25.125, then the number of shares you purchased would be 3,000/25.125 = 119.40.

Perform the same calculation for all five companies you choose, and enter these starting numbers in the table below, next to the $3,000 initial net worth. Update the prices once a week for five weeks. Calculate the net worth of your investment each week by multiplying the week's stock price by the number of shares you originally purchased. For example, if the price of the stock dropped to $25.00, then your stock's net worth that week would be 25 × 119.40 = $2,985.

Stock prices are reported in eighths of a dollar. So, if a price is listed as 25-1/8, the amount is equal to $25.125 dollars. Yep, it's kind of crazy, but they calculate to the half penny.

After five weeks, how did your portfolio fare?

Stock (Ticker Symbol)	Date	Price per Share	Number of Shares	Net Worth
1.				$3,000
2.				$3,000

Stock (Ticker Symbol)	Date	Price per Share	Number of Shares	Net Worth
3.				$3,000
4.				$3,000
5.				$3,000

ADVANCED NET PROJECT   Tycoon

Take the Net Project one step further by buying and selling shares. If one of your stocks isn't doing as well as you'd like, sell your shares and invest in another stock that's doing better. The only catch is that you cannot invest new money beyond what your stocks earn. If a stock has made money and you decide to sell those shares and invest in something else, then you can use whatever money you gained. If your stock is losing money and you sell, then you will have lost some of your original investment and consequently have less to reinvest.

NET PROJECT TEAMWORK   Team Stock Competition

With your teammates, create a stock portfolio by selecting five stocks. With the agreement of the team, invest $1,000,000 of GreatApplications' money and buy the stocks. Watch the prices go up and down for seven days, and then sell on day seven. Compare the performance of your team's five stocks with that of the other teams. The group that creates the biggest gain and earns the most money from the mythical sale wins. These team members will then be promoted to become the next vice presidents of GreatApplications, Inc.

WRITING ABOUT TECHNOLOGY   Online Security

With more business transactions occurring online, major issues have surfaced surrounding the security of these transmissions. Unencrypted data transfers can be hacked into or intercepted by other people. How do you know that your credit card number is safe as it's flying through cyberspace? Do some research and write a 100-word report, on a separate piece of paper, about what is being done to ensure online security.

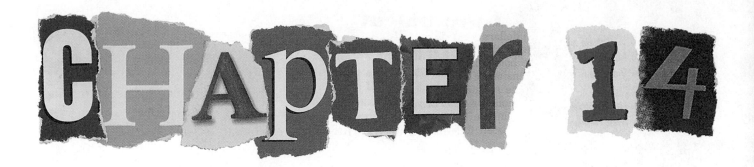

CHAPTER 14

Exploring Government

Chapter Objectives:

In this chapter, you will find out how to be more informed about important issues facing your country. After reading Chapter 14, you will be able to:

1 locate information on bills going through Congress and locate government-related sites.

2 locate information about Supreme Court justices and decisions.

3 discuss network computing and find information about current issues to help you make informed decisions.

4 identify several organizations that influence the operations of the Internet.

Net Terms

network computing

Information Infrastructure Task Force (IITF)

National Information Infrastructure (NII)

National Telecommunications and Information Administration (NTIA)

Good Netizens Make Good Citizens

The Internet offers a unique and exciting opportunity for people to get involved in government. As a concerned citizen and current or future voter, it is your responsibility to become involved. Before you become involved, however, you'll need to be informed. Nothing will get you up to speed faster than your Internet connection. Not only are you able to be updated on current events via the Net, but you can also explore the ramifications of bills before legislative bodies or see what pressing issues the Supreme Court is considering. ■

Objective:
In this lesson, you will learn to locate information on bills being decided in Congress and locate sites related to each branch of the federal government.

Government

Unless you spend the day watching CSPAN, you probably don't know what Congress does all day. Few of us have time to follow Congressional happenings very closely. Still, it's good to know what bills are currently before Congress. This is our country and it's our responsibility to be informed. The actions of our elected officials affect our lives.

Let's see what's going on in Congress right now.

1 Go to *http://thomas.loc.gov* (illustrated in Figure 14.1).

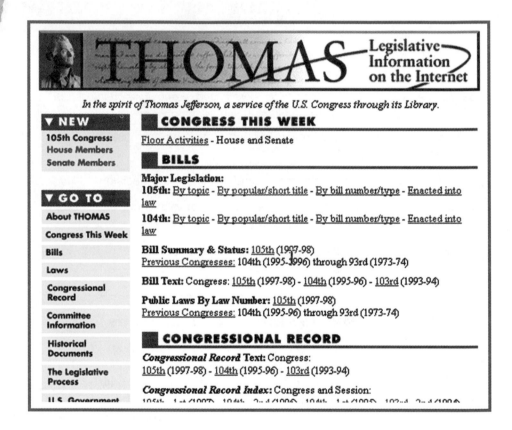

Figure 14.1
The Thomas Internet site provides information about activities in Congress

Netiquette

Writing to Elected Officials

Freedom of speech is a great thing. However, our right to hold and share our own beliefs doesn't include being rude, crude, and disrespectful to elected officials in an e-mail message. The Constitution gives us our freedoms, but our moms and grandmas taught us manners. Give every e-mail the mom test.

Sure, elected officials make mistakes and can even be totally wrong on the issues. But reason and good manners must prevail. A congressperson or a

president will be more likely to record your opinion and reconsider his or her views from a short statement that is well-constructed, easy-to-read, reasonable, and of good taste, than from an e-mail full of trash talk.

When you write your elected officials, first send a copy to a couple of higher authorities: your mother and your grandmother. If they approve of your writing tone, then your message is ready for primetime.

② Under *Congress Now*, follow the link to *Floor Activities* to see what Congress is working on. Locate and record the information requested below.

NET TIP
Web Addresses

Note that current links to most Web sites presented in this book can be found on the Internet Concepts and Activities *Home Page. Choose* Resources *at* **computered.swep.com**. *Remember that a Web address may change at any time. An address given in this book as an example may no longer be valid. If this is so, either access the Home Page for the current link or do a search to find a similar site (see Chapter 9 for a discussion of search methods).*

House of Representatives

Name (number) of bill   What is it about?

1. _____   _____

2. _____   _____

Senate

Name (number) of bill   What is it about?

1. _____   _____

2. _____   _____

③ Locate two additional sites for each branch of the federal government (executive, legislative, and judicial) and record below the kinds of information you found at each site.

Executive

Address   What information
                                                         does this site offer?

1. _____   _____

2. _____   _____

Legislative

Address   What information
                                                         does this site offer?

1. _____   _____

2. _____   _____

Judicial

Address   What information
                                                         does this site offer?

1. _____   _____

2. _____   _____

THINKING ABOUT TECHNOLOGY

Will lawmakers act more responsibly if they know they are constantly being monitored by voters via the Internet? What information would you like to find about the government on the Internet?

ACTIVITY
14.2

Objective:
In this lesson, you will learn how to find information about the Supreme Court.

Law

The Supreme Court is the highest court in America. It is responsible for interpreting the Constitution and applying this interpretation to laws that affect us.

How much do you know about the justices who make up the Supreme Court? Can you name any of them? What important decisions have they made in recent years?

1 Search for *Supreme Court Justices.*

2 Identify the current justices who make up the Court. Fill in the following information:

Name of Justice	Appointed (Date)	Appointed by (President)
1.		
2.		
3.		
4.		
5.		
6.		
7.		
8.		
9.		

3 List two recent court decisions:

1. _____

2. _____

Want one of the quickest e-mail replies on the Net? Write a short note to *president@whitehouse.gov.* You will get an automatic reply that will list the important issues facing the President and the country.

4 Select one of the decisions you listed in Step (2) and answer the following questions:

a.   Who wrote the decision?

_____

b.   What is the name of the case?

_____

c.   What is the case about?

_____

d.   What was the ruling of the Court?

_____

e.   Who (if anyone) dissented?

_____

THINKING ABOUT TECHNOLOGY

Supreme Court Justices are not elected by popular vote. They are appointed by presidential recommendation. Once confirmed by Congress, justices serve for life. Supposedly, this keeps them free of outside influences and public opinion. However, as the public becomes more informed via the Internet, newsgroups, etc., they (the public) can raise a louder voice. Will this affect how the Supreme Court does its job? Is it good for the public to be so informed?

NET FACT

Regulating the Expanding Internet

The Net has moved to our television sets and has become more affordable with the development of network computing. **Network computing** is a new system, developed by Oracle, which stores everything—applications, data, and services—on a network of servers and downloads these to users' computers as needed. Oracle sees this new system as "the dawn of the next generation of computing." According to Oracle's Web site, "Inexpensive, easy-to-use computers linked to powerful, professionally managed networks of information are the keys to network computing." [*www.oracle.com*, accessed 11/29/97] Complex tasks, such as updating software and maintaining virus protection, are moved from the end-user to the professionals who maintain the network. Users will no longer have to update software. The most current versions are always available on the network server. To find out more about network computing, go to *www.oracle.com* and follow the links to "*What is network computing?*"

The costs of Net access have dropped remarkably. Suddenly, everyone can afford to be on the Internet. How will this affect such converging technologies as the television and the computer? How will cable and satellite systems be different, now that the Internet can be delivered by systems other than the phone system?

These are interesting questions. Here is another one. Consider the V-chip, designed to protect families from unwanted television programming. The V-chip is the result of a presidential campaign to improve television. Congress enacted the legislation, and the Federal Communications Commission is enforcing the law. How will this V-chip legislation be applied, now that the Internet is available through your television?

The Net facts are that as the Net becomes increasingly available to more users, it will stir up more controversy. This controversy will lead to more efforts to regulate and control the Net, more court cases, and more laws.

ACTIVITY 14.3

Objective:
In this lesson, you will learn to find information about current issues and identify your (informed) stand on these issues.

Political Issues

Every four years we elect a president to govern the country. Before the election, we hear about controversial issues. Then the elections pass and we go back to life as usual. The issues never seem to get resolved. Why is that?

The Internet provides a good forum for people to continue the debate over important issues. It allows people to inform themselves about what is fact and what is fiction. Information empowers people. In this activity you will research a couple of important issues.

1 Before you start, record your knowledge of the following issues:
What do you know about the greenhouse effect and government proposals to help remedy this?
What do you know about the issue of campaign finance reform?

2 Search for the topic *greenhouse effect* or *global warming*.

3 After researching this issue on at least five sites that present differing views, list the critical issues. Fill in the following table:

Critical Issues

Address	Argument
1.	
2.	
3.	
4.	
5.	

4 After reading some of the arguments, what is your position? Is global warming a credible issue? Should the United States take steps to limit carbon dioxide emissions? What might be the cost to the economy? What new information did you learn through your online research that you didn't already know?

_____

_____

Search the Web for the government sites of other countries. What laws are important to them? What laws have they passed concerning the Internet?

⑤ For many years Congress has debated the issue of campaign finance reform. Search for campaign finance reform and find five sites that present differing views on the issue. In the following table, identify the critical issues.

Critical Issues

Address	Argument
1.	
2.	
3.	
4.	
5.	

⑥ Why do you think Congress has not been more successful in implementing reform? What are the best of the reform proposals? What new information did you learn through your online research that you didn't already know?

_____

_____

THINKING ABOUT TECHNOLOGY

Will the Internet help people become more involved in issues like those covered in this activity? Are you more or less likely to act on these issues, now that you have some information? What can you do?

Net **Life** *Executive Branch Agencies on the Net*

*The legislative branch and the courts are not the only government organizations with a big say in how the Internet works. Agencies like the Federal Communications Commission have regulatory power. The Commerce Department also has a say when it comes to Net commerce across state and national borders. It is the oversight agency for the **Information Infrastructure Task Force (IITF)**, a committee put together by the Clinton/Gore administration to implement the administration's vision of how the **National Information Infrastructure (NII)** should work. The NII is an integrated communications system planned by the Clinton/Gore administration that will be based on a nationwide network of networks, and* *will supposedly allow all Americans to take advantage of the country's information, communication, and computing resources.*

*But these are not the only organizations in the U.S. that influence Internet operations. The **National Telecommunications and Information Administration (NTIA)** is the executive-branch agency responsible for domestic and international telecommunications and information policy issues. With nearly three hundred full-time employees, the NTIA is busy tracking business activities on the Net.*

And this is just a short list of the agencies that are impacting life on the Net.

Tracing Illegal Activity

Messages can be tracked from every Internet computer. Within seconds, government policing agencies, like the Secret Service and the FBI, can trace an illegal message back to the computer that sent the message. They can then begin their investigation into the illegal activity.

With a search engine, look for the Senate and the House of Representatives on the Web. Find out if your two senators and one congressperson have Web pages and e-mail addresses. How can these sites help your representatives as they bid for re-election?

Netiquette

Stand by Your E-Mail

It is considered good netiquette to put your name on any e-mail you send to your elected officials. This sends the message that you stand by your position. It also says that you are a responsible person and that this e-mail message isn't a hoax written to stir up controversy. (This rule applies to newsgroup discussion groups as well.)

NET VOCABULARY

Define the following terms:

1. network computing

2. Information Infrastructure Task Force (IITF)

3. National Information Infrastructure (NII)

4. National Telecommunications and Information Administration (NTIA)

NET REVIEW

Give a short answer to each of the following questions:

1. Why is it important to be informed about the House and the Senate?

2. Do you think that network computing is "the dawn of a new generation of computing," as Oracle asserts? Why or why not?

3. Why is it important to be informed about the latest Supreme Court decisions? What can you learn from the Web sites about Supreme Court decisions that you probably won't find in your local newspaper?

4. An issue will be on the ballot next week, asking voters to approve voting rights for farm animals. You want to be an informed voter before you go to the polls. Explain how you would go about researching the pros and cons of this issue on the Internet.

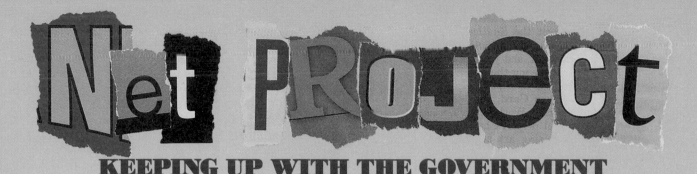

KEEPING UP WITH THE GOVERNMENT

GreatApplications, Inc., needs to stay up to date on legislation that can affect the software business. Search the Web's legislative, executive, and judicial sites and use Usenet political discussion groups to find the important issues related to software and Internet regulation. Make a list of sources that can help you stay on top of the latest laws and court rulings that affect your company's business. Save this information in your *Research* folder.

NET PROJECT TEAMWORK   E-Mail Your Senator

Get together with your team and agree on the three most important issues facing the software industry and the Internet community today from among those you uncovered in the Net Project. After you narrow your list to three, discuss these issues as a team and pick one topic as the most important. Draft a team e-mail to your state's senator, presenting the team's position on the issue. Work together to craft a well-written, well-researched e-mail. Keep it to less than 150 words. Put all team members' names on the message, and e-mail it to your state's senator.

WRITING ABOUT TECHNOLOGY   The Internet's Impact on Government

Write a 100-word response, on a separate piece of paper, to one of the following questions:

Option 1. How will access to Congress, the House, and the Supreme Court change how students view the workings of our government?

Option 2. The Net allows us to take a more active role in government. If our founding fathers were here, how would they react to this new development?

Option 3. It is possible to view your elected official in action—then e-mail your pleasure or displeasure? How do you think our representatives would like this "instant playback" from the voters?

CHAPTER 15

Movies, TV, Music: The Web's Got You Covered

Chapter Objectives:

In this chapter, you'll find resources to help you relax. After reading Chapter 15, you will be able to:

1 find movie reviews and showtimes.

2 find television-related sites.

3 discuss some new technologies that enable you to enjoy audio, video, and animations on the Web.

4 locate sports-related sites.

Net Terms

network computer (NC)

plug-in

Shockwave player

streaming

Web TV

All Work and No Play . . .

All work and no play makes for a pretty dull day. Even the scientists who invented the Internet thought so. Remember the first newsgroup? It wasn't about the project the scientists were working on. It was a group for people to talk about science fiction books.

In this chapter, you'll discover some of the resources available to help you make the most of your recreation time. The Internet isn't going to replace all other forms of media or entertainment, but it will add to your fun. New technology and new data handling processes are making your Web browsing a full multimedia experience. ■

ACTIVITY
15.1

Objective:

In this lesson, you will learn how to find Siskel & Ebert's movie reviews and look up movie showtimes.

Let's Go to the Movies!

The Internet is becoming a marketing vehicle for the movie industry. Months before a movie is released, a Web site can be set up to increase the hype.

Reviews of current and past movies are posted all over the Web. You can even find (subjective) lists of the best, and worst, movies ever made. More and more theaters are posting movie times on the Web, which is great. No more busy signals when you're trying to find out when a show is playing.

Let's evaluate our movie choices.

1 In a search engine, key in *Siskel and Ebert.* Follow the link to Buena Vista Television's *Siskel & Ebert* site.

2 If your computer has audio capabilities, check out Siskel & Ebert's *Revolving Cube Sound Reviews*, illustrated in Figure 15.1.

NET TIP
Web Addresses

Note that current links to most Web sites presented in this book can be found on the Internet Concepts and Activities *Home Page. Choose* Resources *at* **computered.swep.com**. *Remember that a Web address may change at any time. An address given in this book as an example may no longer be valid. If this is so, either access the Home Page for the current link or do a search to find a similar site (see Chapter 9 for a discussion of search methods).*

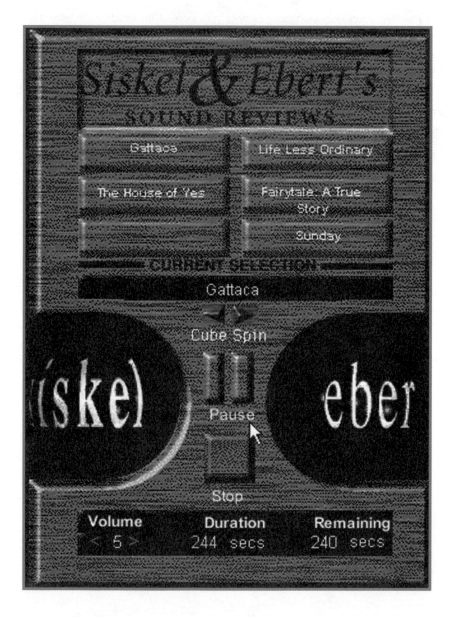

Figure 15.1
Siskel & Ebert's Revolving Cube Sound Reviews

③ Now search the site for *Siskel & Ebert's Best and Worst* list.

④ Fill in the table below with information from the "Best and Worst" list.

    a.   How many times did Siskel and Ebert agree on the best film of the year in the last 10 years? Write down the year(s) and the film name(s).

_____

_____

_____

_____

    b.   How many times did Siskel and Ebert agree on the worst film of the year in the last 10 years? Write down the year(s) and the film name(s).

_____

_____

_____

_____

Internet Milestone

Network Computers

In Chapter 14, you learned a little about network computing, a new concept introduced by Oracle Corporation for simplifying computer use. Larry Ellison, founder of Oracle, wondered why people needed to buy expensive personal computers with lots of software to meet their computing needs. If the information and resources are already on the Net, all users should need is an access terminal that can surf, search, access and use software, watch movies, play online interactive games, and listen to Internet radio. Ellison turned his vision into the **network computer (NC)**, which is a computer that accesses resources from a professionally managed network server linked to the Internet to provide computing services to customers instead of requiring the programs and capabilities to reside on the local computer. Since NCs only need to access computing capabilities rather than contain them, then NCs can be sold at a fraction of the cost of a traditional personal computer, making Internet access more affordable and therefore available to more people.

The network computing idea was so compelling that other companies like Microsoft and Intel quickly jumped on the bandwagon. Network computers lowered hardware and software costs, since all the necessary software components are on the Internet. There is no need for an expensive 8 megagigasuperbyte hard drive, Windows or Macintosh software, or a host of other expensive pieces of software and hardware. All you need is your login access information, and you can access your data and the software you need from any network computer.

Busy shopping and need to pick up some tickets quickly for the game tonight? Log onto any network computer at the mall and order your tickets. Leave your research paper at home? No problem. Log onto the nearest NC at school, access your Net files, and print it again.

⑤ Now let's see what's playing. Go to *www.movielink.com*.

⑥ Click the *Search by Theater* ticket. Enter the Zip code where you live (see Figure 15.2). (Note: Not all theaters are publishing their showtimes online yet, but keep trying.)

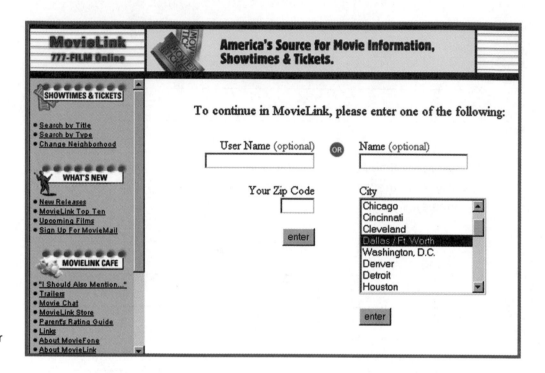

Figure 15.2
Look up movie times in your area at www.movielink.com

⑦ Record below the movie times and theaters for four movies you want to see.

Movie	Theater	Showtimes
_____	_____	_____
_____	_____	_____
_____	_____	_____
_____	_____	_____
_____	_____	_____

THINKING ABOUT TECHNOLOGY

Why do you think movie makers are so eager to have a presence on the Net? Do you think there is a correlation between box-office sales and a Net presence? What other entertainment businesses do you think could increase their sales by offering a Web site?

Couch Potato's Guide to TV

Web sites for TV shows are extremely popular. While only one site can be the "official" site, hundreds of unofficial sites are likely to spring up all over the Internet. You can find everything from lists of past episodes to sound bites and pictures from the latest episodes of popular shows.

Let's do a little searching.

Objective:
In this lesson, you will learn to find television-related information, such as trivia about old and new TV shows, and check out some wacky new plot ideas for Seinfeld on the Seinfeld-O-Matic.

1 Most search engines feature large categories devoted to television, usually located in the recreation or entertainment sections. In Yahoo!, click on the *Entertainment* section.

2 Next, click on *Television* and then *Shows.* You will then see a menu of TV-show categories, as illustrated in Figure 15.3.

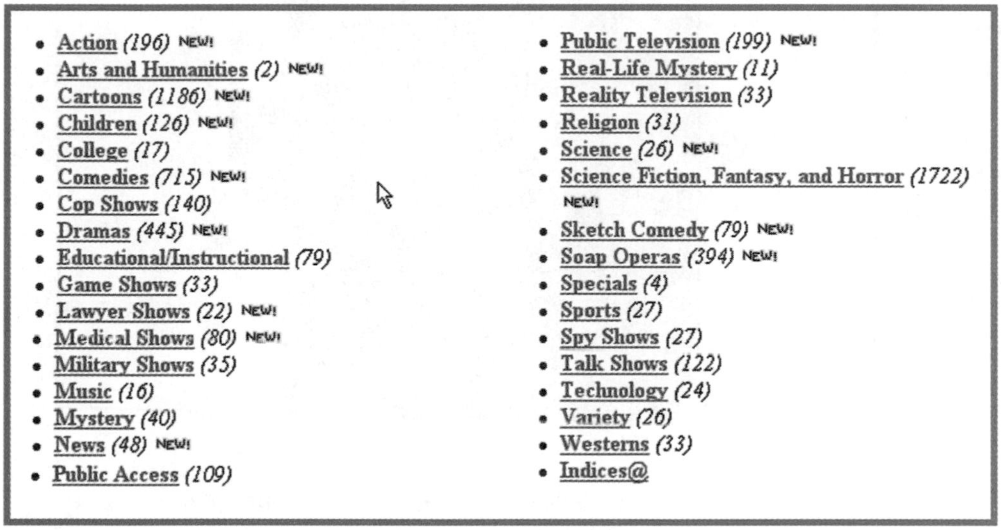

- Action *(196)* NEW!
- Arts and Humanities *(2)* NEW!
- Cartoons *(1186)* NEW!
- Children *(126)* NEW!
- College *(17)*
- Comedies *(715)* NEW!
- Cop Shows *(140)*
- Dramas *(445)* NEW!
- Educational/Instructional *(79)*
- Game Shows *(33)*
- Lawyer Shows *(22)* NEW!
- Medical Shows *(80)* NEW!
- Military Shows *(35)*
- Music *(16)*
- Mystery *(40)*
- News *(48)* NEW!
- Public Access *(109)*

- Public Television *(199)* NEW!
- Real-Life Mystery *(11)*
- Reality Television *(33)*
- Religion *(31)*
- Science *(26)* NEW!
- Science Fiction, Fantasy, and Horror *(1722)* NEW!
- Sketch Comedy *(79)* NEW!
- Soap Operas *(394)* NEW!
- Specials *(4)*
- Sports *(27)*
- Spy Shows *(27)*
- Talk Shows *(122)*
- Technology *(24)*
- Variety *(26)*
- Westerns *(33)*
- Indices@

Figure 15.3
Menu in the television shows section of Yahoo!

3 Find an episode guide to *M*A*S*H*, one of the longest-running, most-watched television shows in history, and answer the questions below.
- a. When did the first episode air? _____
- b. When did the last episode air? _____
- c. How many episodes total were aired? _____

NET FACT

Experience Multimedia on the Net
To fully experience the really cool animations and multimedia effects on most entertainment Web sites, you need to have the Shockwave player plug-in installed in your browser. A **plug-in** is an auxiliary program that works with a major software package to enhance its capability. The **Shockwave player** is a multimedia viewing plug-in that often comes already installed in newer versions of Internet Explorer and Netscape Navigator. But if your browser doesn't have the Shockwave player or you want to update your version of it, go to *www.macromedia.com* and download it!

NET FACT

Streaming

Audio and video streaming is a process for compressing audio and video signals so they can be sent over the Net. The compressed signals are then captured in a buffer, decompressed, and turned into continuous sound and video. The players that made streaming popular are StreamWorks (from Xing) and the RealAudio/Video player from RealAudio. Other companies like Geo Publishing have added their versions. Visit their sites and download the players. Experience streaming. You'll like it.

RealAudio:
  www.realaudio.com
StreamWorks:
  www.streamworks.com
Emblaze:
  www.emblaze.com

Figure 15.4
The Seinfeld-O-Matic

4 Now find the show called *The X-Files* and answer the questions below.
 a. How many categories at Yahoo! are dedicated to the X-Files?

 b. What is the address of the official Web site of the X-Files?

5 For something truly different, see if you can find the *Seinfeld-O-Matic*, illustrated in Figure 15.4. This whacky site developed by (who else?) college students further underscores the need for more homework and less free time in college.

Reload this page to get another possible plot!

Welcome to the Student.Net Seinfeld-O-Matic. The Seinfeld-O-Matic generates millions of possible Seinfeld plots from its extensive database. Send Us nouns, verbs, people, or sentences to add to our plot database at seinfeldomatic@student.net!

6 Pull the lever on the Seinfeld-O-Matic and check out some possible plot scenarios. Record your favorite five plots below.
 a. _____
 b. _____
 c. _____
 d. _____
 e. _____

THINKING ABOUT TECHNOLOGY

Since there is so much Internet interest in TV programming, how much attention do you think producers pay to Internet activity? Do you see a time when Internet feedback will affect programming? Plots?

Music—Lyrics, Shopping, What's Next?

New processes for transferring data are improving the distribution of audio and video on the Internet. **Streaming** is a data handling process that enables data to flow continuously, allowing Web site audio and video to play without requiring file downloads. The sound quality can't match a good FM radio signal, but it's getting better all the time. Many people expect the Internet to become a primary source of distribution for music in the near future.

Let's see what the Net has to fit your musical tastes.

1. Using the *Entertainment* category of a search engine, search for sites that contain lyrics to popular songs.

2. In a text file, record the following information for four songs that you pick.
   a. Song title
   b. Artist's name
   c. A few memorable words in the lyrics

3. Save the file in your *Personal* folder.

Many sites on the Internet are now offering previews to popular music CDs. Most are commercial sites, trying to sell CDs to you. They offer previews as a way of enticing you to buy. All in all, it's a pretty good deal for you: you get a quick preview of the music before you buy, and it's a lot of fun to see what's out there.

4. Search for *music previews.*

5. Follow a link to one of the many music preview sites available.

6. Listen to some of the samples. You can usually find samples by clicking on a speaker icon, like the one illustrated in Figure 15.5.

◀)) = Click for Sound Samples

Figure 15.5
Speaker icon denoting sound samples

ACTIVITY
15.3

Objective:
In this lesson, you will learn how to find music lyrics and music preview sites, and listen to previews of music before you buy.

THINKING ABOUT TECHNOLOGY

Streaming is one of the more exciting data transferring processes developed for multimedia on the Internet. Sound and movie files tend to be large and require a lot of time to download before they can be played on your computer. Streaming allows them to play as they download, resulting in a shorter wait. However, streaming can fall apart when Internet traffic is too high. How was your experience? Could Internet radio ever become a reality?

ACTIVITY

15.4

Objective:

In this lesson, you will learn how to locate sports-related sites for many popular sports and for some lesser-known sports as well.

Sports for the Armchair Quarterback

The Internet is a great place for sports. You can find schedules, stats, records, reports from last night's big game, and player profiles. And don't forget sound and movie bites of Michael Jordan hitting yet another last-second shot to win the game.

But what if you like obscure sports, like camel racing, Danball, or curling? Or what if you want to find out the best places in the country to fly fish? The Internet probably has a page for you to visit, too. Do the following activities and find some of the many resources available for sports fans.

1 Find five sports sites (with information about several sports).

Site sponsor or owner   **Address**

1. _____   _____

2. _____   _____

3. _____   _____

4. _____   _____

5. _____   _____

2 Find five sites related to specific sports.

Address   **Sport**

1. _____   _____

2. _____   _____

3. _____   _____

4. _____   _____

5. _____   _____

Internet Milestone

Web TV

Web TV is the first attempt to merge the Internet and your TV set. Using just an Internet TV terminal and your phone line, you can get online without a computer! Not a big seller in its first years, Web TV is starting to take hold. Web TV provides another great entertainment option for less cost than a traditional computer system. For more information about Web TV, check out *www. philipsmagnavox.com.*

Net **Life** *Tracking Sporting Events Live*

You can now track all the major sporting event scores live on the Web! For example, at www.nfl.com, *you can keep track of every NFL* game as the games progress. (See Figure 15.6.) As video compression improves, you will be able to watch several games at a time on your computer.

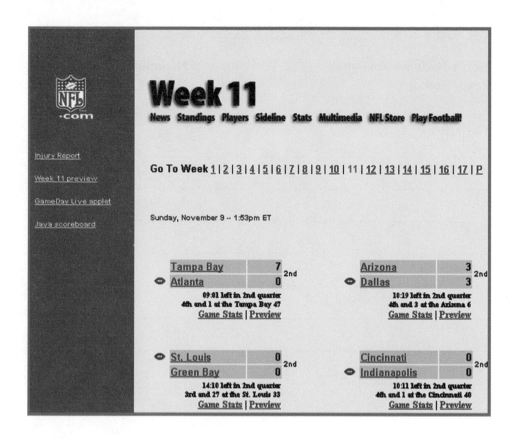

Figure 15.6
Track sports live online

3 Locate schedules for the following organizations:

Professional Organization	Schedule located at:
Women's Professional Volleyball Association	
Ladies Professional Golf Association	
National Basketball Association	
National Football League	
Women's Tennis Association	

Open your favorite search engine and search for a new movie that is coming out soon. Movies aimed toward ages 13 to 25 are likely to have Web pages.

4 Find a current roster for the U.S. National Volleyball Teams.

**Men's National Volleyball
Team Roster**

**Women's National Volleyball
Team Roster**

_____   _____

_____   _____

_____   _____

_____   _____

_____   _____

_____   _____

_____   _____

_____   _____

_____   _____

_____   _____

_____   _____

THINKING ABOUT TECHNOLOGY

How will user interaction affect organized sports? Will sports that haven't been as popular, like ping pong or badminton, gain a larger following?

Net Ethics   *Gambling*

Gambling always presents some intense political and ethical debates. Some states and communities allow gambling; others do not. While gambling in the past was largely a local issue, it has now gone global with the Internet. Here are some ethical issues to debate with your team:

* Should gambling be allowed over the Internet in places where gambling is illegal?
* Who should regulate or control Internet gambling?
* Since legal gambling is usually taxed, who should collect gambling taxes when the cybercasino is international?

Net **Life** *Fantasy Sports Leagues*

So you think you can do it better than the real owners and coaches? Well, you're not alone. So does everyone else. Fantasy sports leagues put you in charge of your favorite team. Pick the roster and see how your team does against other fantasy owners. You can make trades, change your starting lineup, even see stats for your team, but watch out for injuries!

Many fantasy leagues are pay-for-play. But if you look around, you'll find some for free. Have fun.

NET VOCABULARY

Define the following terms and explain their impact on the entertainment value of the Web:

1. network computer (NC)
2. plug-in
3. Shockwave player
4. streaming
5. Web TV

NET REVIEW

Give a short answer to the following questions:

1. Explain how a network computer differs from a traditional personal computer.

2. You are on a business trip to Boulder, Colorado. You have finished your business for the day, but it's still early, so you thought you'd take in a movie. After a long day, a good comedy will help you relax. Explain the steps you would follow on your laptop computer to select a comedy movie to see.

3. You have always liked the TV show "Frasier," and you'd like to find out what other shows Kelsey Grammer has acted in. How would you find this information?

4. More and more the Net is being used by the entertainment industry to promote its products. Is this increasing commercialization a good thing or a bad thing? Who benefits from this commercialization: the entertainment companies, Net users, or both?

MOVIE CRITIC

The office isn't all work. Most of the folks at GreatApplications, Inc., are movie goers. Several of your friends at work have asked you to circulate a weekly newsletter containing movie reviews that they can read on their lunch break. Find reviews for new movies being released this week. Summarize the reviews or paste them into your document called "Movie Reviews." E-mail this document to your team.

NET PROJECT TEAMWORK   Games Debate

Debate the ethical issues of playing games on the job. Should employees be allowed to use the company computers to play games? If so, when and under what conditions? Summarize your team's discussion in a short report saved in your common team folder.

WRITING ABOUT TECHNOLOGY   Unofficial Web Sites and Copyright Protection

Many Web sites post screenshots and sound bites from favorite TV shows. The problem is that this material is copyright-protected property of the network that owns the show. These unofficial sites can be shut down, and the site owners can be prosecuted for breaking the law. Some people argue that posting small pieces of TV shows on a Web site shouldn't be illegal. After all, these sites are fueling the popularity of the show. What do you think about this issue? How can it be resolved fairly for both sides? Write a 100-word response, on a separate piece of paper.

Sprechen sie Internet? How the Internet Speaks

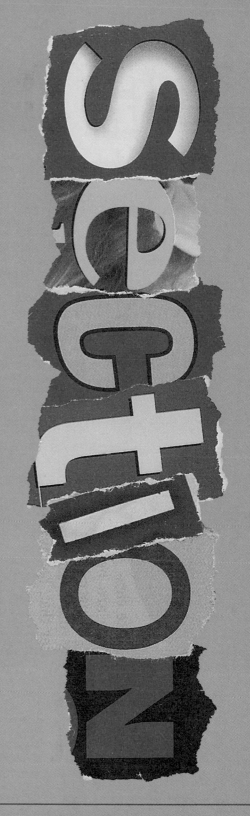

The Internet has a language all its own. In fact, it speaks many tongues. The primary language is *HTML* or *HyperText Markup Language*. This simple language tells the browser how to display the information. For the most part, these instructions work on any browser.

Other languages, with more powerful capabilities, are coming into play on the ever-evolving Internet. Java is causing the most stir in computer circles because of its ability to run on any platform. Many feel Java is *the* programming language of the future.

VRML, or *Virtual Reality Modeling Language*, is the incarnation of virtual reality on the Internet. It permits three-dimensional objects to be displayed and allows users to navigate in and around the image. Users can also "pick up" and manipulate these objects.

Many other languages and scripting tools are making the Internet more interactive and user-responsive than ever. We don't have the space to explore them all, but we'll present a few of them and leave it up to you to explore the vast space that is the Internet.

Chapter 16 will teach you how to create your very own Web page. It's not very difficult to learn. With your own Web page, you'll finally be a true netizen!

Chapter 17 will introduce you to some of the most important languages emerging in the wake of HTML. These include Java and VRML. You'll get a chance to save Duke from the Hangman and meet Floops. You can even drive a Pathfinder around Mars or take a walk through a Vermeer art gallery. The path you take is up to you in virtual space.

Chapter 16 Your First Web Page: Your Parents Will Be
So Proud 180
Chapter 17 The Many Languages of the Internet 194

CHAPTER 16

Your First Web Page: Your Parents Will Be So Proud

Chapter Objectives:

In this chapter, you will learn the basics of HTML coding. After reading Chapter 16, you will be able to:

1 view the source code of an HTML page, identify parts of an HTML page, and define simple HTML tags.

2 create a simple HTML page with ordered and unordered lists.

3 insert a graphic on an HTML page.

The Language of the Web

As you learned in Chapter 4, HTML (HyperText Markup Language) is the standard document format for creating Web pages. HTML commands define how Web pages will look, including text styles, graphic artwork, and hyperlinks to other documents on the Web. A great advantage of HTML is that all browsers can read it. And guess what? It's not complicated to learn, either!

Basically, a page is created as an all-text file with an *.htm* or *.html* extension that Web browsers use to identify it. The file itself contains **tags** that tell the browser how to format the information between the tags. The browser simply displays the information according to the tags' instructions. ∎

Net Terms

tags

bulleted list

unordered list

anchor tag

hypertext reference (HREF)

image source tag

numbered list

ordered list

Understanding Tags

HTML tags usually act like light switches that must be turned on and off. The tags tell the browser how to display the text that lies between the "on" tag and the "off" tag. Tags are written inside of brackets ⟨LIKE THIS⟩. The "on" tag appears where the browser should begin applying the format instructions. The "off" tag, which includes a backslash ⟨/LIKE THIS⟩, appears at the end of the text to be formatted, telling the browser to stop applying the format instructions at this point.

Now let's look at some real HTML.

1 In your browser, go to your home page.

2 In IE 4.0, select *Source* from the *View* menu. In NN 4.02, select *Page Source* from the *View* menu, as shown in Figure 16.1a. Or right-click in either browser and select *View Source.* The source code will look something like Figure 16.1b on page 182. Don't worry. It's not as confusing as it looks.

ACTIVITY
16.1

Objective:
In this lesson, you will learn how to view the source code of a Web page and identify and define basic tags.

NET TIP
Web Addresses

Note that current links to most Web sites presented in this book can be found on the Internet Concepts and Activities *Home Page. Choose* Resources *at* **computered.swep.com**. *Remember that a Web address may change at any time. An address given in this book as an example may no longer be valid. If this is so, either access the Home Page for the current link or do a search to find a similar site (see Chapter 9 for a discussion of search methods).*

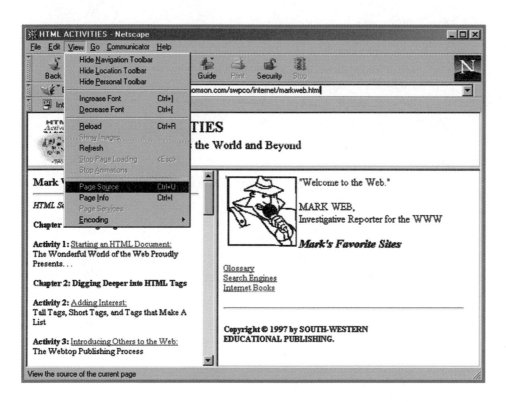

Figure 16.1a
View Page Source command in Netscape Navigator

3 Viewing the source code of a complex page may be overwhelming at first, but try looking for these tags first:

⟨html⟩ ⟨/html⟩	This tag is loaded first and indicates the beginning and end of an html file.
⟨head⟩ ⟨/head⟩	Includes information about the Web page.
⟨title⟩ ⟨/title⟩	Identifies the title that appears in the title bar of your browser.
⟨body⟩ ⟨/body⟩	Identifies the body or main portion of text.

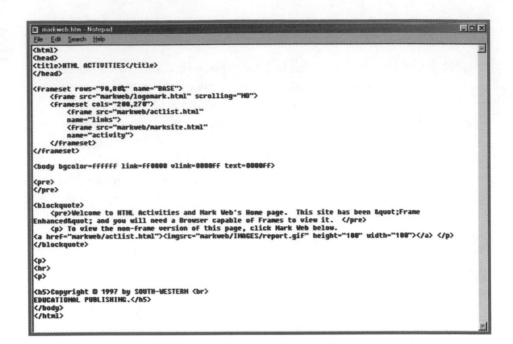

```
□ markweb.htm - Notepad                                            _□X
File  Edit  Search  Help
<html>
<head>
<title>HTML ACTIVITIES</title>
</head>

<frameset rows="90,80%" name="BASE">
    <frame src="markweb/logomark.html" scrolling="NO">
    <frameset cols="200,270">
        <frame src="markweb/actlist.html"
        name="links">
        <frame src="markweb/marksite.html"
        name="activity">
    </frameset>
</frameset>

<body bgcolor=ffffff link=ff0000 vlink=0000FF text=0000FF>

<pre>
</pre>

<blockquote>
    <pre>Welcome to HTML Activities and Mark Web's Home page.  This site has been &quot;Frame
Enhanced&quot; and you will need a Browser capable of Frames to view it.  </pre>
        <p> To view the non-frame version of this page, click Mark Web below.
<a href="markweb/actlist.html"><imgsrc="markweb/IMAGES/report.gif" height="100" width="100"></a> </p>
</blockquote>

<p>
<hr>
<p>

<h5>Copyright © 1997 by SOUTH-WESTERN <br>
EDUCATIONAL PUBLISHING.</h5>
</body>
</html>
```

Figure 16.1b
HTML source code

4 Many other tags indicate changes in font styles, underlining, paragraph breaks, headings, lines, and lists. Look for the following tags:

⟨H1⟩ ⟨/H1⟩   Heading—the number indicates level of importance, with 1 being most important and 6 being least important. Other examples: ⟨H2⟩⟨/H2⟩, ⟨H6⟩⟨/H6⟩.

⟨B⟩ ⟨/B⟩   Bold text.

⟨U⟩ ⟨/U⟩   Underline text.

⟨P⟩   Begins a new paragraph. This tag doesn't need an off tag.

⟨BR⟩   Breaks a line and starts a new one. This tag doesn't need an off tag.

⟨HR⟩   Draws a horizontal line (rule) across the page. This tag doesn't need an off tag.

⟨font⟩ ⟨/font⟩   Indicates change of font (or type) style.

⟨fontsize=⟩   Indicates change in font size.

⟨I⟩ ⟨/I⟩   Italicize text.

5 Tags can be combined. For example, to do text with bold and italics, begin with ⟨B⟩⟨I⟩ and end with ⟨/B⟩⟨/I⟩ to produce bold italic text between those on and off tag combinations.

View the HTML tags found on your favorite Web pages. Locate your favorite sites, and then choose *View, Page Source* in NN and *View, Source* in IE. Kind of weird looking, isn't it?

6 Switch back and forth between your browser and the source page. What do other tags do? See if you can identify 10 additional tags and what they do.

Tag   **Function**

1. _____   _____

2. _____   _____

3. _____   _____

4. _____   _____

5. _____   _____

5. _____   _____

6. _____   _____

7. _____   _____

8. _____   _____

9. _____   _____

10. _____   _____

Don't be discouraged if the page you are looking at seems hopelessly complex. HTML is a language that is constantly evolving to do more powerful things. You should still be able to find very basic tags. Be patient and look through the source, identifying what you know. Pretty soon, HTML will seem pretty simple.

THINKING ABOUT TECHNOLOGY

While computers and computer languages seem to get more complex all the time, HTML stands out as a fairly simple method of communication. Why do you think HTML is so simple? What advantages does it have? What disadvantages does this simplicity bring?

ACTIVITY
16.2

Objective:
In this lesson, you will learn how to create your own Web page.

Create a Simple Web Page

Now that you've seen the basics of a Web page, it's time to create your own.

1 Open a text editor, like Notepad in Windows or SimpleText in Macintosh.

2 Key in the information shown in Figure 16.2, inserting your own information where asked.

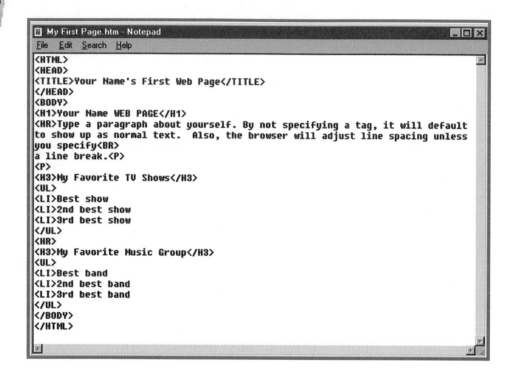

```
My First Page.htm - Notepad
File   Edit   Search   Help
<HTML>
<HEAD>
<TITLE>Your Name's First Web Page</TITLE>
</HEAD>
<BODY>
<H1>Your Name WEB PAGE</H1>
<HR>Type a paragraph about yourself. By not specifying a tag, it will default
to show up as normal text.  Also, the browser will adjust line spacing unless
you specify<BR>
a line break.<P>
<P>
<H3>My Favorite TV Shows</H3>
<UL>
<LI>Best show
<LI>2nd best show
<LI>3rd best show
</UL>
<HR>
<H3>My Favorite Music Group</H3>
<UL>
<LI>Best band
<LI>2nd best band
<LI>3rd best band
</UL>
</BODY>
</HTML>
```

Figure 16.2
The contents of your first HTML file

Internet Milestone

Tim Johann Berners-Gutenberg-Lee

Johann Gutenberg created a printing press with movable metal type containing letters, numbers, and symbols, and in 1454, printed multiple copies of a letter. The invention of the printing press allowed millions of inexpensive paper copies to be made quickly and easily. Gutenberg's press was the photocopy machine of the 15th century. His invention started revolutions. Not only was there a revolution in mass communication, but the availability of inexpensive books greatly increased literacy and improved education. Guten-

berg's invention made the Protestant Reformation possible, by allowing the people of the time to share their new philosophies and ideas. Inexpensive printing allowed American and later French revolutionaries to share their ideas with the masses. The Gutenberg press had a major impact on the course of history.

One can only speculate on the impact the World Wide Web will

have on the history of the planet. When Tim Berners-Lee invented his simple HTML version 1, he sparked a massive communications revolution that can only be compared to Gutenberg's invention in the scope of its impact.

One hundred years from now, the names Gutenberg and Berners-Lee may stand side-by-side in the history books as the two most significant individuals in the history of written mass communication. How will the world be different as a result of HTML?

(3) Did you notice you learned another tag while you were keying the file? Let's save the document and see what the ⟨LI⟩ tag is for.

(4) Choose *Save As* from the *File* menu.

(5) In the *File Name* box, key *My First Page.htm* in Windows 95 or Windows 98. On your Macintosh, key *My First Page.html.* On older Windows 3.1 systems, key *MFP.htm.* (Old Windows computers can't handle long file names.) Windows generally prefers the *.htm* extension, and Macintosh prefers the *.html* extension.

(6) Click *Save* and close the text editor.

(7) In your browser, select *Open* from the *File* menu.

(8) Locate the file you just saved and open it. Does your new Web page look similar to Figure 16.3?

Figure 16.3
Example Web page

(9) Notice that the ⟨LI⟩ tag created a bullet, or raised dot. You can think of "LI" as meaning "list item." A **bulleted list** is a list in which each item is preceded by a bullet character. A bulleted list is also an **unordered list**, because it indicates no particular order of importance among the listed items. Generally, unordered lists use the ⟨UL⟩ tag at the beginning and the ⟨/UL⟩ tag at the end of the list of items. When the list is designated as "UL" or "unordered list," then the "LI" command creates a bullet. As you will see in the next activity, the "LI" or "list item" command does something different in an ordered list.

Print out your Web page to hang on the refrigerator at home. Your parents will be so proud!

What if the Gutenberg Press had never been invented? What if HTML had never been invented? Would your really cool Web page have been possible?

Net Life *SGML + TB-L = HTML*

In the beginning there was GML, or the Generalized Markup Language. GML was created by IBM in the 1960s as a way to share and edit documents. In 1986, SGML was born as Standard Generalized Markup Language. SGML was adopted by ISO, or the International Organization for Standardization. Tim Berners-Lee used SGML to help him create HTML. HTML is maintained by the ERB (Editorial Review Board) of the W3C, or the World Wide Web Consortium. The W3C continues to organize, maintain, and publish improvements to HTML, which has various versions: HTML 1, HTML 2, HTML 3, HTML 4, and so on.

If you followed all of this, then you will be able to follow this sentence:

IBM created GML which was improved as SGML and adopted by the ISO. TB-L used SGML to guide the development of HTML 1, 2, 3, 4, which is maintained by the ERB at the W3C.

And people actually speak like this! What is the W3 coming to?

We realize this is your first Web page, so try this only if you are brave. Replace the ⟨BODY⟩ tag with this line in your Web page:

```
⟨BODY BGCOLOR=ffffff LINK=ff0000 VLINK=0000ff
TEXT=0000ff⟩
```

What did this new tag do?

Advanced Web Page Design

ACTIVITY
16.3

Objective:
In this lesson, you will learn how to add hyperlinks and graphics to your Web page, and you will learn some advanced HTML tags.

Now that you've created a simple Web page, let's spice it up with some graphics. We'll also make it more useful by adding hyperlinks. You can even make this your home page with links to all of your favorite spots on the Internet.

But first you need to learn a new tag. An **anchor tag** is the HTML codes that define a hyperlink to another document or Web page. The anchor tag begins with ⟨A and ends with ⟨/A⟩. The text or graphic between ⟨A and ⟨/A⟩ is the link's hot spot that, when clicked, transports the user to the linked location. An anchor tag is a little bit longer than the tags you have learned so far, but it is simple when you understand the parts. Here's an example:

⟨A HREF="http://www.thex-files.com"⟩The X-Files⟨/A⟩

The *HREF* code stands for **hypertext reference**. This code within an anchor tag, followed by an equal sign, signifies to the browser that the address of the target document follows. After the equal sign, in quotation marks, is the URL, or address of the location you are linking to. Place a closing bracket after the URL. Then give your link a name. The name you key in after the URL will show on your Web page as the underlined hyperlink. The ending ⟨/A⟩ code, then, terminates the anchor tag.

Now let's add hyperlinks on your Web page to your favorite TV shows.

1 Search the Web for sites dedicated to each of your favorite TV shows, and write down the URLs.

2 Open your Web page in your browser.

3 Open the HTML source file for your page either through the *View* menu or by right-clicking on your page and selecting *View Source*, as you learned in Activity 16.1.

4 Using the example above, create anchor tags for each of your favorite shows. Your source file should look similar to Figure 16.4a.

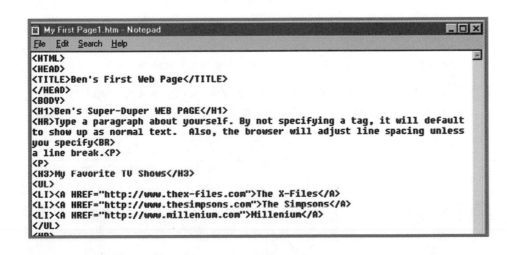

```
My First Page1.htm - Notepad
File  Edit  Search  Help
<HTML>
<HEAD>
<TITLE>Ben's First Web Page</TITLE>
</HEAD>
<BODY>
<H1>Ben's Super-Duper WEB PAGE</H1>
<HR>Type a paragraph about yourself. By not specifying a tag, it will default
to show up as normal text.  Also, the browser will adjust line spacing unless
you specify<BR>
a line break.<P>
<P>
<H3>My Favorite TV Shows</H3>
<UL>
<LI><A HREF="http://www.thex-files.com">The X-Files</A>
<LI><A HREF="http://www.thesimpsons.com">The Simpsons</A>
<LI><A HREF="http://www.millenium.com">Millenium</A>
</UL>
```

Figure 16.4a
Source file containing anchor tags

5 When you have finished adding the tags, save your file. Switch to your Web page in your browser and click the *Refresh* button to view your changes. Did your hyperlinks appear underscored, as in Figure 16.4b?

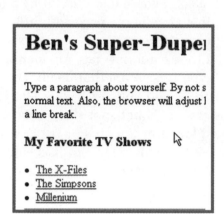

Figure 16.4b
Your Web page now has hyperlinks

Now let's add a picture to your page. It's very important to be organized with your image files. Ideally, you should keep them in the same folder as your HTML file, so you can locate them easily.

An **image source tag** is the HTML code that inserts a graphic image on a Web page. The image source tag begins with ⟨*IMG SRC=* followed by the address of the image's file location and ends with a closing bracket. The tag looks like this:

⟨IMG SRC="*location/filename.extension*"⟩

Notice that you have to insert the location and exact file name of the image, so that your browser can identify it. If your image is not in the same folder as your HTML file, you must be sure to include the full path to your image file, or it will not display.

First let's download an image from the Internet to add to your page.

6 Go to *www.thomson.com/swpco/internet/markweb.html.*

7 Right-click on a picture or hold down the single mouse key on your Macintosh and choose the *Save Picture As* command (see Figure 16.5). Save the picture in the same folder as your Web page and write down the name you give it and its extension.

8 Now go back to your Web page and open your source file.

9 Following the example given earlier, key an image source tag into your source file to insert the picture you just downloaded. Make sure to put in the precise path to the image, including the drive letter. If you stored the image in your C drive, then the path should begin *C:/* followed by the names of each folder you must open, in sequence, to get to the image file.

10 Now save your source file and go back to your Web page. Click the *Refresh* button on your toolbar, and see your Web's page's new look!

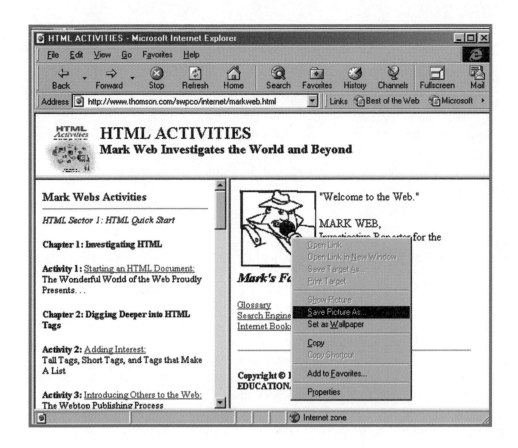

Figure 16.5
Downloading a picture from a Web site

We're on a roll now, so let's make one more change to your Web page. You got a quick preview of bulleted lists in the last activity. As you recall, bulleted lists are unordered—they do not indicate any particular order of importance among the bulleted items. However, the items in a **numbered list** are numbered sequentially to indicate an order of importance. Therefore, a numbered list is an **ordered list**, with the tag code of ⟨OL⟩.

Let's change your favorite music groups list to a numbered list.

⓫ Go to your Web page's source file and change the unordered list code above your music group list to the ordered list code ⟨OL⟩, as shown in Figure 16.6a. Also change the ending code to the ordered list ending code ⟨/OL⟩. Note that you don't have to change the list item code ⟨LI⟩. The code for an ordered or unordered list tells the browser whether to use bullets or numbers for the list items.

⓬ Save your changes to your source file and refresh your Web page. You now have a numbered list of your favorite music groups, similar to Figure 16.6b.

Have fun adding to your page. You can use this page as your home page to access your favorite parts of the Internet. You can expand from a page to a "site" by creating

```
<H3>My Favorite Music Groups</H3>
<OL>
<LI>Pink Floyd
<LI>Tori Amos
<LI>Primus
</OL>
```

Figure 16.6a
Creating a numbered list

My Favorite Music Groups

1. Pink Floyd
2. Tori Amos
3. Primus

Figure 16.6b
Ordered list tag becomes a numbered list

other pages that have hyperlinks to each other. If your school has a Web server, you can post this page (or site) for others to see.

THINKING ABOUT TECHNOLOGY

Many software products on the market can make HTML coding very simple. Using these products, you might not even have to see the HTML tags. Is it still valuable to understand something about the way tags work? Why or why not?

Net Ethics   *Stealing Pictures*

It is easy to "liberate" pictures off the Web. A couple of mouse clicks and it's yours. But should you take an image from the Web without permission? We were allowed to download the image for the last activity because it belongs to the publisher of this book. However, we found a really cool image of the Simpsons that we had to leave behind and not use in this book because . . . well, you know.

Some unethical people have taken copyrighted images, distorted them, and reposted the mangled images back on the Web. A Mickey Mouse vampire comes to mind. (Although a vampire Bart Simpson does seem in character.)

Disney, among others, has taken legal action against Web publishers who have used and misused their images without their express written consent. And a lawsuit is what such people deserve. What cyber-sick-o would deface images meant for the child in all of us for the sake of a cheap joke? Come on . . . show some class!

Netiquette

Helping Older Browsers Across the Web

Today, browsers are more powerful than ever. They add capabilities to Web pages that go far beyond HTML. Tools like JavaScript, Java, and Shockwave add interest to Web pages.

Still, Web page creators often create two or three versions of Web pages to help out the folks in cyberspace who may not be able to upgrade to the latest and greatest browser. This is why you may be asked to select between a *Text* version and a more enhanced *Java* or *JavaScript* version of a Web page. This is the highest form of Netiquette—going the extra mile to provide for the browser-impaired.

NET VOCABULARY

Define the following terms:

1. tags

2. bulleted list

3. unordered list

4. anchor tag

5. hypertext reference (HREF)

6. image source tag

7. numbered list

8. ordered list

NET REVIEW

Describe the function of the following tags and show how each is used:

1. ⟨B⟩

2. ⟨LI⟩

3. ⟨IMG SRC⟩

4. ⟨H1⟩

5. ⟨H2⟩

6. ⟨HR⟩

7. ⟨P⟩

8. ⟨HTML⟩

9. ⟨BR⟩ _____

_____

10. ⟨HEAD⟩ _____

_____

11. ⟨BODY⟩ _____

_____

12. ⟨I⟩ _____

_____

13. ⟨UL⟩ _____

_____

14. ⟨FONT⟩ _____

_____

Net Fun

Okay, so this lesson is really basic and you are looking for the *really* cool stuff. For a step-by-step course in HTML, buy *HTML Activities: Webtop Publishing on the Superhighway*. For information see the South-Western Educational Publishing Computer Education Web page at **computered.swep.com**. Or key *HTML* into any search engine. You can find a thousand guides to HTML for free on the Web!

PLUG IN YOUR CREATIVITY
FOR AN EFFECTIVE WEB SITE

The Board of Directors at GreatApplications, Inc., has been watching you. The board members are impressed and have assigned to your group the daunting task of developing the company's Web strategy.

Using the information you've gathered in the previous Net Projects, begin thinking about how your company could best profit from a Web site. Try sketching some ideas for page design. Will you use a lot of graphics? What about fonts? How will you organize the page?

If you need more ideas, visit more sites on your lists. Look for "Top 5%" sites, or sites that have won Internet awards. Follow some links from sites you've visited to find out where they lead.

Make a tree diagram of your Web site. Remember, good organization is the key to creating an effective Web site.

NET PROJECT TEAMWORK Web Site Hardware

The computer guru at GreatApplications, Inc., just took a job at Microsoft. The boss is in a bind and has asked your group to identify what hardware the company needs to present Web pages for its millions of customers. As a group, research the specifications and requirements for the new company Web server. What kind of equipment is necessary to set up and run a Web server for a large company like GreatApplications, Inc.?

Prepare a Web site proposal with sketches and diagrams clearly labeled. Include information about what equipment will be needed and how much it will cost. Save your work in your common folder with an additional copy in your personal research folder as a backup.

WRITING ABOUT TECHNOLOGY Doing Business on the Web

From your experiences so far on the Internet, select one of the following questions and write a 100-word response, on a separate piece of paper.

Option 1. How important is it for a business to have a Web site?

Option 2. How important is a Web site as a sales tool for business?

Option 3. How can a poorly organized Web site harm a business?

CHApTER 17

The Many Languages of the Internet

Chapter Objectives:

In this chapter, you'll learn about some of the other tools that will drive the Internet into the next century. After reading Chapter 17, you will be able to:

1 discuss Java and run Java applets.

2 identify and discuss several Internet programming languages and graphics file formats.

3 explore VRML worlds.

4 search for information about other Web technologies.

Net Terms

Java

platform

applets

JavaScript

CGI

Perl

ActiveX

.gif

.jpg or .jpeg

DHTML

Hot Languages for Cool Web Effects

In the last chapter, you learned about the main language of the Internet, HTML. You even made your own Web page. As you may have noticed, your page wasn't quite as exciting as some of the pages you've visited.

HTML is a very simple language. Although it is evolving and new capabilities are added to it all the time, it can only go so far in presenting information.

Now there are some new kids on the block, and they are turning the Internet upside down. Perhaps the most important of these newcomers (at least for the moment) is Java. **Java** is a complex programming language that allows a program to be written once

and used on any operating system. This fundamental difference from most software on the market saves software vendors a lot of money, since they don't have to rewrite their software for every platform they wish to sell to. A **platform** is the operating system a program runs on. For example, Macintosh is one platform and Windows is another. **Applets** are tiny programs written in Java that can be embedded in HTML pages. Examples include animated characters, scrolling text, and simple games.

JavaScript is a less-powerful programming language than Java, but it is easier to use. Instead of creating programs that are run by the browser, JavaScript places its

commands directly on the HTML Web page in the form of a list or scripted set of commands and processes. JavaScript requires less software to create and works very well for certain specialized tasks.

Older scripting languages are also popular, including CGI and Perl. **CGI** (Common Gateway Interface) is a recognized standard for interfacing applications, like database programs, with Web servers and Web pages. CGI allows users to interact through Web pages. For example, with CGI you can create a form in which site visitors enter data, and the data will go to the server for processing. **Perl** (Practical Extraction and Report Language) is a programming language designed to handle a variety of system administrator functions. Both CGI and Perl can link programs and databases together with Web pages to perform lots of complex functions.

ActiveX is Microsoft's answer to the problem of linking traditional software to the Internet. ActiveX transforms applications like Word or Excel into powerful Web tools.

Another important newcomer, though it has been around for a couple of years, is VRML. As you learned in Chapter 11, VRML (Virtual Reality Modeling Language) is the language used to create 3-D "worlds," where you can interact with objects or with other Net users in a virtual setting that seems almost real. As with HTML, VRML pages use plain text files to define shapes, lights, and textures. In a virtual VRML phone store, you could walk through the store, pick up a phone, and "manipulate" it (look at it from any angle) in virtual-reality (VR) space. Using VRML, architects can show clients their building designs from above, behind, the right side or left side, inside or out. Seeing the building in 3-D before it is built helps the architects and clients see where adjustments are needed before the design is literally "set in stone." Links can be added to these worlds to take you from VR space to VR space and even out to plain old two-dimensional HTML pages.

You may need to install a plug-in to use Java applets in your browser or to maneuver through VRML worlds. Check with your instructor if you are having problems. Upgrading your software is the best way to keep up with all these new enhancements to HTML. ∎

ACTIVITY

17.1

Objective:
In this lesson, you will visit Java-enabled sites and learn what Java applets can do.

Java—What Can You Do for Me Today?

Java was created to (believe it or not) enable household appliances to communicate with each other. Although the development of these smart appliances didn't go very far, Java programmers found another way to keep the language alive: the Internet.

Because all kinds of computer platforms have access to the Internet, it made sense to create a language that would allow programs to only be written once and played or executed via a Web browser on any kind of computer system. This feature is called "write once, deliver anywhere."

Although Java applications are still in their infancy, we'll visit a few sites that use Java, so you can see how Java enhances your Internet experience. Let's go!

1 Start at the source, *http://java.sun.com.*

2 Click the link to *Applets.*

3 Read about applets available online and describe below what two of them do.

1. _____

2. _____

4 Click on the link to *applets written here at JavaSoft.*

5 Play a game of hangman and see if you can make Duke dance with glee. (See Figure 17.1.) After you watch Duke dance for a couple of minutes, you may not *want* to save him.

NET TIP

Web Addresses

Note that current links to most Web sites presented in this book can be found on the Internet Concepts and Activities *Home Page. Choose* Resources *at* **computered.swep.com.** *Remember that a Web address given in this book as an example may no longer be valid. If this is so, access the Home Page for the current link.*

Net Ethics   *Competition or Standardization?*

It always happens. A healthy competition between companies causes them to create differences in their products. Product differences runs counter to the spirit of the Web and of HTML—which stresses a common set of standards that everyone can use and access.

However, businesses must look for ways to improve their products against the competition in order to attract customers. To take advantage of some of these improvements on the Internet, you may need to install plug-ins or upgrade your browser software.

Because of the browser wars, Microsoft, Sun, Oracle, and Netscape have added all sorts of enhancements to HTML. These exciting new features go way beyond the carefully constructed open standards produced by the Executive Review Board (ERB) at the World Wide Web Consortium (W3C).

New features force people to upgrade their software or miss out on the special effects the new features provide. Should companies be allowed to go beyond the recognized Web standards? Should they be able to push users into new products and software? Are companies free to compete, to innovate, and to create a better mousetrap? Can competition produce better browsers, better Web features, and a more exciting and powerful Internet? Would anyone really want to hold Microsoft, Netscape, Oracle, SUN, and other companies back as they seek to gain a competitive edge?

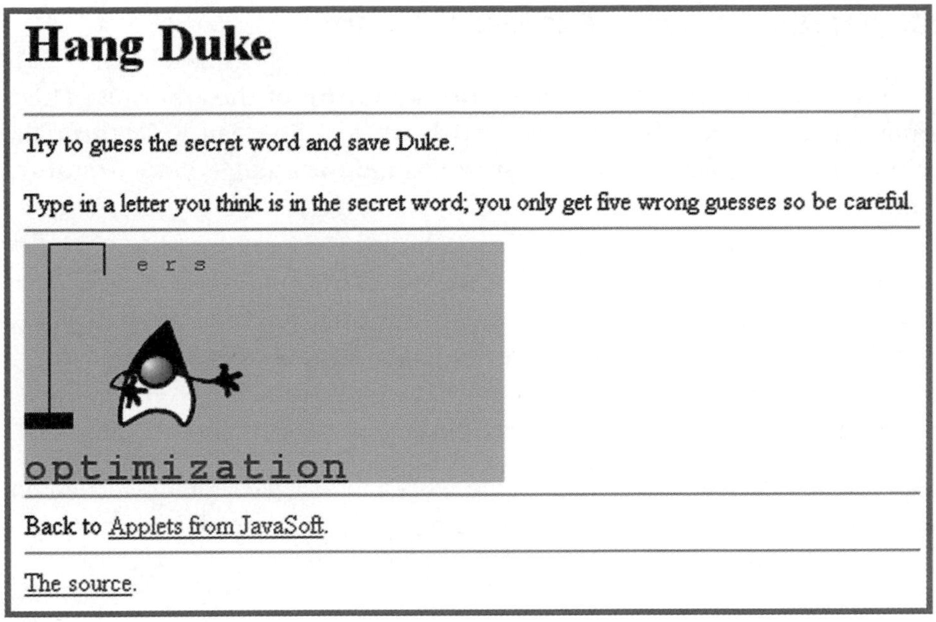

Hang Duke

Try to guess the secret word and save Duke.

Type in a letter you think is in the secret word; you only get five wrong guesses so be careful.

e r s

optimization

Back to Applets from JavaSoft.

The source.

Figure 17.1
Duke survived...this time.

6 Now check out some of the other applets. Although these applets may seem limited, they actually do a lot in very little space. And as developers get used to the language, more powerful applications will emerge.

THINKING ABOUT TECHNOLOGY

What are your first impressions of Java? Does it really live up to all the hype? What advantages do you see with a Java-enabled Internet? Surf around and find other Java pages.

Internet Milestone
Sun's Java Language

Java was created by Sun Microsystems (*http://sun.com*) as a compact programming language for electronic appliances, such as VCRs, satellite receivers, and microwaves. First called "Greentalk" and later "Oak," Java was apparently named after a type of coffee several of the Sun developers were drinking one day. Little did the creators at Sun know that Java would become the next big milestone in Internet history.

Java solves the problem of how to create software programs that can be delivered quickly and easily through the Web to any kind of computer. Java is to programming languages what HTML is to publishing. The theory is that you can write one program and have any computer—Macintosh, Windows, or Unix—run the program with the help of a "just in time" (JIT) compiler built into a Java-enabled Web browser. To see samples of Java code, or to try a sample test delivered using the Java programming language, visit the *Java: Programming Basics for the Internet* book's Web site at *www.studio-jplus.com/appletto.html.*

ACTIVITY

17.2

Objective:
In this lesson, you will learn how to locate and navigate through VRML worlds.

A Walk in the Virtual Park

VRML offers an exciting view into the future of the Internet. This language allows for the creation of 3-D worlds. You can walk through these worlds, look up or down, turn around, or change your camera angle.

Many believe that the Internet of the future will be a true virtual-reality experience. You will be able to walk in buildings and open doors or drawers to pull out files with information you are searching for. Hollywood has certainly provided some interesting views of the possible future. Will it ever be like that? Only time will tell. Meanwhile, find out what VRML is being used for here in the present.

1 First, let's meet Floops, one of the most interesting VRML characters on the Internet. Go to *http://vrml.sgi.com.* Figure 17.2 explains the buttons that control movements through this virtual world.

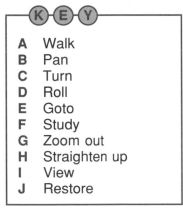

KEY

A	Walk
B	Pan
C	Turn
D	Roll
E	Goto
F	Study
G	Zoom out
H	Straighten up
I	View
J	Restore

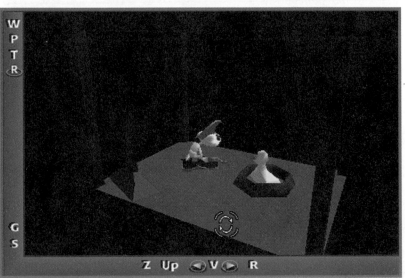

Figure 17.2
Meet Floops!

2 Click the link to *Floops Greatest Hits.*

3 Pick one of the Floops scenes and click to load the *.wrl* file. VRML uses *.wrl* files for its "worlds." These files tend to be rather large and can take a while to download. Be patient.

4 When the Floops scene is finished loading, click inside the frame to start the animation. What do you think of the little guy?

5 Check out other sites in the *VRML Gallery.*

6 Now locate five other cool VRML sites and record below what you found at these sites. Have fun exploring!

Address	**What does the site contain?**
1.	
2.	
3.	
4.	
5.	

THINKING ABOUT TECHNOLOGY

Now that you've had a chance to look at some of the cool VRML sites out there, what do you think the future of the Internet holds? Will VRML play a significant part? Why or why not? Can businesses make use of virtual reality worlds? How?

Net Fun

Microsoft has taken the lead in extending HTML in new directions. One new innovation is called *Dynamic HTML* or *DHTML*. Dynamic HTML allows users to move and manipulate objects around a Web page as easily as they manipulate icons on their Windows computer screen. Visit Microsoft's site at *www.microsoft.com* and use the *search* feature to find *DHTML* or *Dynamic HTML*. Try some of their interactive demos.

CHAPTER REVIEW

NET VOCABULARY

Define the following terms:

1. *Java*

2. *platform*

3. *applets*

4. *JavaScript*

5. *CGI*

6. *Perl*

7. *ActiveX*

8. *.gif*

9. *.jpg or .jpeg*

10. *DHTML*

NET REVIEW

Give a short answer to the following questions:

1. *What is the main advantage of the Java programming language?*

2. *What is VRML and how does it differ from HTML?*

3. *How would you go about searching for VRML sites?*

4. *How does an applet work? What is the difference between an applet and an application?*

While Java, JavaScript, and Shockwave make a lot of pages interactive, there are other ways to get movement on a page. *Animated Gifs* are picture files that move, like cartoons. Type *Animated Gif* or *Animated Gifs* into your search engine and see what's shaking in the world of animation.

A VIRTUAL-WORLD SITE FOR GREATAPPLICATIONS, INC.

You've already given a report to the board of directors at GreatApplications, Inc., about how to build an effective Web site for the business. You've even helped to design the site. Now you've been introduced to Java and VRML and have gained a vision of the future of the Internet.

Locate Java and VRML sites that are being used for commercial purposes and download them for a new presentation to the board of directors. You may want to include a couple of the fun sites you've seen, but only do so to illustrate ways of making this site practical in a business setting.

Remember that the board of directors is openminded as long as the company makes more money. They want to be sure that whatever money they spend setting up Web sites or creating VRML worlds is going to come back in increased revenues.

NET PROJECT TEAMWORK   Web Technologies for the Future

The board of directors of GreatApplications, Inc., was not pleased with your earlier report about Java and VRML. The report came back with a huge "INCOMPLETE" stamped over the cover page. A note was attached stating the following:

> We have heard of other technologies that may serve our company's needs better than Java and VRML. Please investigate the following: *JavaScript, JScript, DHTML, Animated Gifs, ActiveX, VBScript, Perl,* and *CGI.* If you find any Net technologies worth knowing about, put them in your report. Please be ready to provide a more complete report at the next meeting of the board.

Oops. Time to get the team together and fix the mistake. This task is too big to do alone. Divide up the list and learn as much as you can about the technologies listed by the board. Add to the list *Push* and *streaming* technologies. That should impress them. Also, don't leave out *Shockwave.*

Prepare a report listing the following:

1. Describe what the technology can do. What are its major effects on the Net and how can it help customers of GreatApplications, Inc.?
2. Explain how it can be helpful to a business. How can business use the technology?
3. Explain who invented or created the technology and who supports this technology.
4. Describe its potential five years from now. Will the technology still be in use?
5. Define what would be needed, in terms of personnel, money, equipment, software, and resources, to use this technology. Is this technology cost effective?
6. What other companies use this technology?
7. How does this technology compare with Java and VRML? What are its strengths and weaknesses when compared to Java and VRML? What does it do or not do in relation to Java and VRML?

There are some obvious places to start looking:

Microsoft	*http://www.microsoft.com*
Sun Microsystems	*http://sun.com*
Netscape	*http://www.netscape.com*
Oracle	*http://www.oracle.com*
Lan Times Parts	*http://www.ltparts.com*

Try searching technical magazines and techie Web pages. Don't forget to use your search engine. You may not be able to find good information on all of the technologies, but if you do your homework, you can make an impressive report at the board meeting.

The Lan Times Parts Web site, illustrated in Figure 17.3, offers top-quality reviews of Internet technologies. This site will help you research some of these difficult technical topics.

Figure 17.3
Technology reviews on Lan Times Parts site

Save your research in your common team folder and in your own personal research folder.

WRITING ABOUT TECHNOLOGY   The State of the Internet

You've seen a lot of exciting things through the course of this book. You've also learned valuable skills that will help you through college and in the working world. For your last assignment, evaluate the current state of the Internet. How was your experience? Will the Internet be helpful and useful to you in the future, or will it be merely entertaining? What technologies do you think will be more developed in the future? What is missing from the Internet that could make it a better experience? Can we live without it? Write a 100-word response and save it in your personal research folder.

Active server pages   Web pages that allow you to change their appearance by resizing pictures and moving things around.

ActiveX   Microsoft software that allows traditional applications to work on the Web.

Address or Location box   The box on a Web browser where you enter and access URLs.

Anchor tag   HTML codes that define a hyperlink to another document or Web page. The anchor tag begins with ⟨A⟩ and ends with ⟨/A⟩. The text or graphic between ⟨A⟩ and ⟨/A⟩ is the link's hot spot that, when clicked, transports the user to the linked location.

Applets   Tiny programs written in Java that can be embedded in HTML pages.

ARPANET   Advanced Research Projects Agency Network, the earliest ancestor of today's Internet. This network was created to maintain some way of communicating in case a nuclear war or natural disaster knocked out a large section of communication lines.

Attachments   Files linked to an e-mail message so that they travel to their destination together. Any type of file can be attached, but usually database, spreadsheet, graphics, or program files are sent as attachments.

BITNET   One of the earliest mail systems serving educational users.

Short for "Because It's Time Network," BITNET was created by academic researchers who were tired of waiting for electronic mail and file transfer capabilities.

Black Thursday   November 3, 1988, the day of the Internet worm, when one-tenth of all Internet servers were forced to shut down as a result of this malicious attack.

Boolean logic   System of logic invented by George Boole, a nineteenth century mathematician. This system uses operators to manipulate data, based on a simple yes or no ranking system. The primary operators in Boolean logic are AND, OR, and NOT.

Boolean operators   The operators such as AND, OR, and NOT used in search strings to refine the scope of the search.

BTW   Internet lingo for "by the way."

Bulleted list   Unordered list in which raised dots or "bullets" precede each item.

Bulletin board system (BBS)   A computer system used as an information source and message system for a particular interest group. Users dial into the BBS, read and leave messages for other users, and communicate with other users who are on the system at the same time. BBSs are often used to distribute shareware.

CGI (Common Gateway Interface)   Recognized standard for interfacing applications, like database programs, with Web servers and Web pages. CGI allows users to interact through Web pages. For example, with CGI you can create a form in which site visitors enter data, and the data will go to the server for processing.

Click and drag   Use of a pointing device, such as a mouse, to latch onto an object on screen and move it to some other location. Place the pointer over the object you want to move and click the mouse button to grab it. Then hold the button down while you slide the object to its destination. Release the mouse button.

Client   A personal computer that is part of a server-client network.

Compressed files   Files that are compacted from their normal size to save space. These files are smaller and therefore can be transferred over the Net at faster speeds.

Cookie   Information created by a Web site and stored on the user's hard disk. It provides a way for the Web server to keep track of the user's patterns and preferences and, with the cooperation of the Web browser, to store them on the user's own hard disk in a cookies.txt file.

Data   Individual pieces of information that a computer processes. Data are stored in computer files, and can be in any form: numbers, text, images, and even voice and video.

DHTML (Dynamic HTML)   Microsoft's extension to HTML that allows users to move and manipulate objects around the Web page as easily as they manipulate icons on their Windows computer screen.

Dialog box   A box or window in which you are required to enter information before the software can execute a command.

Directories or folders Simulated file folders that hold data, applications, and other folders. Folders are logical places to put related files.

Domain name A description of a computer's "location" on the Internet.

Domain Naming System (DNS) computer A computer with software that enables it to compare domain names that people can remember, like *www.disney.com*, with the actual IP (Internet Protocol) number that defines a server on the Internet. The DNS computer makes the association and the requested server can be found.

Dow Jones Industrial Average A measure of stock performance of 30 large U.S. companies, often used by investors as a benchmark, or standard, against which to judge performance of individual stocks.

Download To transmit a file from one computer to another. Generally, "download" means receive and "upload" means transmit.

Drivers Programs that allow hardware, like printers and sound cards, to communicate with a computer's operating system. The operating system calls the driver, and the driver "drives" the device.

Drives Places on the computer that store data.

E-book Book that has been digitized and put into online libraries for public use.

Ellipses Three little dots following some command options that indicate that a dialog box will appear if this command is selected. You will see them in pull-down menus.

E-mail Electronic mail; memos, messages, and attachments transmitted over a network.

Emoticons Keyboard symbols arranged to express emotions.

Extensions File types, or file categories, added to the end of file names, preceded by a dot, as in the following form: filename.doc.

FidoNet A 1980s e-mail protocol that was most used for its bulletin board capabilities.

Files Data storage areas created and named using an application program.

File Transfer Protocol (FTP) A program that allows you to move files from place to place on the Internet.

Flaming Emotional electronic communication. In other words, online cursing.

Folders or directories Simulated file folders that hold data, applications, and other folders. Folders are logical places to put related files.

Freeware Any software on the Net that you never have to pay for.

.gif (Graphics Interchange Format) Widely used Web graphics format developed by CompuServe.

Gopher Document cataloguing system on the Net, popular during the late 1980s. Still around today, gopher uses long descriptive file names and a hierarchical menuing system to catalogue millions and millions of documents, but has been in decline with the rise of the World Wide Web.

Graphical user interface (GUI) The use of pictures or icons to communicate commands from the user to the software. Click a GUI icon with your mouse and something happens. For instance, click the Print button, and your document will print.

Hard drive The primary storage area on your computer. It offers a large storage capacity and fast retrieval.

Header First part of an e-mail message, which contains controlling data, such as who sent the e-mail, who it was mailed to, who should receive copies, priority level, and the subject of the message.

History folder Folder in which your browser keeps track of the most recent URLs you've visited. Entries in the History folder show the name of the page that appears in your Title Bar and the Internet address of the sites you visited.

Hits The number of times a Web page has been accessed or the number of items found in response to a search query.

Home page A page of information that appears in a Web browser window. Often called a "Web page," the home page is usually the first page that users see when they come to a Web site. However, some people call all Web pages home pages.

Hyperlink A link between one object and another. The link is displayed either as text or as an icon. On World Wide Web pages, a text hyperlink displays as underlined text, typically in a different color, whereas a graphical hyperlink is a small image or picture.

Hypertext Links that, when chosen, transport you to the selected information. Hypertext can link to information within a document, in another document on the same computer, or in a document residing on any Web server on the Internet.

HyperText Markup Language (HTML) The standard document format used on the World Wide Web. The HTML commands define how the Web page will look, including text styles, graphic artwork, and hyperlinks to other documents on the Web.

Hypertext reference (HREF) HTML code HREF = within an anchor tag that signifies to the browser that the address of the target document follows.

HyperText Transport Protocol (HTTP) The communications protocol used to connect to servers on the World Wide Web. Its primary function is to establish a connection with a server and transmit HTML pages to the client browser. Addresses of Web sites begin with an http://prefix.

Image source tag HTML code that inserts a graphic image on a Web page. The image tag begins with ⟨IMG SRC = followed by the address of the image's file location and ends with a closing bracket.

IMHO Internet lingo for "in my humble opinion."

Information Infrastructure Task Force (IITF) Committee put together by the Clinton/Gore administration to implement the administration's vision of how the National Information Infrastructure (NII) should work.

Interface System of interaction between the user and the computer.

Internet service provider (ISP) A business that physically connects its customers to the Internet.

Internet worm Program unleashed on the Internet on November 3, 1988, that infected host computers by finding security holes, and then overloaded system resources by replicating itself. The program infected over 6,000 computers, which was about one-tenth of the number of computers on the Internet at that time.

InterNIC (INTERnet Network Information Center) The organization that assigns and registers Internet domain names.

IP (Internet Protocol) number A number that uniquely identifies a specific server on the Internet. IP numbers appear as four numbers separated by periods, like 193.45.67.123.

Java A platform-independent programming language. Java programs only have to be written once and can play on any platform.

JavaScript Programming language that is easier to use than Java, but not as powerful. JavaScript uses the HTML page as its interface, whereas Java can generate a completely customized interface.

.jpg (or .jpeg) Standard graphics format developed by the Joint Photographic Experts Group. Its compact nature makes it ideal for the Internet.

List box A list of options that you can scroll through to make your selection.

LOL Internet lingo for "laughing out loud."

Maximize button A button in a corner of your Windows screen that will make a window larger, usually to fill the entire screen. This button is called the "zoom box" on a Macintosh.

Minimize button A button in a corner of your screen that will make a window smaller. In Windows, clicking the minimize button shrinks the window down to a button and puts it on the taskbar, out of the way.

Mirror site Copy of the original site that resides in a computer in another location. The purpose of a mirror site is to lessen Net traffic to the original site and speed up transmission by allowing users to go to the site closest to them.

Mosaic The first GUI Web browser, created by the National Center for Supercomputing Applications (NCSA). This browser made the World Wide Web popular. Mosaic was user-friendly and free to users.

National Information Infrastructure (NII) An integrated communications system planned by the Clinton/Gore administration that will be based on a nationwide network of networks, and will supposedly allow all Americans to take advantage of the country's information, communication, and computing resources.

National Telecommunications and Information Administration (NTIA) The executive-branch agency responsible for domestic and international telecommunications and information policy issues.

Natural language searching A search method, still in its developmental stage, in which the query is expressed in English, French, or any other spoken language in a normal manner.

Netizen A citizen of the Net, or a fellow traveler on the Information Superhighway.

NetNews All the news that runs over the Internet.

Network A group of computers that can communicate or "talk" to each other through connections or links. The Internet is the largest computer network ever created and is often called "the network of networks."

Network computer (NC) Low-cost computer that accesses resources from a professionally managed network server linked to the Internet to provide computing services to customers instead of requiring the programs and capabilities to reside on the local computer.

Network computing   System developed by Oracle which stores everything—applications, data, and services—on a network of servers and downloads these to users' computers, as needed. Complexity such as updating software and maintaining virus protection are moved from the end-user to the professionals who maintain the network.

Network drives   Drives that are shared by a network of computers.

Network interface card (NIC)   A circuit board that connects your computer to the others on the network, so that the computers can exchange information.

Newbies   New users of the Internet.

Newsgroup   Collection of messages on the Internet about a particular subject. People subscribe to newsgroups to meet and talk electronically with other people interested in the same subjects.

NSFNET   The National Science Foundation network of supercomputers established in the 1980s for scientific research. This network became the foundation for today's Internet.

Numbered list   List in which the items are sequentially numbered, indicating an order of importance among the listed items.

Operating system (OS)   The master program that runs the computer. All applications must be able to "talk" to the operating system.

Operators   Symbols used to perform computer operations, such as to filter data in a query.

Ordered list   List in which the items are displayed in order of importance.

The tag ⟨OL⟩ denotes an ordered list in HTML.

OWLs   Online writing labs established on many university Web sites to help people improve their writing.

Patches   Fixes to bugs in software that has already found its way to the customer.

Peer-to-peer network   A network in which every computer has access to every other computer's resources—drives, folders, and files.

People finder   Search feature provided by search services on the Internet that helps you find people's e-mail addresses, street addresses, and phone numbers.

Perl (Practical Extraction and Reporting Language)   A programming language designed to handle a variety of system administrator functions.

Phrase searching   Searching for exact sequences of words in a query by enclosing the words in quotation marks.

Platform   Operating system.

Plug-in   An auxiliary program that works with a major software package, such as a browser, to enhance its capability.

Proprietary software   A program owned and controlled by a company or person.

Protocol   A communications system used to transfer data over networks. It is like a language that both computers can speak and understand.

Pull-down menu   A bar displayed usually at the top of the program screen that lists options from which the user can select. Once an option is selected by a mouse-click, a vertical list opens, giving the user a choice of commands.

Pull media   Internet content delivery system in which users access content

one site at a time by clicking a link or entering a URL.

Push media   Internet content delivery system in which the user specifies the information to be delivered, and the system searches and downloads the information automatically to the user's computer.

Query   Method of filtering data to find information that meets the search criterion.

Remote access   Contacting a computer from a remote location, usually with a modem over phone lines.

Rich text format (RTF)   Text format that enables the use enhancements, such as bold, italic, and different fonts and colors. You can also insert pictures, sound, and video clips or documents created in a variety of programs.

ROTFL   Internet lingo for "rolling on the floor laughing."

Scroll bar   A bar, with a small box in it, located at the side or bottom of a window, or both. Clicking and dragging the small box allows you to slide around the window to view contents that were previously hidden. Clicking one of the arrow boxes allows you to move a little at a time in the arrow's direction. Clicking the gray area inside the bar moves a new screenful of material into view.

Search engine   Computer software that searches for data, based on some criterion, such as a key word.

Search services   Web sites, such as Yahoo! and AltaVista, that maintain a directory database of other Web sites. You can look for information on the Web by entering a search criterion, such as a key word, where indicated on the search service Web site.

Self-extracting files   Executable files that decompress themselves automatically when run.

Server   A high-speed computer on a server-client network that stores information and distributes it to requesting clients.

Server-client network   A network of clients sharing information distributed by servers. This is the type of network on which the Internet system is based.

Shareware   Software that you can download for free, try out for a certain length of time, and then purchase if you find it valuable.

Shockwave player   A multimedia viewing plug-in for a Web browser that allows users to experience the animations and full multimedia effects on some Web sites.

Spam   Unwanted and unsolicited advertising or other messages, such as political or social commentary.

Streaming   A data handling process that enables data to flow continuously, allowing Web site audio and video to play without requiring file downloads.

Subject line   Place in an e-mail header where the sender inserts a brief description of the message contents.

Tags   HTML instructions that tell the browser how to display the Web page information. Tags are enclosed in brackets ⟨LIKE THIS⟩.

Taskbar   A toolbar that displays the applications (tasks) that you currently have running. Clicking on a taskbar

button restores the application to its previous size.

Thread   Several newsgroup postings related to the same topic.

Ticker symbol   A two-to-five letter abbreviation that represents a company in stock listings.

Toggle   A control that allows the user to alternate between two options.

Toolbar   A bar of GUI icons that usually provide one-click access to frequently used commands.

Uniform Resource Locator (URL)   The Internet addressing scheme that defines the route to a file or program. The URL is used as the initial access to a resource.

Unordered list   List that shows no particular order of importance among its items. The tag ⟨UL⟩ denotes an unordered list in HTML.

Usenet   Comes from USEr NETwork. A giant public-access network on the Internet, maintained by volunteers, that provides user news and e-mail. Newsgroups get their messages from the Usenet network.

User-friendly   Easy to learn and use.

Virus   A program written to alter the functioning of the infected computer. The virus code is buried within an existing program. When that program is executed, the virus code is activated and attaches copies of itself to other programs in the system. The virus may be a prank that causes a small annoyance, or it may be malicious vandalism that destroys programs and data.

VRML (Virtual Reality Modeling Language)   Language used to simulate 3-D objects, lights, and textures, viewable using a VRML viewer within the Web browser. This language can create 3D "worlds," where users can interact with objects and other netizens in a virtual setting. After downloading a VRML page, its contents can be viewed, rotated, and manipulated, and simulated rooms can be "walked into."

Webmasters   People who create, organize, and manage Web sites.

Web servers   Computers on the Internet that allow others to access their drives, folders, and files. They accept requests from Web browsers to transmit HTML pages and other stored files.

Web TV   An Internet TV terminal that allows you to access the Internet through your TV and phone line, without a computer.

Workgroup   A smaller network within the larger network. The computers of the people in the workgroup are linked together, so that they can share resources to accomplish group tasks.

Zoom box   A box in a corner of your Macintosh screen that will make your window larger, usually to fill the entire screen. This box is called the "maximize button" in Windows.

INDEX

Acropolis, tour, 118
active server pages, 6, 203
ActiveX, 195, 203
address book, 89
Address/Location box, 30
advertisement-based e-mail, 81
Al Gore's information
   superhighway, 120
Aladdin Systems, Inc. on the Web, 72
AltaVista home page, 37
Amazon.com, 149
anchor tag, 187, 203
AND/OR/+ operators, 106
applets, 194, 203
applications, switching between, 10
ARPANET, 5, 203
astronomy, 128
attached files, 88
attachment button, 87
attachments, 83, 87, 203
back buttons, 33

binary systems, 110
biology, 130
BITNET, 137, 203
Black Thursday, 127, 203
bookmark folder, creating, 40
bookmarks/favorites, 36–37
books online, 116
Boolean logic, 105, 203
Boolean operators, 105, 110, 203
browser, 186
   primer, 27
   window elements, 28
   wars, 6
BTW, 143, 203
bulleted list, 185
bulletin board system (BBS), 137, 203
business, 146

capital ideas, 139
Census Bureau Web page, 54
CGI (Common Gateway
   Interface), 195, 203
click and drag, 7, 203
client, 4, 204
color, 62
communicating, 2
competition or standardization, 196
compressed files, 71, 204
compression programs, 73
computer numbers, 53
cookie, 34, 204
copy, 10
couch potato's guide to TV, 171
cyberwords, 143

data, 16, 204
Declaration of Independence, 140
decompressing files, 72
dialog box, 3, 204
directories, 16, 204
domain names, 50, 52, 53, 204
Domain Naming System (DNS)
   computer, 53, 204
double-arrow pointer, 7
Dow Jones Industrial
   Average, 151, 204
download, 68, 204
downloading FTP software, 74–75
dream browser, 57
drivers, 69, 204
drives, 16, 204

e-book, 115, 204
e-mail, 80–83, 85, 90, 162, 204
economic forecasts by the CBO, 148

economics, 147
Egyptology, 98
elected officials, 158
ellipses, 3, 204
emoticons, 87, 204
executive branch agencies, 163
Explorer, 17
extensions, 71, 204

fantasy sports leagues, 176
favorites/bookmarks, 36–39
FidoNet, 137, 204
File Transfer Protocol, *see FTP*
files, 16, 22, 204
   attached, 88
   compressed, 71
   decompressing, 72
   self-extracting, 73
flaming, 98, 205
folders, 16, 20, 205
   mail, 86
font options, 60–61
forward buttons, 33
fractal, 134
fraud, 150
freeware, 152, 205
FTP, 19, 205
   software, downloading, 74–75
funding, 63

gambling, 176
games, 70
.gif (Graphics Interchange Format),
   199, 205
gopher, 137, 205
government, 158
graphical user interface (GUI), 2, 205
graphics on the web, 199

hard drive, 16, 205
header, 83, 205
history, 140
    folder, 34, 205
hits, 104, 205
home buttons, 33
home page, 30, 205
    AltaVista, 37
    Paris Musee du Louvre, 32
    Yahoo!, 36
HREF, 180, 187, 205
HTML, 47, 205
    source code, 182
HTTP, 49, 205
hyperlink, 46–48, 205
hypertext, 27, 205
    Markup Language, *see HTML*
    reference, *see HREF*
    Transport Protocol, *see HTTP*

IITF, 163, 206
image source tag, 188, 205
IMHO, 143, 206
Information Infrastructure Task
    Force, *see IITF*
interface, 57, 206
Internet
    addresses, 30, 49
    and business, 146
    lingo, 143
    Public Library lobby, 115
    service provider, *see ISP*
    sources, 139
    worm, 127, 206
Internet Explorer
    History option, 35
    icon, 4
    toolbar, 32
    window, 28
InterNIC (INTERnet Network
    Information Center), 50, 206
    page, domain name owner, 52
    registration service Web page, 51
IP (Internet Protocol number), 53, 206
IRS forms, 148
ISP, 8, 88, 206

Java, 194, 196, 206
JavaScript, 194, 206
journalism, 142
.jpg or .jpeg, 199, 206

language, 194
    of Web, 180
law, 160
list box, 60, 206
log on, 33
LOL, 143, 206

Macintosh browser, 3
Macintosh folder structure, 16
mail button, 84
mail folders, 86
mailbox icon, 84
math, 131
maximize button, 6, 206
menu, pull-down, 3
message, 83, 85
meteorology, 125
Microsoft FTP site, 19
minimize button, 6, 206
mirror site, 118, 206
Mosaic, 27, 29, 206
movies, 168
multimedia on the net, 171
Musee du Louvre home page, 32
music—lyrics, 173

names, 51
NASA's Cool Websites image
    map, 128
National Information Infrastructure
    (NII), 163, 206
National Museum of Natural History,
    tour, 117

National Telecommunications and
    Information Administration
    (NTIA), 163, 207
natural language
    searching, 110–111, 207
NEAR/ADJ operators, 108
net, 129
    addresses, 46
netizen, 33, 157, 207
NetNews, 96, 207
Netscape
    Communicator icon, 4
    FTP site, 18
Netscape Navigator
    History option, 35
    toolbar, 32
    window, 29
network, 4, 207
    communications and
        cataloguing, 137
    computer (NC), 169, 207
    computing, 161, 207
    drives, 16, 207
    interface card, *see NIC*
    of networks, 7
newbies, 47, 207
news, 142
newsgroup(s), 93–95, 97, 99, 207
    posts, 96
NIC, 4, 27
NII, 163
NOT/- operators, 107
NSFNET, 21, 207
NTIA, 163
numbered list, 189, 207

offline, 115
one-click commands, 32
online
    encyclopedias, 117
    resources, 114
    shopping, 149
    writing labs (OWLs), 136
operating system (OS), 63, 207
    know-how, 2
operators, 105, 207
    AND/OR/+, 106
    NEAR/ADJ, 108
    NOT/-, 107
ordered list, 189, 207
OWLs, 136, 207
    Internet Public Library, 137

parentheses, 109
paste, 10
patches, 69, 207
peer-to-peer network, 4, 207
people finder, 114, 119, 207
Perl (Practical Extraction and Report Language), 195, 207
personal interface, 57
PGP (Pretty Good Privacy), 120
phrase searching, 110, 207
platform, 194, 207
plug-in, 171, 208
PointCast push system, 142
political issues, 162
POP (Post Office Protocol), 90
posting, 98–99
POTS (Plain Old Telephone System), 64
Project Gutenberg, 117
proprietary software, 81, 208
protocol, 49, 208
public debt, 147
pull media, 142, 208
pull-down menu, 3, 208
push media, 142, 208

query, 104, 208

refresh/reload buttons, 33
regulating, 161
remote access, 21, 208
rich text format (RTF), 87, 208
ROTFL, 143, 208
RTF, 87

scroll bar, 8, 208
search engine, 104, 106, 208
comparison, 111
search services, 36, 208
Security First Network Bank, 153
Seinfeld-O-Matic, 172
self-extracting files, 73, 208

server, 4, 208
server-client network, 4, 208
SGML + TB-L + HTML, 186
shareware, 68, 70, 208
dilemma, 73
Shockwave player, 171, 208
Siskel & Ebert's Revolving Cube Sound Reviews, 168
source file containing anchor tags, 187
Southern California Earthquake Center, 119
space exploration, 128
space-out, 124
spam, 82, 208
spelling, 141
sports, 174
live online, 175
status bar, 58
stealing pictures, 190
stock prices, 151
stop buttons, 33
streaming, 172–173, 208
subject line, 83, 208
subscribing, 94–95
Sun's Java language, 197
switching between applications, 10

tags, 180–181, 209
taskbar, 6, 209
Thomas internet site, 158
thread, 96, 209
3D pyramid, 131
3D view of weather, 127
ticker symbol, 152, 209
Tim Johann Berners-Gutenberg-Lee, 184
toggle, 58, 209
toggling multimedia options, 64
tool, 136
toolbar, 3, 32, 58, 59, 209
tracing illegal activity, 164

U.S. Postal Service Web page, 42
Uniform Resource Locator, *see URL*
UNIX operating system, 63
unordered list, 185, 209
unsubscribing, 94–95
URL, 30, 209

Usenet, 96–97, 209
user-friendly, 27, 209

virtual degree, 118
virtual encyclopedias, 116
virtual filing cabinet, 15
virtual frog dissection kit, 130
virtual library, 114–115
virtual museum, 117
virtual park, 198
virus, 34, 209
Volcano World, 48
VRML (Virtual Reality Modeling Language), 131, 209

Web, 129
addresses, 5, 30, 93, 107, 126, 138, 147, 159
browser, 28
language, 180
servers, 49, 209
TV, 174, 209
Web page, 184
design, 187
example, 185
Webmaster, 105, 109, 209
window size, 6
Windows Explorer, 17
Windows file and folder organization, 17
Windows Web View, 3
WinZip on the Web, 72
workgroup, 4, 209
World Wide Web (WWW) (W3), 8
writing, 137

Yahoo! home page, 36

Zen and the Art of the Internet, 125
zoom box, 6, 209